D0975690

LOST OR DAMAGED LIBRARY MATERIALS

THE CARE OF LIBRARY MATERIALS IS THE RESPONSIBILITY OF THE BORROWING PATRON. TAX DOLLARS SHOULD NOT BE USED TO REPLACE OR REPAIR MATERIALS ABUSED BY INDIVIDUALS. A FEE SCHEDULE HAS BEEN SET TO REFLECT THE COSTS TO THE LIBRARY OF REPLACING OR SPECIAL HANDLING OF LOST AND DAMAGED MATERIALS.

MATERIALS WERE SELECTED AS AN INTEGRAL PART OF THE LIBRARY COLLECTION, AND FOR THE USE OF ALL PATRONS. IF A BOOK IS OUT OF PRINT, THE SUBJECT AREA WILL STILL NEED TO BE RESTORED DUE TO THE LOSS OF THE MATERIAL.

FEES WILL BE CHARGED AS FOLLOWS:

DAMAGE

1. VISIBLE DAMAGE (WATER, COFFEE, INK, ETC.) WHICH REDUCES LIFE OF MATERIAL BUT STILL CAN CIRCULATE...................$2.00

2. DAMAGE REQUIRING ANY SPECIAL HANDLING (SAND, PENCIL MARKS, ETC.)....................$3.00

3. DAMAGE REQUIRING THE BOOK BE REBOUND...................$6.00

LOSS

THE REPLACEMENT COST OF THE MATERIAL WILL BE CHARGED, PLUS A $2.00 MATERIALS AND HANDLING FEE.

IF THE MATERIAL ITSELF CANNOT BE REPLACED:1.) THE PRICE WE PAID WILL BE CHARGED PLUS A $2.00 PROCESSING AND HANDLING FEE FOR A NEW BOOK. 2.) A FLAT FEE OF $10.00 WILL BE CHARGED TO REPLACE THE LOSS TO THE COLLECTION.
(THE AVERAGE PER-VOLUME COST OF A BOOK IS $23.00)

Parents' Guide to Raising a Gifted Child

Parents' Guide to Raising a Gifted Child

Recognizing and Developing Your Child's Potential

James Alvino and the
Editors of Gifted Children Monthly

Little, Brown and Company   Boston — Toronto

FIRST EDITION

Much of the material in this book was previously published in
Gifted Children Newsletter, now called *Gifted Children Monthly*.

Library of Congress Cataloging in Publication Data
Alvino, James, 1947–
     Parents' guide to raising a gifted child.
     Bibliography: p.
     Includes index.
     1. Gifted children — Addresses, essays, lectures.
     2. Child rearing — Addresses, essays, lectures.
     3. Gifted children — Education — Addresses, essays,
lectures. I. Gifted children monthly. II. Title.
HQ773.5.A58   1985   649'.155   85-10363
ISBN 0-316-03727-3

Designed by Patricia Girvin Dunbar

Published simultaneously in Canada
by Little, Brown & Company (Canada) Limited

PRINTED IN THE UNITED STATES OF AMERICA

C.1

For Jaimi,
my nine-year-old daughter, who makes me increasingly
aware of the need for and value of books like this

Preface

PHILOSOPHERS, psychologists, scientists, and educators continue to debate the age-old problem of the origin of intelligence: is intelligence determined primarily by one's genes or by one's environment? Invariably it is the result of both — working together. Neither raw potential nor all the advantages of an enriched environment is alone sufficient to guarantee that a human being becomes an intelligent person, develops his or her potential to the fullest, and succeeds in life as he or she could.

However, parents can make a tangible difference in the growth and development of their children in those everyday areas in which they interact, guide, admonish, teach, provide for, and otherwise rear their children to the best of their knowledge.

Expanding parents' knowledge about what's best for their children is what this book is all about.

Parents' Guide to Raising a Gifted Child is for *all* parents interested in recognizing and developing their children's potential from the years of preschool through junior high school. Whether your son or daughter has already been identified as "gifted," or whether you want to give your child an extra edge that could make a difference in the child's potential, what you do at home and what takes place at school are of the utmost importance.

Parents' Guide is a resource of highly practical and specific parenting advice, consumer tips, troubleshooting techniques, and enjoyable and educational family activities offered by experts in education for the gifted and by parents who have "been there." Not everything will fit your situation or work for you, but you won't find a more comprehensive variety of time-tested ideas and suggestions anywhere.

Acknowledgments

THIS BOOK is a compilation of three years' worth of the best articles, research, parenting advice, and other material gleaned from *Gifted Children Newsletter* (now *Gifted Children Monthly*), the multiaward-winning publication "for the parents of children with great promise."

Much of the actual editing was done by the former managing editor of *Gifted Children Newsletter*, Jeanette Moss, who masterfully blended the discrete elements into a unified voice without destroying their integrity. The manuscript was typed by Carolyn Baker, who saw to it that each of several hundred pages of raw copy was miraculously transformed into something clean and readable.

A countless number of authors have unwittingly contributed to this tome by virtue of their previously published material in *Gifted Children Newsletter*. Their special insights add depth and variety to each chapter. Thus, in addition to other individuals and publications actually cited in the text itself, the following persons have made contributions in one form or another: Steve Allen, comedian, author, composer; Dr. Alexinia Baldwin, Associate Professor of Curriculum and Instruction, State University of New York; Robert Baum, managing editor, *Gifted Children Monthly*; Dr. Carolyn Callahan, Assistant Professor of Educational Psychology, University of Virginia; Misty Chamberlin, Medford, Massachusetts; Jeanie Chandler, personnel director and flutist, Marin Symphony Orchestra, Marin County, California; Bernie DeKoven, Phil Wiswell, Ruth Roufberg, Sid Sackson, game reviewers, *Gifted Children Monthly*; Dr. James R. Delisle, Assistant Professor of Special Education, Kent State University; Diane Divoky, Sacramento; Barbara Elleman, coeditor of *Booklist*, American Library Association; Dr. Virginia Ehrlich, president of New York State's Advocates for Gifted and Talented Education; Helene West-Feldman, psychologist and family counselor, Beverly Hills; Jan K. France, microbiologist, Natchez; Sandra Fujita, San Francisco; Richard P. Gallagher, educational consultant, Philadelphia; David Grady, former editor of *Learning* magazine; Bruce Grefe, painter, illustrator, art teacher, Camden, New Jersey; Mary Lou Jones, Clarksburg, West Virginia; Barbara Kent, Yuba City, California; Anne Lewis, editor, *Education USA*; Anni J. Lipper, advertising director, *Gifted Children Monthly*; Susan Meyers, San Francisco; Patricia Bruce Mitchell, National Association of State Boards of Education, Washington, D.C.; Lewis Nordan, Fayetteville, Arkansas; Susan Perry, Los Angeles; Dr. Donna Rand, Talcott Mountain Academy of Science and Mathematics, Avon, Connecticut; Dr. Sandford Reichart, Distinguished Professor Emeritus, Case Western Reserve University; Dr. Sally M. Reis, coordinator of gifted programs, Torrington, Connecticut; Dr. Joseph S. Renzulli, Professor of Educational Psychology, University of Connecticut; Dr. E. Susanne Richert, director of Gifted Education, Educational Information and Resource Center, Sewell, New Jersey; Gina Ginsberg-Riggs, executive director, Gifted Child Society, Glen Rock, New Jersey; Fred Rogers, creator of *Mister Rogers' Neighborhood*; Phyllis Rosser, contributing editor for *Ms.* magazine; Bill Schlesinger, patent attorney, Arlington, Virginia; Dr. Dorothy Sisk, Professor of Exceptional Child Education, University of South Florida; Samuel and Alice Steinruck, Clementon, New Jersey; Nancy Stuart, vice-president, Gifted and Talented Publications, Inc., Sewell, New Jersey; Dr. E. Paul Torrance, Alumni Foundation Distinguished Professor of Educational Psychology, University of Georgia; J. Pansy Torrance, evaluator, Future Problem Solving Program, Athens, Georgia; Cynthia Turnock, circulation manager, *Gifted Children Monthly*; Jerome Wieler, Children's Hospital, Boston; Dr. Frank Williams, educational consultant, Newport, Oregon; Paul Zeh, Wichita; Ron Zucca, media specialist, Educational Information and Resource Center, Sewell, New Jersey.

And finally, a very special thank-you goes to Arthur Lipper III, founder of *Gifted Children Newsletter* and chairman of *Gifted Children Monthly*, without whom there would be no book at all.

                                        J.A.

Contents

Parents' Guide to Raising a Gifted Child

Do You Have a Gifted Child?

I⊤ WASN'T long ago that being "gifted" only meant having a high Intelligence Quotient (IQ). This notion is associated with the psychologist Lewis Terman, who developed the first broadly used tests of comparative intelligence and studied gifted children and genius over a period of nearly sixty years. In fact, use of the IQ as a chief means of identification of the gifted is still prevalent despite a broadened definition, ushered in by the federal government, which included academics, creativity, the arts, and leadership along with strong intellectual ability (IQ) as categories of giftedness.

While there is much controversy about the definition of "gifted" and how to determine which youngsters can be so categorized, studies have shown that parents — not teachers — most often identify gifted children first and most effectively. If these findings are valid, it is important that parents be aware of relevant facts, fictions, and current debates concerning identifying giftedness.

DEFINING AND IDENTIFYING GIFTEDNESS

The 1972 report to the United States Congress, *Education of the Gifted and Talented,* by Sidney P. Marland, Commissioner of Education, established the federal definition of giftedness, which was to influence the field from then on. It said:

Gifted and Talented Children are those identified by professionally qualified persons and who, by virtue of outstanding abilities, are capable of high performance. These are children who require differentiated educational programs and/or services beyond those normally provided by regular school programs in order to realize their contributions to self and society.

These are children with demonstrated and/or potential high performance in the following areas:
— *General intellectual ability*
— *Specific academic aptitude*
— *Creative or productive thinking*
— *Leadership ability*
— *Ability in visual or performing arts*

This broadened definition distinguishes between "gifted" and "talented," a distinction that plagues the field's most noble efforts to integrate the two under one definition. Sometimes the two terms are used interchangeably. The implicit distinction is that "gifted" refers to intellectual abilities and "talented" to artistic abilities. But in most cases, "talent" — encompassing the fine and performing arts — is, at best, relegated to second-class status and, at worst, not even considered in the same league as "gift," as if the two were mutually exclusive.

The federal definition also recognizes that gifted children require special educational attention and includes potential as well as actual performance as a criterion. When framing the 1978 Gifted and Talented Children's Education Act, Congress used it in requiring schools to identify and provide activities for children with "demonstrated" or "potential" capabilities in the five areas Marland specified.

IDENTIFICATION PRACTICES

A survey in the *National Report on Identification* (1982) shows that almost half of the states have adopted Marland's definition of giftedness. Most of the other states use IQ and academic aptitude criteria only, and several states still have no definition of giftedness at all. Other surveys show, however, that in practice almost all states still rely on test scores — IQ and achievement — to identify students for placement in special programs. Just emphasizing actual school performance goes against the federal specification that children "capable [who have potential] of high performance" be considered.

A trend away from use of the federal government's broad definition of giftedness shows up in the dwindling allocation of funds for education. Programs for the gifted are often the first to go, and when they are retained, cutbacks can take the form of excluding children who would have been included the previous year.

To sum up the current situation, the federal government attempted to broaden the definition of giftedness and succeeded to some degree. Nevertheless, some states pay only lip service to the guidelines, and financial constraints have brought about a regression in identification practices.

Despite the confusion in the gifted and talented field today, considerable agreement among the experts does exist. They recognize that research is still needed to clarify the complex elements of giftedness, heredity, environment, achievement, potential, and creativity.

One myth that has retarded the development of the special education gifted children need is that "if these kids are so smart, they'll do fine on their own." On the contrary, Marland's 1972 report to Congress cited a number of studies showing that gifted children who are not challenged with programs tailored to their needs become underachievers. The report said that if they are to reach their full potential, gifted children must have special education.

Another myth about gifted children is that they are always well behaved. On the contrary, often those children who are not challenged enough and are bored at school develop characteristics wrongly associated with the nongifted and even with slow learners.

The following negative characteristics often actually reflect giftedness, but ironically screen appropriate children out of programs: boredom with routine tasks, refusal to do rote homework; stubbornness about moving on to a new topic; self-criticism, impatience with failures; criticism of others, including teachers; vocal disagreement with others, including teachers; joking or punning at inappropriate times; emotional oversensitivity, overreaction, becoming angry or crying easily if things go wrong; lack of interest in details; messy work; refusal to accept authority; nonconformity; general stubbornness; a tendency to dominate others.

Critics of the Marland report's definition say that its categories are limiting, confusing, and without clear specifications concerning performance levels that indicate giftedness. Also, they say, the categories overlap. Creativity, for example, is in every category.

An alternative to the federal definition of giftedness, the "three-ring conception," was developed in 1977 by Joseph Renzulli of the University of Connecticut. Renzulli's system, using three interlocking criteria (creativity, above-average ability, and task commitment), cuts across all curriculum and talent areas. It deemphasizes IQ, states that three characteristics must come together in a child's area of interest. Renzulli's work with children has shown that a child's intense interest and motivation in an area indicate possible giftedness. His model for identifying the gifted has been adopted by hundreds of school districts around the country and can be interpreted to fulfill the federal requirements.

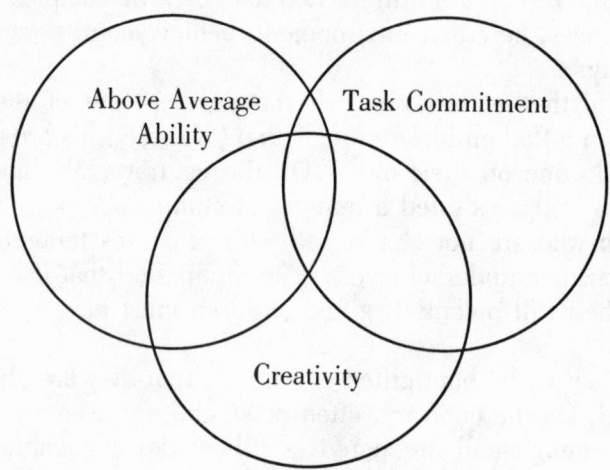

If parents are aware that IQ is still the most widely practiced method of identification of the gifted, they can advocate broader techniques. Even Terman's own samples and studies do not validate the idea that IQ is *sufficient* to identify the gifted. An eighth assessment, in 1982, of the same subjects first identified as gifted in 1921 indicates that those identified as gifted by IQ fell into two groups — an "A" group, whose members made exceptional achievements and outstanding contributions to their fields, and a "C" group, whose members did not. The former, among them Isaac Asimov, for example, are generally recognized by society as being gifted, while the latter are not.

A system such as Renzulli's "triad model" encompasses the broad definition of giftedness and provides a more effective method of identification at the same time. Studies of eminent children and adults regarded as gifted show that they have the three traits of the triad in common. This would include Terman's "A" group. The "C" group apparently lacked — or did not demonstrate — creativity and/or task commitment. Renzulli's model and the most recent data from the studies of Terman's successors illustrate how measurements of ability can differ from applied performance. Task commitment — high motivation, perseverance, and just plain hard work — is apparently an extremely powerful factor in giftedness.

Most experts think that using a variety of formal and informal methods of identification is most effective. They contend that validated scales and checklists for self, peer, parent, and teacher nominations — though "subjective" in nature — are good indicators of exceptional behavior. It is important to keep in mind, however, that many locally developed instruments are poorly designed and don't measure what they say they do. Also, *stages* of identification should be recognized. Different identification tools are needed for initially nominating students to the program and for assessing the needs and abilities of students once they are in the program.

The Debate about Testing

Standardized testing has been around since the beginning of the century, and despite continued criticism of the inherent limitations and shortcomings of norm-based test instruments, some form of standardized testing seems destined to remain a widely used tool in evaluating student progress and identifying the comparative levels of capability and development for individual students.

Though most experts advocate the use of standardized testing along with other means to select students for gifted programs, there is disagreement about the extent of the value of these tests. Those who strongly support the method say that it is especially effective in the areas of mathematical and/or verbal reasoning ability. Another important reason for testing the gifted is for diagnostic purposes. Achievement tests, for example, can help determine what information a student already has acquired in a given subject, so that the student may proceed at a pace and level commensurate with his or her ability to learn. Some believe that nonstandardized assessments such as checklists and rating scales are less than adequate to identify the gifted, that such measurements are often costly, that they lack validity and replicability, and in many cases deal with learned skills and not potential.

Those who emphasize using alternatives to test scores contend that standardized testing is not sufficient to identify the gifted and that such a use is based on a narrow definition of giftedness. They point out that highly creative thinkers — which in the estimation of some experts best describes gifted individuals — are often stifled by the need to focus on the single "best" answer to a standardized test question. Consequently, many gifted children do not score high on such tests and therefore go unidentified. Another disadvantage to the tests is their tendency to reinforce a conformity of thinking to the detriment of originality. Instead, experts advocate evaluation of student products and performance-based assessment, which involves original applications of knowledge and skills to achieve goals in real life or simulated exercises.

It has also been in vogue for some time to point out the cultural factors in IQ tests — for example, the triviality and irrelevance of many test items, their sampling of a narrow spectrum of human cognition, their utter inappropriateness in most contexts of human behavior, and, finally, the labeling and stigmatizing of children that happens when we use them.

Despite such warnings, the science of psychometry continues to plod along, concerning itself most with such things as content and construct validity, reliability and units of measurement, standard error, and the like. Psychometrists seldom seem to question the real foundations of the testing industry — which is, after all, a multimillion-dollar business — or the consequences to children of such testing.

Thus, the ironic fact that standardized tests often handicap intellectually gifted children and prevent them from being identified continues. One of the most flagrant deficiencies in standardized testing is neglect of the thinking *process* children use in reaching their answers. The importance of converging on a psychometrist's "correct" answer can predetermine and stifle a child's creativity and authentic discovery. Doing well requires being able to make one's thinking conform to psychometrically determined "systems of relevance."

Here is an example. In a preschool test from "Sesame Street," children were presented with a group of four objects and were asked to choose the item that did not belong. The set consisted of a yellow rain hat, an orange baseball cap, a red mitten with a white stripe, and a white hard hat. Subsequently it was explained that the correct answer was the mitten, because it was the only object that was not a hat.

In this example we witness an impoverishment of possible embryonic systems of relevance in the child's world. The "correct" grouping is not the only valid three-object class among the four objects. The same result (mitten) could be arrived at through the recognition that only one of the objects has two colors. Thus the *same* result can be derived from two schemes of relevance, or from both simultaneously. *Different* results are possible and valid as well. On the other hand, coming from an implicit organizational scheme of "mine or Dad's," the child of a construction worker might answer that the hard hat does not belong. Or the items might be classified into hard and soft. Interest structures and cognitive operations are never completely disentangled, even by adults.

The process of analyzing and evaluating the test question itself can be an application of higher cognition, but this process does not show up on a standardized test, especially not in the scoring. The Marland report reflected the limitations of standardized testing for the gifted. The report found that:

• As many as 50 percent of all gifted children may go unidentified if group tests alone are used.

• Individual tests are more accurate than group tests in identifying the gifted.

• In some cases, ratings on group tests tend to be higher for below-average students and lower for above-average students.

• The discrepancy between group and individual test scores increases in direct proportion to levels of intelligence; thus, the most highly gifted children can be penalized the most severely.

Problems and Progress

"We have continued to view giftedness as an absolute concept," Renzulli says, "something that exists in and by itself without relation to anything else. . . . Most of our identification efforts are directed toward uncovering the magic piece of evidence that will tell us if a child is 'really gifted.' "

The magic evidence in most procedures for identifying the gifted continues to be a score of at least 125 to 130 on an intelligence test. Because of its apparent objectivity, this measure offers educators a simplified and traditionally uncontested criterion — a welcome justification when a child's exclusion from a program is challenged.

"Parents seem to wear their kids' IQ scores like a badge, without realizing that the score itself tells us very little," says Donald Treffinger, professor of creative studies at the State University of New York in Buffalo.

Publishers of intelligence tests claim that their products measure general intellectual ability, but most psychologists and educators agree that the tests measure only certain areas of intelligence — logical or analytical reasoning abilities — that relate to success in schoolwork. "There are hundreds of different mental functions," says one educational psychologist, "but we're only tapping about ten of them. . . . Creativity and problem solving abilities are not measured by any of the tests."

Even in performing the more limited task of identifying children with logical reasoning ability, IQ tests are known to do a faulty job. An elementary school principal, JoAnn Shaheen, described one of her pupils — a little boy who was a natural leader with an outstanding sense of fair play. His achievement test scores (99th percentile in reading and 95th percentile in math) put him at the top of every teacher's list of academically gifted children. But at the end of third grade, his IQ score was 125 in the verbal section and 81 in the performance (nonverbal) section.

Children like that little boy are forcing parents, educators, and even the federal government to look closely at a value system that places extraordinary importance on intellectual performance as measured by IQ tests. Even though exceptional academic aptitude would seem to be easily "testable," it may or may not show up on IQ tests because, among other things, measurement is not precise at the extreme ends of the ability curve.

Leadership: A Special Concern

Leadership is an important characteristic in the broadened definition of giftedness — one of the five areas specified by the 1972 federal definition — and one that certainly cannot be identified by use of an IQ test! But what is leadership? How can you identify, nurture, and develop it in your child? These questions take on a special significance for parents of gifted children. The answers could determine to a considerable degree the role your child assumes in the future.

A single, all-inclusive definition of leadership, however, is difficult — perhaps impossible — to find. It meant different things to different people. However, most definitions involve the ability to influence others and bring about change.

Beyond the definition, what is the precise relationship between leadership and giftedness? Experts in the field continue to view leadership in different ways. Some ask whether leadership potential can exist in people who are not otherwise identifiable as gifted. After all, communication skills, insight, ability to solve problems creatively, and decision-making are often among those intellectual qualities cited as inherent to leaders.

Other experts would argue that leadership ability is not dependent upon the presence of other gifts, because some of the characteristics of leadership — such as social skills — are not necessarily found in people gifted in other areas. It would appear that some combination of abilities characteristic of giftedness in other areas is necessary to be a gifted leader, but no single ability is sufficient or can be equated with the gift of leadership.

Despite the inability to find a universally accepted definition of leadership, and despite differing viewpoints about the relationship of leadership to other areas of giftedness, various characteristics of leaders — both skills and styles — can be discerned. Those traits frequently cited as common to leaders are independence in thought and action, or a certain degree of nonconformity. Self-confidence is another commonly mentioned characteristic, as is a willingness to take risks (i.e., risking failure in order to achieve success). Psychosocial skills — empathy, sensitivity, and all the "humanitarian" concerns — seem always to be included when talking about leadership.

WHAT PARENTS CAN DO

One study on identifying the gifted, conducted by Virginia Ehrlich when she was with the Astor Program in New York, found that there are at least forty-six broad traits commonly cited in the literature as being associated with intellectual giftedness at all ages. Of these, from one to fifteen, or an average of four or five, out of thirty-five are usually cited by parents of young children (up to age seven). The brighter the child, the more traits they mention.

For the young child, aged three and a half to five and a half, those that turned out to be significantly associated with intellectual giftedness were vocabulary, thinking ability, capacity for symbolic thought (mathematical skills), insight (capacity to see relationships), early physical and social development, and sensitivity.

The ability to read was mentioned more frequently than any other trait, but this information was valuable in discriminating between children of high and low IQs and only when the parent was able to cite a specific level of reading ability: for example, "She's seven and reading at the fourth grade level."

Except for the seven cited above, there is no clear pattern of traits that one can use as a measure. A parent may observe only a few traits and yet conclude, justly, that the child is gifted. Much, much more research will be required before we can rely exclusively on any checklist for positive identification.

Following are some other characteristics that parents can use in estimating whether their child is gifted:

Verbal facility	Facility in writing
Good memory	Ability to learn easily
Flexibility of thought	Abstract reasoning
Complexity of thinking	Planning and organizational
Energy	ability
Creativity, imagination	Originality
Curiosity	A sense of wonder
Range of information	Broad range of interests
Aesthetic interests or talents	Attention to detail
Outstanding performance	Scholastic achievement
Leadership	Attention and concentration
Persistence	Self-criticism
Responsiveness	Strength of character
Candidness	Dependability
Social responsibility	Cooperation
Enthusiasm	Sense of humor
Ability in spatial relation-	Emotional stability
ships	Self-sufficiency and self-
Good health	confidence

Favorable comparison with siblings, others

Preference for older play-mates

Judgments about their gifted children are inevitably affected by the parents' own level of education, community demographics, and intrafamily experiences. Bright, well-educated parents sometimes expect their children to exhibit bright behavior, so they consider it "normal." In families with several bright children, expectations for the younger children are high and thus their behavior may not be recognized as being superior. In areas where unusually well trained personnel congregate, a child's superior performance may not be recognized simply because it does not differ markedly from the local norm. On the other hand, in the general population, many parents do not recognize intellectual giftedness simply because circumstances do not permit a display of such abilities.

What parents need most is confidence in their own skill in evaluating their children. Regardless of all the objective criteria psychologists, educators, and others may wish to cite, parents seem to have an intuitive sense about their own children. They know, frequently without being able to explain how they know, that a child has unusual ability. During interviews this is often stated as "I don't know why, but I just know this child is different!"

In order to persuade school authorities that a child is gifted, it is wise for parents to present convincing evidence that is acceptable to the educator. Following are a few suggestions.

1. Obtain a psychologial evaluation, including an *individual* IQ test and at least a reading or vocabulary test.

2. Obtain recommendations from former or present teachers and principals.

3. Present a list of descriptive behaviors that are associated with giftedness (see pages 15–17), *with examples*.

4. Use school records of achievement, including both classroom grades and results on standardized tests stated in terms of norms, such as grade equivalents or percentiles. (Raw scores and standard scores are not as easy to interpret.) Question any *marked* discrepancies in the records.

5. For children whom you believe to be gifted but who show such "negative" traits as misbehavior, impatience with classroom activities, boredom, refusal to do homework, lack of interest, or frequent absence from school, several steps may help. First, dis-

cuss the situation with the child. Then consult the teacher, guidance counselor, school psychologist, or the principal. Find out what provisions are made in class to challenge a gifted child. Look for discrepancies between scores on standardized achievement tests and classroom grades. Is the teacher grading behavior or achievement? Ask for a psychological evaluation of the child's abilities. If the school cannot provide it, seek it elsewhere (at the local university, a guidance clinic, or psychological service).

6. Work cooperatively with the school. Avoid adversarial situations.

7. *Always* give your child your protective and moral support. You are his or her first and best line of defense.

8. Help your child unlock leadership potential by supporting existing leadership training programs in his or her school and encouraging their establishment where such programs don't exist.

At home, a good initial frame of reference might be the list of traits, skills, and characteristics contained in the Leadership Identification Checklist that follows. Observing how often your child exhibits leadership-associated behavior actually yields an informal, but empirically based, profile of demonstrated or potential leadership ability. Hence, the checklist can be used to assess relative areas of strength and weakness and indicate what skills you can help your child develop further.

A LEADERSHIP IDENTIFICATION CHECKLIST FOR PARENTS

Derived from the definitions, issues, and characteristics associated with leadership ability and its use, the following list of traits and behaviors may indicate strong leadership potential in your child. They are applicable to all age groups, but are also relative to your child's age group. (For example, exceptional communications skills in a three-year-old will be different, of course, from exceptional communications skills in a twelve-year-old.)

This list has not been "statistically validated," but it does include portions of another list that has been validated for its predictability, as well as the views of several recognized leaders with high credibility on the subject.

This list is in no way exhaustive of leadership characteristics, but includes most of what appear to be essential ones. And remember, most children — no matter how gifted — will not display all these traits and behaviors. You may observe them in your child at home or school, at work or play. Check the appropriate column.

	Seldom or never	Occasionally	Considerably	Almost always
Leadership Characteristics*				
• Carries responsibility well, can be counted on to do what he has promised and usually does it well.	——	——	——	——
• Is self-confident with children his own age as well as adults; seems comfortable when asked to show work to the class.	——	——	——	——
• Seems to be well liked by his classmates.	——	——	——	——
• Can express himself well; has good verbal facility and is usually well understood.	——	——	——	——
• Adapts readily to new situations; is flexible in thought and action and does not seem disturbed when the normal routine is changed.	——	——	——	——
• Tends to dominate others when they are around; generally directs the activity in which he is involved.	——	——	——	——
Other Psychosocial Skills				
• Has strong interpersonal skills; can influence others to adopt some view, course of action, or direction.	——	——	——	——

	Seldom or never	Occasionally	Considerably	Almost always
• Shows understanding, empathy, and sensitivity to others' needs; expresses ethical or humanitarian concerns.	___	___	___	___
• Is acknowledged by peers as a role model; sets and demands high standards for self and others.	___	___	___	___

Other Cognitive/Academic Skills

• Sets goals and priorities; can plan and strategize, organize, and coordinate activities.	___	___	___	___
• Solves problems creatively; often called on by peers or teachers for ideas and suggestions.	___	___	___	___
• Shows good judgment, decision-making capacity; able to anticipate consequences of actions.	___	___	___	___

Other "Personality" Characteristics

• Is charismatic, magnetic, spontaneous, insightful; others seem to gravitate toward him or her.	___	___	___	___
• Shows independence, nonconformity of thinking; willingness to take risks.	___	___	___	___

	Seldom or never	Occasionally	Considerably	Almost always
• Is task-oriented in certain situations; shows discipline, persistence, and commitment in contexts and areas of high interest.	___	___	___	___

If you observe in your child several of these traits or behaviors marked in the third or fourth columns, there is indication of strong leadership ability, demonstrated or potential. Parents should not push their children to be leaders, however. The object is to provide opportunities and experiences for leadership to emerge.

*(From *Scales for Rating the Behavioral Characteristics of Superior Students* by Joseph Renzulli et al. The first six items were excerpted from Part IV: Leadership Characteristics. The full scale is available from Creative Learning Press, Mansfield Center, CT 06250.)

GIFTEDNESS IN SPECIAL POPULATIONS

Certain subpopulations of students bear special care in the identification process or they are likely to be missed and their giftedness to be unrecognized. Among these groups are the learning disabled and handicapped, minority children and the disadvantaged, and bilingual students.

Learning Disabled and Handicapped Students

Gifted children with learning disabilities may be labeled as "handicapped," and their giftedness can go unnoticed as a result. At best, they appear to be average students who are not recognized for special gifts, particularly in a school environment where administrators, teachers, and individual students find it hard to believe that a learning disabled student can, indeed, be "gifted."

Reporting in the *Journal for the Education of the Gifted,* Joan

Wolf and Janice Gygi of the University of Utah carefully document classification discrepancies found among learning disabled students. The findings of a study made in Illinois in 1980 show that out of 5,140 children screened through either a verbal or performance IQ test, 118 scored 120 or higher.

Examples given by Wolf and Gygi include a student of high intellectual ability unable to read at his grade level. A child may be in seventh grade, for example, struggling with mastery of second grade concepts and really be interested in a tenth-grade discussion of Shakespeare.

The authors refer to the book *Cradles of Eminence,* biographical accounts of four hundred twentieth-century world leaders, scholars, and other eminent persons, and note that more than half of these persons had difficulties in formal classroom settings. "Some of the 400," Wolf and Gygi point out, "were learning disabled students who found ways to compensate for their disabilities outside of the classroom." School experiences related by these world figures included "poor curriculum, dull, irrational or cruel teachers, abuse from other students, and classroom failure." Many of them, the article states, "avoided school whenever possible, finding that learning on their own was more rewarding."

George Patton, an example of such a student, didn't attend school at all until he was twelve years old and never read well. His parents and other members of his family spent hours reading to him. He was able to graduate from West Point Military Academy by memorizing entire lectures and texts. Another was Adlai Stevenson, who "avoided school whenever possible, preferring the education he received from an enriched home environment." And Pablo Picasso "felt he had no reason to study with teachers who had nothing to teach him."

Wolf and Gygi define gifted students as those who perform in the top 3 to 5 percent of the population. Giftedness is obvious, they feel, when a learning disabled student excels in visual or performing arts, but "problems arise when the student is gifted in the area of general intellectual ability" and exhibits behaviors associated with a specific learning disability. "Many students are incorrectly labeled as learning disabled," they state. "It has become popular to use the term for those who do not perform well in school for any reason."

They suggest use of parent reports and students' self-evaluations to assist in detecting areas of strength. In addition, they feel "the increasing use of observation and the development of behavioral checklists may be helpful in identification." Parents and teachers may tune in to the child's exceptional abilities during free time when the choice of a selected activity is the child's.

All the areas that indicate giftedness with non–learning disabled children — superior problem-solving skills, acute intellectual curiosity, high task commitment, superior reasoning ability — should be looked for to identify the gifted among the learning disabled, Wolf and Gygi conclude. It's a matter of seeing through the camouflage.

Creative or imaginative behavior that would be reinforced in most children might be deemed aberrant in an emotionally disturbed child. Efforts may be made to stifle those creative abilities rather than to encourage them. It is easy to see how these children would become frustrated when adults continually focused on what they are unable to do, rather than recognizing that the children also have talents and need to have the opportunity to practice and develop those talents.

Thus the "gifted handicapped" child is perhaps best regarded as neither gifted nor handicapped, but a unique individual who has a broad range of educational needs not satisfied by traditional programs in special education or traditional programs for the gifted. Unfortunately, because of the widespread influence of special education programs, the educational program for the gifted handicapped child is often characterized by strategies that address only the problems presented by the handicap. These programs fail to allow the child to maximize the potential areas of giftedness. The frustrations that face the child, the parents, and the schools stem from the fact that the handicapping conditions often mask the potential that the child may have, and the strategies appropriate for dealing with children who have similar handicaps may further mask the abilities of the gifted.

For parents of the gifted handicapped child to work effectively with the school in providing appropriate programs, it is important that the parents first recognize that most regular classroom teachers do not have the resources to recognize either handicapping conditions or giftedness beyond the most obvious and uncontested cases. Second, the typical special education teacher has been carefully trained to deal with a population that has characteristics so different from those of the gifted that most of his or her teaching strategies are not likely to be appropriate for a gifted child. Parents must make the school aware of the specific talents that the gifted handicapped child possesses, and then help the school identify appropriate intervention strategies that will meet the needs of the child.

In most cases, alerting the school and the child's teacher to the special abilities of a handicapped child is not approached so as to be received positively by school personnel. Assertions that the child is also gifted are often read as denial of the child's "real" problem. It is, therefore, important that carefully documented evidence of a child's special abilities be presented. Of course, a psychologist's evaluation that indicates talents is a valued piece of information, but testimony from former teachers, the presentation of products that indicate giftedness, and/or other performance data can be used to support the case.

In the process of attempting to alert the school personnel to potential giftedness in a handicapped child, use the provisions of Public Law 94-142 to your advantage. First, there should be a careful documentation of your child's performance and potential abilities. You may ask whether the tests that have been used to assess potential and performance may have been biased because of the child's handicap. For example, a child who has a motor coordination problem may perform poorly on a test requiring writing skills, or a child who is emotionally disturbed may refuse to cooperate with the examiner. A well-trained psychologist will recognize the influence of these variables and account for them in the interpretations of test scores.

It may be necessary to make the school aware that the child *can* be both handicapped and gifted at the same time. The teacher or school psychologist may be unfamiliar with the literature in this field. You should also contact the person in your school district who is responsible for programs for gifted children. These individuals are often able to provide information which will be useful in identifying the special abilities of a child and can suggest appropriate goals, objectives, and teaching strategies to be incorporated into an individual educational plan for your child.

Further cooperation with the school can be based on your experience and that of previous teachers with your child. If a teacher has been particularly successful in bringing about outstanding achievement with your child in some area, ask that teacher to identify ways that seem to elicit appropriate and productive behaviors. Identify settings in which the child performs at maximum efficiency. Help the teacher identify the preferred learning style of the child. Ask questions of friends about the relative effectiveness of teachers in recognizing special abilities.

Minority Children

One of the most sensitive and complex issues in the field of gifted education centers around the identification of children from minority cultures. The federal definition of giftedness, supported by considerable research, recognizes no racial or cultural bias in intelligence and talent. However, procedures for recognizing the gifts and talents of minority children are problematic; standardized measures, such as IQ and achievement tests, are fraught with sometimes subtle, sometimes overt, cultural bias.

Alexinia Baldwin, State University of New York at Albany, lists several variables that can influence the "functioning level" of minority children. Although all of these factors will not apply to all minority children, they can help illuminate a specific child's performance.

• The parents may not speak English, thus they cannot converse with the child in the language needed for upward mobility nor can they answer many of the child's questions.

• The home may not provide for normal stimulation because of lack of playthings designed for this purpose.

• The predominant discipline is external; that is, codes of behavior are dictated by parents or older brothers or sisters and are expected to be followed without question. An independence is not encouraged; thus children often lack self-motivation and problem-solving skills.

• The pragmatic nature of home activities and the acceptance of mature responsibilities out of necessity for survival do not allow for fantasy as a way for children to explore possibilities or develop flexible thinking.

• Out-of-school experiences are limited in variety, leading to

environmental isolation and a lack of the interactive skills associated with leadership ability.

Despite the factors that mitigate against a minority child's functioning as well in school as "majority" children, youngsters from
culturally different backgrounds often show evidence of high-level
ability to process information. Parents and teachers who are asked
to nominate children for a gifted program should be able to recognize certain "nonstandard" behaviors as signs of exceptional
ability.

Baldwin lists some things to look for: colorful, persuasive language skills with a peer group; ability to use commonplace items
for purposes other than intended (dolls and toys made from tin
cans, wagons and sleds made from packing boxes); capacity to
remember and report detailed information of events occurring in
the community (the story of tragedy or triumph of an individual
"outside the law"); ability to judge environmental situations (an
upcoming storm, danger signs) by cues and perceptions not usually
taught in school.

Bilingual Students

It has always seemed ironic that "bilingual education" began
with the premise that children in such programs came to school
with deficient intellectual skills. Of course, this is a natural conclusion where cognition is measured almost solely by standardized
tests requiring mastery of the English language.

It would seem, though, that bilingual students, by virtue of
being able to speak two languages, may have an advantage over
other students who cannot. Some research now supports this view.

According to Anne Gallegos of New Mexico State University,
research on bilingualism and cognition has suggested that bilingual
students "have a more flexible cognitive structure." Gallegos says
parents should be aware that learning a second language can
increase children's ability for divergent thinking.

Speaking primarily of Mexican-American children, Gallegos urged
the California State Federation of the Council for Exceptional
Children to bypass the standard guidelines when defining giftedness of minority children. Those guidelines, she said, were derived

from studies of Anglo children from middle or upper socioeconomic classes.

For example, Mexican-American children tend to display traits of giftedness behaviorally, Gallegos says, rather than on traditional intelligence measures. Data collected in Mexican-American communities indicate that a child's interaction with an adult at an adult level is a good indication of giftedness.

Citing research by Teachers College, Columbia University, Gallegos tells minority parents they may recognize giftedness in their children based on the following ten behaviors: unusual talents in music, drawing, rhythms, or other art forms; many "intelligent questions" about topics in which young children ordinarily have no interest; keen perception about things observed and retaining of that information; ability to concentrate for a longer period of time than other children of the same age; an interest in and comprehension of clocks and calendars at an early age; a large vocabulary and the use of entire sentences at an early age; telling of stories and recounting of events with great detail at an early age; conversing intelligently with older children or adults; ability to read with little or no formal teaching; writing short stories, poems, or letters.

Gallegos advises that minority parents who observe any of these traits in their children should request assessment of their children's abilities for "possible placement in a gifted program."

Taking Charge of Your Gifted Child's Education

THE EXPECTATIONS parents have for their gifted children demonstrate the need for parents to give careful consideration to, and be in control of, their children's education and development. Parents of gifted children cannot abdicate these responsibilities to the schools — or to dumb luck. The children may be "smart" and "supertalented," but they are still children — and "different." They need the guidance, support, and strong nurturing of parents and other members of the family. Parents must also get the children themselves involved in appreciating and using their gifts well. All must act on the basis of an informed awareness.

This chapter will provide some of the information parents of gifted children need: the child's point of view and being responsive to it; the parents' — and grandparents' — influence and roles in cultivating giftedness; the special challenges to single parents of gifted children; the dilemmas and choices surrounding early childhood education — day care, preschool, and the Super Baby phenomenon; and, finally, the consideration of private schools.

GIFTED CHILDREN SPEAK OUT!

Despite our heightened awareness about the needs of bright children, and despite our best intentions and efforts as parents and teachers, gifted children can *still* lose out on a full education. Perhaps we disregard a strong interest of theirs or maybe we fill their school days and years with items that we, not they, deem important. Instead, the key to success in working with gifted youngsters — or at least one of the keys — might be to ask them what it is they need or want to get from school.

In a recent survey by James R. Delisle of Kent State University, more than six thousand gifted children, aged five to thirteen, in the United States, Canada, and Europe, responded to questions about their perceptions of giftedness and the "high points and hassles" of being bright. The collective and typical responses to these questions represent a good cross-section of perceptions and attitudes of gifted children from such diverse geographic regions as British Columbia and Puerto Rico, Kentucky and California, and may provide other gifted children — and their parents — with some valuable insights. Starting with the obvious, they were asked, "Are you gifted?"

Some answers were:

• "I think I'm smarter than other kids my age because when my teacher gives a spelling test and it's time for me to go to my gifted program, she speeds up for me and the other kids can't keep up." — A girl, nine, Alaska.

• "I don't think I'm gifted because I can always learn something from others." — A girl, ten, Connecticut.

• "It depends. I *am not* what you'd call brilliant, but I'm not dumb either. I do get some nice comments on my reading abilities, though." — A girl, eight, Illinois.

• ". . . in a sensitive way, yes, I am gifted." — A boy, twelve, Georgia.

Children also responded to questions about the definition of giftedness, the pros and cons of special programs, and the term *gifted* itself (most children don't like it; they prefer the word *talented*). A consensus shared these views:

If I'm gifted, tell me in what way. "Sometimes I feel pressured into *always* being better than average." — A girl, twelve, Kansas.

Talk to me about my talents. "My parents have helped me feel OK about being intelligent. This gave me self-confidence." — A boy, eleven, West Germany.

Help me to put my talents into a real-world perspective. "I'm just different because I'm a little smarter, but that's not to say I'm *better* than anyone else." — A boy, nine, Georgia.

Friends and Classmates

Another area of concern to gifted children and their parents involves friendship. Many children report that intellectual differences make no difference in beginning or maintaining friendships ("My friends don't really seem to care, unless they're just keeping it inside them," said a twelve-year-old girl). Others find that academic talents tend to stifle relationships with anyone except other gifted children — a reaction many bright children attribute to jealousy from less able agemates. Still others hide their abilities in the hopes of being accepted as "just another kid." For example:

"Sometimes we'll do an easy thing, and I'll take my time to look like I'm just as puzzled as everyone else," a nine-year-old girl said.

"There are times I try to act dumb so that my friends who aren't so bright won't feel uncomfortable," said a twelve-year-old boy.

However, just as many children refuse to hide their lights under a bushel, as one comment illustrates: "I don't think I should ever hide my abilities. You should never hide what you are because then people will never know what you are inside."

Overall, gifted children seem content with their talents, despite the occasional gibes from classmates who don't realize that "being bright" is not something done to spite others.

Schools and Programs

Schools can help and hurt. To listen to the children tell it, it seems clear that someone is doing *something* right — and very often it's a teacher.

"Teachers encourage originality and creativity, stimulate your imagination and care about you personally as well as schoolwise. They understand you're not perfect and they make you feel good and happy. Teachers *can* help," said an eleven-year-old boy.

The most often stated desire of gifted children regarding learning is that they want hands-on activities, applied information. Despite the fact that many gifted children have high verbal skills and can relate their ideas using an impressive vocabulary, they *still* want to manipulate objects as well as ideas.

"I like learning by doing experiments and playing Mrs. Aaron's math and reading games," said a seven-year-old. "It's more fun than memorizing and doing workbooks."

"I enjoy hands-on activities most of all, because they allow you to discover for yourself. Nothing is more strange than finding that all those words and figures in your text actually mean something," a twelve-year-old girl commented. If only this one change were made in today's school curricula, a full half of the school-related complaints registered by the children surveyed would be remedied.

Another area where bright children believe that schools are already succeeding is in the establishment of programs for the gifted.

"Gifted programs help students to learn more and to 'keep up' with their brains," a girl in Puerto Rico said.

"I like to be around children who are as intelligent as I am," said an eleven-year-old boy.

For some children, the appeal is the work that can be done in such programs.

"We should learn how many inches from the Earth it is to the moon," a seven-year-old girl said.

"We should use computers, play advanced games, and learn a lot about ourselves and how to deal with the fact that other people will always expect more out of us," another girl, aged ten, observed.

However, not all is well in schools. In fact, the children are quite specific about those aspects of education that, for them, stifle learning. For example:

". . . Most of the time it's just review, review, review."

"I sit there pretending to read when I'm really six pages ahead."

"The work isn't challenging a lot of the time."

". . . the teachers often have me do extra things, like move desks or go get their coffee."

In summary, it appears that gifted children's needs at school will be met if the following points are considered:

• Give bright children credit for what they know. ("If you do something right once you won't have to do it again.")

• Offer bright children the chance for hands-on explorations. ("I'd like a science lab table, a planetarium and an invention room.")

• Remember that school is also a place for learning social skills.

("Teachers shouldn't say, 'There was only one A and so-and-so got it,' because the class snickers.")

• Allow the teacher to humanize the classroom. ("Once I told my teacher I was bored and *she* even admitted that it was boring. Somehow, that made it more bearable.")

Parents, as well as teachers, receive high grades from their children for the jobs they are doing — which, in this case, is child rearing. High on the list of children's compliments are those strategies parents have used to interest their youngsters in new topics:

"They have challenged me to do things that I don't even like to do just to prove that I don't really know the good from the bad . . . and again, they prove themselves right."

"My father teaches me everything in math before I even know what he is talking about. This helps me to get interested in new topics."

Regarding parental "weak spots," it is ironic that the area of greatest concern for gifted children is that they may not be "good enough" to please Mom or Dad. Such concerns lie in two areas: expectations of parents for their children and comparisons of siblings by parents.

"My mother expects me to be smarter than before I was labeled 'gifted'."

"I think my parents want me to do better even at home just because I'm gifted in school. I think they expect too much."

"I'm compared to my brother and sister by my father. It makes me feel like I have to do everything they did — like winning spelling bees and science awards."

Nevertheless, a large number of children reported that home-based expectations are neither too high nor too low, and that they are pleased to know that their talents are appreciated.

COPING WITH HIGH EXPECTATIONS — YOURS AND THEIRS

As Linus once remarked to Charlie Brown after reading a ringing note of encouragement that his mother had placed in his lunch, "There is no heavier burden than a great potential." Being the parent of a gifted student, you may sometimes feel that the burden is also yours and, in a way, it is. Joy and disappointment are part and parcel of being a parent, yet having a child with significant intellectual ability does bring special satisfactions and concerns.

When a child is identified as gifted, parents' and teachers' expectations almost always go up. Predictably, heightened expectations often result in intensified pressure on the student. And although gifted children acknowledge that the unbelievable pressure to achieve is mostly self-imposed, some of it is generated by the school and reinforced by the parents.

A high school boy said, "I try to take a challenging curriculum, but it's time-consuming, and there's so much pressure to get A's. I get a B and right away my parents think something's wrong."

Describing her own similar experience, one girl commented, "When my report card came home with a few more B's than I'd like, my mother said, 'What's wrong?' I told her, 'Mother, I'm not a machine.' But she kept at me with remarks like 'You got a B in that class, how come you're still talking to your friend on the phone?' "

A contrasting, but equally common, parental response is "Why do you study so much? You work too hard. Go out in the sun." You may think that it's supportive to say, as one mother did, "Honey, you're putting too much pressure on yourself. So you got a C on the test. You're still a fine person." Yet this daughter complained, "My mother meant well, but it's not helpful to tell me that it doesn't matter when it does matter — at least to me."

While you are trying to help your child, you may unwittingly complicate or even thwart the effort because of your strong identification with him or her. When children get good grades, their parents glow with pride. When gifted students receive a C or a D, it's only natural for everyone to be disappointed. However, when children have to cope with their parents' feelings as well as their own, the problems and the pressures are compounded. While students are struggling with their own self-criticism and disappointment, you may be adding to their burden by taking the matter too personally and becoming too actively involved in seeking a solution.

How can you help? Let your child feel that it is safe to vent unfiltered frustrations, anxieties, and disruptive emotions at home without jeopardizing the relationship with you or stimulating a diatribe. For example, you might say, "Billy (Joyce), am I on your back too much about your schoolwork and grades?" "Do you feel that I'm putting too much pressure on you or am expecting too much of you in school?" Give your son or daughter prime *listening* time and try to withhold your judgments — supportive, benign, or critical. If it's appropriate to comment, simply let your remarks reflect that you understand your child's feelings. For example, "I see, you are feeling a bit overburdened, then, and would prefer that I don't place so much emphasis on your grades." This is an open-ended remark that invites further comment from your child.

In general, gifted students tend to be highly self-critical, sensitive, and intense. If you tend to be a critical parent, your child may become defensive and actively or passively resistant. Gifted children may express their anger by getting poor grades or defying rules. They strike back indirectly at your pride in their accomplishments. They resist your efforts by proving that they, not you, control their fate, even if it means risking failure.

A gifted child who is not doing well in school often conceals a poor self-image under a veneer of braggadocio. He or she requires special support to develop a better sense of self-worth. As a parent, what you say and how you say it do matter. Frequent negative, sarcastic, or critical judgments can become self-fulfilling prophecies. Rather than offer criticism, listen to your child's rationalizations, such as blaming the teacher or even you for not helping. Talking about the matter can help your child develop insight and recognition of personal responsibility. For example, "Sue, I understand that you don't feel your teacher gave you enough guidance on this project and that you may have a personality conflict with him. But it's your job to ask for help when you need it. We all need help from time to time." Remember, gifted children don't need you to tell them that it takes studying to get good grades; they already know that. So work together to uncover the reasons behind the resistance and to understand the personal anxieties and ambitions that influence specific behavior. Your goal is to create an atmosphere in which it is safe for your child to share strengths and weaknesses without fearing ridicule, criticism, or even undeserved praise. The best way to do this is to be open about your own strengths and weaknesses whatever the context of the discussion is — school, work, athletics, for example. You want to convey to your child that not being perfect is OK, that it's human. You're not perfect either and you don't expect the child to be.

It's important for you to be especially thoughtful when your children encounter problems stemming from their own extraordinarily high standards. Gifted children often don't like to acknowledge that they don't know something about a subject, for example. This is really a matter of self-acceptance. They need to understand that denying imperfections and errors is detrimental. Learning to recognize one's personal strengths and shortcomings is a valuable lifelong skill.

As parents, we sometimes see our children as the most significant measure of ourselves. We look to their accomplishments to enhance our self-esteem, or we let their lack of achievement generate within us feelings of frustration and failure. Your reputation as a parent or as a person should not depend on your child's grades, appearance, or number of college acceptances; yet, as one high school senior said, "You should see the competitiveness among parents. They compare the number of honors or advanced placement classes we take. It's an ego boost to them that we're gifted or that we get into Harvard or Stanford. They feel 'special' because of us."

This reverse dependency can be one of the causes of conflict and pressure. Realistically, you cannot always expect appreciation from your children for giving them opportunities and a home base from which they achieve. Just as you hope that your child will make an honest effort at school and accept the consequences without guilt or arrogance, you must be content with the knowledge that you are doing what you believe is best.

Respecting your child's achievements, even though they may not be what you had hoped for, will foster your youngster's self-respect. Perhaps if you look past a disappointing report card, you will find your gifted son or daughter persistently and tenaciously pursuing a special personal interest that is unrelated to but just as worthy as your dreams and the aspirations of your friends.

THE PARENTS' AND GRANDPARENTS' ROLES IN CULTIVATING GIFTEDNESS

Quite a bit has already been mentioned in this chapter on the parents' collective role in helping their bright children develop well. However, a few studies and insights on the separate maternal and paternal roles are worth noting. The role of the grandparents is one that is considered less often but deserves special notice, too. And as the divorce rate continues to climb, single-parenting gifted children is also an area of tremendous importance.

Mothers

A question of increasing concern is whether it is essential for mothers to stay home with their young children. Mothers who do decide to stay home, believing that it's better for their youngsters' development, now have some new research to back up their instinct. Frances F. Schachter, clinical psychologist at Queens College and Coney Island City Hospital, maintains that the mother's presence at home encourages the development of the child's intellect, particularly if the family is a middle-class one.

Children with superior intellects have always been well represented in middle-class families, but often this abundance has been attributed to more resources within the home, greater communication among the children and adults, or wider experiences — opportunities to travel, for instance — as family members. Schachter, however, says that it may be the result of more attention given by mothers to very young children, from birth to age three.

In her study as reported in *Today's Child*, 70 preschoolers matched for age, sex, and background all attended the same "toddler center" in New York City part-time each week. The 32 middle-class working mothers in the study were "particularly intelligent and well educated, and their offspring could have been expected to score higher on intelligence tests than the children whose middle-class, *non*-working mothers had less education." However, the children whose mothers had full-time jobs scored significantly lower on IQ tests than those whose middle-class, less-educated mothers stayed home during the first three years.

Furthermore, Schachter says, it is only in the middle class that this phenomenon occurs. Other research shows the opposite effect with children from lower-class backgrounds whose mothers work. These children tend to do better on IQ tests than children from lower-class families where the mothers stay home.

Although the children with working mothers tended to be more self-sufficient, in other ways the study showed little difference between the children of working and nonworking middle-class mothers. They had similar language development and no obvious differences in emotional development.

Schachter claims that the important ingredient of middle-class mothering may be the speciality of the "tuning in" to young children, which substitute caretakers may not supply. Mothers with a choice, she advises, should consider not working or working only part-time during a child's very early years: "Independence is fine, but too much too soon can produce . . . a phony poise that can cover up real gaps in development."

Another study concerning maternal influence showed that gifted children achieve better in school if their mothers have high expectations for them. In a survey conducted by Idell Natterson, the home-school coordinator for Beverly Hills High School, a total of 22 mothers of high- and low-achieving gifted high school boys were asked about their child-rearing practices, particularly their expectations of academic performance. Natterson found that mothers of the high-achieving boys encouraged high academic performance beginning early in their children's lives. These mothers were strong educational models who stressed structured and goal-oriented educational activities.

The mothers of the low-achieving boys, on the other hand, were less committed to high academic achievement and more interested in their children's self-actualization and spontaneity. Although perturbed by their sons' poor classroom performance, these mothers tended to value equally their children's talents and achievements in nonacademic areas.

Although the Natterson study leaves many questions unanswered, and other studies have demonstrated that high achievement in academic subjects does not guarantee happiness or success in the "real world," it does validate the premise that practices in the home can influence school achievement. However, it is also acknowledged that an overemphasis on the academic side, with neglect of the personal and emotional side of a gifted child's development, can be detrimental to long-term growth and future success. It is important to encourage your child in his or her interest areas — not just your interest areas — and to respect him or her when these do not coincide with your own.

Fathers

How do fathers contribute to their children's intellectual growth? Can fathers actually make the difference in the cognitive development of a gifted child? Can they be the catalyst that sparks their sons' or daughters' giftedness? Recent studies suggest that the answer is "yes" to both questions.

While it is obvious that both mothers and fathers influence their children's intellectual growth, it is becoming clearer that they do so in different ways and that they influence boys' and girls' intelligence differently as well.

In his book *Fathers*, Ross D. Parke reports that as early as infancy male babies are affected by the presence or absence of their fathers. Those whose fathers do not live with them tend to score lower on cognitive development measures than male babies who have frequent contact with their fathers. The main predictors of male children's cognitive development appear to be the father's prowess as a playmate and his expectation of independence for the child.

With female infants, on the other hand, neither the father's absence nor the extent of his involvement, if present, seem to affect the child's early cognitive progress. A father's influence on his daughter's intellectual growth apparently comes a bit later in her development.

By late infancy and early childhood, the pattern of parental influence on their children's intelligence becomes well defined, Parke says. "Both mothers and fathers influence girls through verbal interaction and warmth and boys through physical interaction." However, which specific cognitive skills are affected by each parent is still unknown.

With school-age children Parke reports that fathers' presence and availability affect both boys' and girls' academic performance. Citing findings from "father absence" studies, Parke writes that "the sons of highly available" fathers attain superior academic performance and reach their full intellectual potential compared to boys from fatherless families.

Girls' cognitive development also seems to be adversely affected by the absence of fathers. Girls from intact nuclear families tend to have higher IQs, better achievement test scores, and higher grade-point averages than those from fatherless families.

Much speculation surrounds the "how and why" of paternal influence on children's cognitive development. Some researchers point to the father as a model of perseverance, achievement, and motivation. Children pick up their fathers' behavior patterns and values and assimilate them as their own. Others explain that the lower levels of cognitive ability of children from single-parent households are due to lesser amounts of attention and interaction than are found in two-parent families.

And what about nontraditional two-parent families? Parke cites a study, conducted by Norma Radin, that focused on American families of preschool children whose fathers were the *primary* caregivers. A significant conclusion drawn from this research showed that boys and girls raised primarily by their fathers scored higher in verbal ability than children raised in traditional family settings. Where fathers were the primary care-givers, both boys and girls showed a higher belief in their own ability to control and determine their fate than did children who were raised in traditional families. Girls, in particular, seemed to fare well from the influence of the child-rearing fathers. This appeared to be related to the fathers' awareness of "sexist influences" in society and their concern for their daughters' future success.

Adding to the complexity of parental influence on children's cognitive development is the issue of socioeconomic status. A study reported in *Child Development* suggests that a father's salary may have more influence on his children's IQ scores and educational achievement than his physical presence. A research team from Indiana, Purdue, and Cornell universities found that kids who were fatherless as a result of *divorce* performed nearly as well intellectually and academically as those with fathers, as long as the household was socially and economically stable.

Despite somewhat conflicting research findings — the jury is still out — it is apparent that in many cases the father, by virtue of his presence and availability, is a significant environmental influence on his son's and daughter's intelligence. And this can mean the difference between "average" and "gifted." It's not that fathers are more important than mothers (or vice versa, for that matter), but it is now acknowledged that having a father in the traditional role of "breadwinner" exclusively is not sufficient for children's optional cognitive development.

Grandparents

Grandparents have played significant roles in the lives of eminent personalities, and usually in positive ways. Adlai Stevenson's grandfather used to "coax the children into the library with milk and cookies, then read to them there while they enjoyed their refreshments," according to his biography in *Cradles of Eminence*. The grandfather read to them from *Hamlet*, and stimulated Stevenson's interest in history so much that the boy had read "all thirteen volumes of Markham's *The Real American Romance* before he was thirteen."

Margaret Mead devotes a whole chapter of her autobiography, *Blackberry Winter*, to the topic "On Being a Granddaughter." Mead says: "My paternal grandmother . . . was the most decisive influence on my life."

As Erik Erikson stated in a *Psychology Today* interview, "Old people can be generative. . . . They can be good grandparents, and not only to their own grandchildren. I'm convinced that old people and children need one another and that there's an affinity between old age and childhood that, in fact, rounds the life cycle."

There are several specific positive roles that grandparents can serve in gifted children's lives: as listeners, as storytellers and sources of information, as mentors, as identifiers of giftedness, as reinforcers of social values and standards, as guides to social living, and as sources of love, comfort, and security.

Grandparents as Listeners: Gifted children love to talk, to share their ideas and discoveries, and they frequently prefer older children or adults as an audience. For the very young, the talking (frequently more of a monologue) can just be the endless chatter of the child expressing wonder at natural phenomena. For the older child, it may be a description of a current school project, a special hobby or achievement.

Grandparents make ideal listeners. A child can describe an unusual achievement or the receipt of an award "because it will please Grandma or Grandpa to hear it," and not be accused of conceit or showing off. The grandparents can provide an appreciative, attentive audience, genuinely enchanted with the achievements or observations of their young progeny. By their affectionate attentions, grandparents will tend to encourage hobbies and special interests. Freed of the many responsibilities of parents, grandparents often indulge the child and cater to the interest or hobby, not only by purchasing suitable items, but also by sharing treasured collections or seeking out special information to share with the child.

Grandparents as Storytellers: Grandparents are the celebrated storytellers and, most often, the stories are true, rendered a bit romantic and exciting because they happened in that mysterious "long ago and faraway" place. For example, Scott Momaday, Pulitzer Prize winner for his novel *The Way to Rainy Mountain*, recalls the tales his grandmother of the Kiowa Indian tribe told him: "Although my grandmother lived out her long life in the shadow of Rainy Mountain, the immense landscape of the continental interior lay like memory in her blood. She could tell of the Crows, whom she had never seen, and of the Black Hills, where she had never been."

It is evident that a major role of grandparents for gifted children, as well as all children, lies in their capacity for providing interesting and unusual information. Since gifted children have an insatiable thirst for knowledge, this is a particularly significant role, which is usually enjoyable to both. It is often the grandparents, more than any other persons, including the parents, who can provide lessons in genealogy, history, geography, customs, standards, time, and distance. They provide the link between the past and the present, and are perhaps the best interpreters of the significance of time in our lives.

Many children have learned about foreign lands, customs, language, and historical developments through their grandparents. The grandparents like to reminisce and appreciate their receptive audience. The children listen, thinking they are hearing a marvelous story, meanwhile learning many lessons of life. For gifted children, who have retentive memories and a strong capacity to see relationships, these stories form a foundation for future reference.

Grandparents as Mentors: Parents of gifted children should take advantage of the specialized knowledge and skills the grandparents may have. For example, a boy of seven in a class for the exceptionally gifted became intrigued by trigonometric problems. A patient grandfather undertook to teach him, and the boy showed impressive knowledge of the subject for his age. Immigrant grandparents in this country frequently converse with each other in a foreign language and use it with the child as well. A gifted child has no difficulty with the transition from one language to another. Such bilingualism should be encouraged, especially when the child is gifted.

Grandparents happily share the special knowledge they have with these very receptive young pupils and will pursue special interests with them. Realistically, parents frequently are so pressed with other responsibilities that they, too, welcome the time that grandparents make available to the child.

Grandparents as Identifiers of Giftedness: Although no study is available on this subject, the biographical literature and experience with gifted children indicate that grandparents can be significant sources of information. It is likely, because of the constructive roles they play, that they have access to insights about the child that may escape even parental observation. Achievement-oriented parents, for instance, set high expectations for very young children and often take for granted behavior that is far above normal for most children. Grandparents may have a broader base for reference and thus judge the child's abilities more objectively.

Grandparents as Reinforcers of Values and Standards: To the extent that the grandparents have relinquished their supervisory roles over their own sons and daughters, there are distinctions in roles between parents and grandparents. In all situations, these distinctions in roles must be respected.

Grandparents have the obligation to reinforce constructive values established by parents and to maintain a careful regard for the ultimate authority of the parents. Gifted children are quick to sense discrepancies in attitude. These can confuse the child and undermine the parent-child relationship. Casting a child in a mold, by saying "You are just like your father" or "You are just like your mother" when he or she misbehaves, deprives the child of individuality, creates a sense of inevitability that can be harmful, and diminishes the status of the parents. Because the gifted have such retentive memories, they can suffer from such unfavorable comparisons even more than the average child would.

Differences between parents and grandparents should be discussed privately. Certainly, grandparents need to keep in mind changing patterns of behavior as generations change and to focus only on significant differences in values. Parents, on the other hand, can find guidance in grandparents' tendencies to be less restrictive and more tolerant of infractions. The grandparent knows from experience that "looking the other way" or moving to prevent misbehavior can frequently be more productive than observing and punishing every minor fall from grace. The grandparents are not as likely as parents to set a higher standard of behavior for a gifted child than for other children.

Grandparents as Guides to Social Living: Grandparents provide lessons in social living in ways that the child can appreciate and understand. They may have slightly different customs from the parents — the clothes they wear, their values, what they eat — or particular needs that must be respected. The child accepts these differences in their proper context and thus is introduced to the world of cultural diversity. The child with loving and involved grandparents comes to understand something of human frailty, of beginnings and endings, of life and death. A warm bond between a child and grandparent may be the cause for grief at separation, but it also creates a basis of understanding and acceptance of the patterns of life. The gifted, with their insightful view of the world, have much to gain from such experience. Parents should encourage them to develop such understanding and compassion, so that they can transfer these traits to their later roles of responsibility and leadership.

Grandparents as Sources of Love, Comfort, and Security: No child can have too many sources of love and care. The wider the circle, the happier the child. Grandparents should, quite naturally, be an integral part of this network. Because the gifted seem to understand events more readily, and because they seem to be able to take care of themselves with greater ease, they are frequently denied the satisfaction of these emotional needs. Parents frequently respond to these children on the basis of their intellectual capacities rather than in terms of their emotional and developmental needs. On the other hand, grandparents may marvel with frank admiration at a major achievement, but seem to retain a capacity to superimpose a demonstration of affection that may be shunned yet secretly wanted and relished by the child.

The presence, or even the memory, of an understanding, loving grandparent can serve as an emotional bulwark against the slings and arrows of an unfriendly world. Wise parents include grandparents in their arsenal of security and protection for their children.

Single Parents

How are single parents meeting the needs of their gifted children? Do gifted children have more difficulty adjusting to divorce? It is hard to find answers to these questions, but they are becoming increasingly important as nearly one out of every five school-age children lives with a single parent.

Studies have traditionally shown that intellectually gifted children are more likely to come from two-parent homes and that there is a high correlation between performance and family income. Lewis Terman, creator of the Stanford-Binet Intelligence Scale, found that boys whose performance began to drop off in high school were more than twice as likely to come from divorced homes. And Parke reports in *Fathers* that studies show that cognitive development of both girls and boys is adversely affected by the absence of fathers.

On the other hand, highly creative children often have to overcome some kind of problem in childhood, either with parents, siblings, or themselves, according to Max Fogel, formerly director of Mensa's Education and Research Foundation. "As long as children aren't psychologically crushed by problems in the home," says Fogel, "divorce may actually enhance their creativity by heightening the need to find their own way and by giving them more responsibility than is usually allowed in American homes." Though very little guidance or counseling is being offered to single parents of gifted children, single parents who are successfully coping with their gifted children's needs seem to share some common characteristics — a positive attitude and a "we'll make this work" collaboration with their children.

"Gifted children are more perceptive and intuitive," says one mother, "so a parent should be honest about his or her feelings and the financial situation without burdening them with the problems. I told my children we really didn't have a lot of money to work with but that didn't mean we were going to be held down; we'd find ways to do things." Another mother found herself reviewing the household budget in detail with her seven-year-old daughter so she would understand why they couldn't afford the trips that others took. In a nice turnaround on popular wisdom, several children developed their gifts while working — out of economic necessity — in their parents' businesses.

"I let my children see I'm not perfect," says a mother of two young adolescents. This type of honesty is especially important for gifted children in single-parent homes, says Susanne Richert, director of Gifted Education at the Educational Information and Resource Center in Sewell, New Jersey. "They seem to have an obsession with perfection and tend to be highly ethical. They will challenge parents on a moral level which can be especially difficult without the support of another adult." Single parents also tend to look to their gifted children for their own self-esteem, which places an extra burden on them, she says. But "by showing our gifted children we're not perfect, we allow them to let down a bit on themselves."

Many mothers found building their own self-esteem and becoming assertive more painful than the economic hardships they experienced, particularly in the early years of their divorce, but well worth while for themselves and their gifted children. Not only did these parents come to rely less on their children for their own sense of worth, but their children came to see in their mothers a special strength and capacity for rising above adversity. Support groups ranged from Al-Anon and Parents Without Partners to some mothers who formed a "parachute group" inspired by Richard Bolles's *What Color Is Your Parachute?* "We worked our way through the book, looking at our gifts and skills," says one mother. "Then we created a summer camp for our children, producing and filming a puppet show."

Studies of single fathers raising children show they experience guilt and a sense of loss and often seek psychotherapy or counseling during the first two years after divorce. Although single-parenting placed limitations on their earnings, working hours, and work relations because of time constraints, none reported a significant loss of income in assuming their new role.

Most comfortable with the effect of divorce on their gifted children are parents who have arranged joint custody (sharing important decisions about their child's upbringing) or shared custody (sharing physical care). They feel it diminishes their children's greatest fears — that they will be abandoned and that they may be responsible for the breakup — and gives them the support of two parents on a regular basis. "Our children know we are both interested in their intellectual development," says one father.

Joint custody also provides two listeners to children's problems and two points of view, which are particularly important for the gifted child who tends to ask the "hard-to-answer" questions at an early age. One father sees his daughter benefiting from multiple points of view because of what he calls "an opening up" of the family. "She is meeting many more people than before because there are more people in my life now and she attends my film openings — and also spends Saturdays with her mother."

Meeting the young child's needs for intellectual and creative stimulation seems to be the easiest task for the single parent. A single mother says, "We go to the library and read together often. I phone county agencies to find good, inexpensive activities and I look for day care that provides a learning experience." One parent of a nine-year-old son takes advantage of the "teachable moment." "I discuss the meaning of the statistics on the back of a baseball card or what we're hearing on the news, and I include my son in my conversations with others."

But meeting the needs of the preschooler who has a short attention span or who may be "hyperactive," as many gifted children are, is extremely difficult when there is no one to "time share." One mother says, "My three-year-old son was terribly curious and got into a lot of trouble. I tried to allow for his creativity, but I never knew how much space to give him and how much firmness. Finally I found a psychiatrist who showed me how to be firmer in placing limits. My son and I both liked each other better when I had more control."

Susanne Richert counsels single parents to find other parents who have similarly demanding children and "trade time with them." This gives the parent a rest and the child a peer to engage his or her interest. Friends, neighbors, and relatives may also share some of the burden at this time and act as role models. One mother with two children became a Quaker after her divorce and finds that her Friends Meeting provides her with an extended family. "I can borrow a grandparent whenever I need one, and my children have developed a lot of adult friendships."

A number of mothers found family therapy helped their gifted children adjust to the new family structure. Gifted boys were angrier with their fathers for "leaving" them than their gifted sisters were, and sometimes became underachievers, "dropping out" intellectually or developing behavior problems.

One mother talked about her gifted son who was separated from both his father and his stepfather through divorce. "He became severely depressed," she said, "and flunked out of his accelerated class. He writes poetry, reads every book by an author that interests him, but slides through high school without doing any work. He's become highly skilled at programming computers and I hope to find a college-level course that will stimulate his academic interest again."

Another woman turned to the Big Brother organization for a surrogate father when her son was seven. "His 'Big Brother' took him camping and fishing," she said, "but didn't just separate him from my daughter and me. We were all invited to picnics with his family, and our families are still close friends."

Boys from single-parent homes also seem to have more problems dealing with the nonconformist behavior that goes with giftedness. A mother of a twelve-year-old boy says, "It's hard when they go through that time of trying to be like everybody else. My son has finally adjusted to sixth grade by becoming the class clown."

Girls find separation from their fathers most difficult if it occurs when they are in seventh or eighth grade. According to the Philadelphia psychologist Suzanne Schneider, who works with gifted adolescents and adults, the gifted girl needs a father or significant male at this time to validate both her sexuality (to make her feel she is a desirable member of the opposite sex) and her competence. Fearing their daughters would hide their giftedness, which is a common act, mothers reported enlisting the help of male relatives and friends.

Other mothers mentioned the positive effect of mentors. One gifted fourteen-year-old boy found the family veterinarian encouraged his interest in horses. Working for his mentor provided money to buy his own horse and the expertise to become a horse trainer.

Schools with good academic programs and extracurricular activities are vitally important for the gifted child from a single-parent home. "I'm really fortunate to have a good school system that offers science fairs, plays, gymnastics, a school newspaper," says one father. "My seven-year-old daughter signs up for everything." Another mother feels fortunate that her school recognized her twelve-year-old daughter's dramatic talent and offered her the opportunity to participate in many high-quality theatrical productions. Both the drama and voice coaches became her mentors.

Yet another mother says the school let her down. "I didn't know my oldest child was gifted until the school nurse mentioned it to me, rather casually, one day. Sally was never challenged in the classroom and decided if things didn't come easily they weren't worth doing. I wish I'd had the emotional energy to push her more, but I didn't even have enough for myself at that time."

One parent, on the other hand, has complained to the school about her gifted daughter's boredom in algebra class. She arranged a conference with the teacher, the guidance counselor, and her daughter to try to solve the problem. She says she has found it important not to be a "closet single parent," despite the fear that labeling children as coming from a "broken home" can set up negative teacher expectations.

Although single-parenting of the gifted child places extra burdens on the parent, several mothers said their children would never have developed their giftedness if the tension in the household had not been removed. And they attribute their children's maturity and sense of responsibility to the need for them to contribute actively to the family's survival, both financially and emotionally.

Some mothers spend all their free time with their children, feeling they need as much attention as possible, and other mothers and fathers say they need to date in order to restore their emotional energy.

In a recent study of sixty California families five years after divorce, a psychiatrist, Judith Wallerstein, and a psychologist, Joan Kelly, found the children who had made the best adjustment were living with a psychologically healthy parent — the same factor that produces good adjustment to life in the two-parent home.

EARLY CHILDHOOD EDUCATION
FOR GIFTED CHILDREN

Baby talk apparently is a good idea, after all. In fact, talking to your baby right from birth may be one of the most important contributions you can make toward the intellectual development of your children. Two research studies confirm that parents are on the right track for raising an intellectually brighter child if they actively engage their child in early and deliberate communication.

J. V. Carew, as reported in *Young Children* by the early childhood specialist Joseph Stevens, Jr., of Georgia State University has found that verbal interaction is critical to mental development. Carew studied groups of preschool children reared at home and enrolled in day care and discovered for both groups that a high percentage of adult-led language activities was a good predictor of later high IQ scores in these children.

Just routine talk isn't good enough, however. The researchers say that adults must "put out" to stimulate the minds of infants and toddlers. This includes such focused involvement as labeling and describing things, comparing and contrasting objects, classifying things according to kind and function, and questioning activities.

For optimal intellectual growth (again reflected by IQ), the child needs to dominate these "dialogues" starting around eighteen months of age, the study found. No longer merely the "active observer," the child should be allowed to take the lead, while the parent continues to provide rich and substantive talk at the child's cue. In short, what you put in is what you get out.

Not critical, but still intellectually "valuable," according to the study, are other activities usually associated with stimulating intellectual growth. Among them are stacking and building, which involve spatial and fine-motor abilities; reasoning and problem-solving activities, such as "experiments" in which children measure the relative volumes of jars or glasses; and activities that involve large-muscle play, such as expressive-artistic and explorative play (pretending, dressing up). These were not found to have a "decisive" effect on measurable intelligence.

This kind of parenting effort is just the tip of the iceberg with respect to what has been dubbed the "super baby" movement. Thousands of high-achievement-oriented parents are seeing to it that their children start in designer diapers, fine-tune their gross motor coordination at gyms for tots, appreciate classical music (and even play it!) at the age of two, and are enrolled in a top nursery school with a view toward a top college.

This can be rough on children *and* parents. As far as the popular press is concerned, the "burnout" syndrome, so common with teachers, high-powered executives, and athletes, finally has infected parents — especially those trying to raise "super babies."

There is a book out now, *Parent Burnout* by Joseph Procaccini and Mark Kiefaber, and newspaper articles from coast to coast warn parents who are juggling jobs, music lessons, ballet classes, private schools, and waiting lists for the "right" nursery schools that they are headed for a good case of this malaise.

Procaccini says, for example, that parents who haunt the nursery school waiting lists, but find that their children aren't on the one they want, get the attitude that "Well, that's it. It's finished. I might as well just send them to the Salvation Army because that means Harvard's out, that means no Nobel Prize."

In an article in *The Oregonian*, Mary Elizabeth York, coordinator of early childhood education studies at Portland State University, chided parents who request reading and writing at the preschool level for their offspring. That's a "misinterpretation" of research that shows children can learn vast amounts in their first five years, she says. "Parents are neglecting to look at the way preschoolers learn, through play and at their own speed," York said.

The same theme occurred in a full-page feature on gifted children in *USA Today*. As reported there, Columbia University Teachers College offers parent seminars for those trying to raise gifted children and feeling a great deal of anxiety about doing so.

"When parents perceive their child has gifts, they feel an awesome responsibility," says James Borland, codirector of the Columbia University Center for the Study and Education of the Gifted. "They don't want to squander their child's chance for success. Giftedness is not something you pin down easily and it's not going to disappear if you make one mistake." The seminars, he said, reassure parents that "being a good parent for gifted kids is the same as for other children."

Mothers and fathers experiencing "parent burnout" over raising their youngsters — especially infants and toddlers who have come to be called "super babies" — can do something about their situation. With appropriate rest and relaxation, a bit of counseling, and a change of philosophy and attitude, the signs of stress and anxiety may eventually be overcome, giving way to a healthy mind and body once again.

Compare that relaxation with the possible lasting effects of making critical mistakes with your child almost from birth — not by doing too little, but by doing too much!

It can also be detrimental to suggest that unless you do nothing your child will develop emotional maladjustment. Many parents are doing more than just encouraging their children to explore diverse avenues of experience and introducing them to a host of alternatives through which to discover themselves. They're pushing their kids everywhichway for mostly the wrong reasons. Early childhood educators are concerned that, indeed, parents may get results opposite from what they intend. Their children may turn off to learning and become underachievers.

Although the super baby phenomenon, for all its "sensationalized" aspects, does reflect a general acknowledgment of the advances in knowledge of early childhood development and reinstates the value of the intellect in our society, it's an acknowledgment that has gone awry. Also reflected in this phenomenon is insecurity and a lack of confidence in our educational system, a fear of children being ill prepared for an uncertain future, and a feeling that one must "take things into one's own hands" by buying every possible advantage and edge for the child during the formative years. After all, a top nursery school could start the child on the fast track to Harvard.

Parents need to be sensitive, caring, and responsive to their children, never forgetting they are individuals. They need to offer them opportunities, of course, and give them lots of encouragement — and an "out" if they aren't handling what the parents think they should.

Indeed, perhaps far worse and more irrevocable than "parent burnout" is "child burnout."

Day Care

You may not know whether your child is gifted at the age of five or six months, but if you have her or him enrolled in a daycare environment at that age, the outlook is not good for the child's optimal development, according to Burton L. White, director of the Center for Parent Education in Newton, Massachusetts.

White says parents "cheat themselves and their children" by using day care as "storage facilities" during the early months of child development, and that the absence of an optimal rapport between the child and his environment can lead to personality problems and insecurity as the child grows older.

Why can't an "optimal rapport" be established in a day-care

setting? "Because substitute care systems don't attend as much to the child as a parent would," White explains. "These early months are the foundations and precursors to optimal development. . . . It's not an easy adjustment for the child in such a setting."

White recommends that in the majority of cases no substitute care take place for the first six months of the child's life. Afterward, a half day at a time is permissible, White says. If it's impossible to stay home with the infant, then in-home substitute care — by a grandparent or other relative, for example — is the next best thing. A person should be selected for his or her capacity to "tune in" to the needs of the child by playing and talking to it profusely.

Assuming your child develops optimally for the first six months, there are other measures you should take, according to White, to prevent an early loss of potential. By the age of seven or eight months, for example, a gifted child may show signs of precociousness or advanced abilities with language. These skills should be encouraged and reinforced by constantly talking to the child, he says, "but some parents are silent and don't even talk to their children at this age, don't feed into the language system."

To the cognitive development of a child, gifted or not, parental silence can have devastating effects, which may or may not be made up later, White explains. "No one knows for certain."

Another critical period of development takes place at about one and a half years of age, when "nine out of ten children begin to lose their potential and fall back intellectually," White claims. The fact that even gifted children may suffer losses in intellectual capacity results from a conflict between developmental needs and survival needs. White states that parental concerns for the child's safety dominate between seven and eighteen months, a situation that "causes many parents to inhibit their child's movement, creative exploration, and sense of curiosity."

Rather than inhibit developing exploration and curiosity, White insists, "child-proofing" your home — putting breakable objects out of the child's reach, blocking off stairways — is as important for optimal cognitive development as it is for safety.

Preschool and the Transition

It is unfortunate that in an era of computer technology and an explosion of general information, parents remain concerned but uncertain about the benefits or hindrances of preschool learning environments for a gifted child. Some may be concerned about the adverse effects of pushing a child; others may be anticipating problems if the child already has mastered some early subject matter upon entering school. It is quite clear that learning experiences before entry into school are more beneficial than hindering.

Early educational stimulation has long been considered important in this country as well as in others. Research by Benjamin Bloom revealed that between birth and six years of age, children's IQs are about three-fourths crystallized, so that the question of whether or not early schooling is necessary is seemingly moot.

Instead the discussion has centered around the pros and cons of the educational experiences that should occur for preschoolers. There are four basic kinds of schooling available.

Many parents and psychologists have felt that schooling outside the home should occur for part of the day and that its purpose should be for socialization only. For these people, the thought of "burdening" a preschooler with a structured school program is unconscionable. They feel that the child's preschooling must be a very warm and loving environment filled with the rich experiences that come as a part of the family and the community. This type of program is the most child-centered, and directions for activities originate with cues from the children themselves.

There are others who feel that there should be a highly structured environment that will help the child cope with his or her expectations of school. Many parents pursue this type of structure to extend their children's learning and "push" their children ahead. Parents of children with an unusual ability to perceive knowledge far beyond expectations for their age often desperately seek a structured plan to enhance or accelerate their children's knowledge. This type of program is directed by the teacher, and the child has little control over what is learned. These programs lay great dependence upon extensive planning.

A third type of program, which has received wide acceptance, is one that combines elements of both the types listed above. This one combines direction by both teacher and child, and if it is well run, takes away much of the argument against structured programs.

A fourth type of experience or learning situation is an extension of experiences in the home and family environment, just as the occasions arise, without any formal or planned program.

More information on preschool experiences is given in *A Parent's Guide to the Education of Preschool Gifted Children*.

The group of problems the child may encounter upon entry into "regular" school, says Alexinia Baldwin, State University of New York at Albany, will be related in some measure to the type of early program he or she has experienced. For example, a child who is accustomed to exploring many creative answers to a problem may find frustrating the more rigid structure of the school and lack of time with the teacher for exploring these ideas. At the other end of the continuum, a child who has experienced disciplined attention to detail and directions during a preschool experience might suffer and endure many hours of inadequate stimulation in regular school that could squelch any motivation to excel.

Some of the specific problems that parents can expect young gifted children who have had preschool experiences to face when entering school are:

• *Boredom:* Because of the slow pace set by the teacher in order to accommodate the skill level of the other students in the class, a gifted child may find little that is stimulating in the lessons. Parents can expect a resistance to attending school, complaints about being ill, and daydreaming in class. These are some obvious manifestations of boredom, but there is other behavior that can be traced to boredom, such as disruptive activities, sullenness, or withdrawal.

• *Acquiescence:* This is a most disheartening reaction because acquiescence means conforming to the norm in classroom behavior, social attitudes, and levels of achievement. A gifted child who is far beyond the group in knowledge and skills tends to "adjust" to the situation in order to fit the normal pattern. Many will become lazy thinkers and classic underachievers.

• *Superiority Complex:* The high level of knowledge and skill gifted students bring when first they enter school can give them a feeling of superiority to their classmates. This feeling sometimes causes intolerance of others of the same age and subsequent isolation from the group.

• *Aggression:* Some gifted children have a low tolerance for unstimulating or repetitive activities. If the child feels rejection, boredom, or lack of challenge, the frustration can come out in aggressiveness. Attempts to control the behavior instead of looking for the cause can compound the problem.

A look at these problems would suggest that an extension of experiences for the gifted preschooler is a hindrance, rather than a help, and thus a disadvantage. However, in spite of the impending school problems, early learning experiences are an advantage to the child. *The child will be more aware of her capabilities, be better prepared to pursue knowledge independently, have a stronger self-concept, be better prepared to cope with differences that will set her apart from her peer group, and have an opportunity to increase her knowledge in the area she is most interested in.*

It is important that the teacher be made aware of the experiences your child has had in preschool. A conference when the child is enrolled would be helpful. If the school your child is about to enter does not have a plan for meeting the needs of the gifted, then a cooperative effort on the part of parents and teachers to encourage such program attention should be fervently pursued.

PRIVATE SCHOOL

Should you send your gifted child to private school? Well, that depends.

The factors that lead increasing numbers of parents each year to remove their children from public school were the topic of a special seminar sponsored by the Education Writers Association in conjunction with the Johnson Foundation in Racine, Wisconsin.

Although the movement toward private education is by no means epidemic (nonpublic schools constitute about 19 percent of all elementary and secondary schools and contain about 11 percent of all students), there are definite reasons why the statistics are growing. "When concerned parents see their public schools as inadequate," says John Esty, president of the National Association of Independent Schools in Boston, "they'll put their kids in private school."

In explaining the shift from public to private schools, Esty cited concerns over discipline, academic standards, quality of teachers, parental expectations, and ethical issues as the major determinants in parents' decisions.

Church-affiliated schools make up the largest percentage of nonpublic schools and represent their fastest growing segment. However, enrollment in high-tuition schools (over $1,500 per year) has increased significantly since 1966. According to Donald Erickson, director of the Institute for the Study of Private Schools at UCLA, there is usually an inverse relationship between these two categories: the former offer varying degrees of religious identity and doctrine; the latter promise academic superiority.

Studies on demographics and socioeconomic status suggest that "superior academic services" are primarily what motivate upper-middle- and upper-class parents to enroll their children in high-tuition schools. They have exceptionally high aspirations for their children, Erickson says, so they seek out superior services — better teachers, smaller classes, closer supervision, better rapport with parents. He also cites an awareness of the value of good "connections" as entering into their decisions.

Are such academic services of high-tuition schools "superior"? Private schools offer what allegedly cannot be obtained "free" in public school — "responsiveness." (They are usually described by their school as "responsive to them.")

Erickson hypothesizes that the following operating characteristics can reasonably be expected of private schools: greater parent commitment and involvement; social cohesion, a closeness among parents and school staff; a sense of doing something special; a down-to-business attitude; orderly classroom conditions; strong teacher commitment; an emphasis on student learning; and above-average levels of academic achievement.

Specific advantages of nonpublic schools also tend to include specialized programs suited to the ability levels and interests of their students and good student-teacher ratios (on the average fifteen to one in elementary schools) conducive to individual attention.

But not everyone agrees that superlative operating characteristics can be obtained only in private schools. For example, Theodore Sizer, former Harvard dean and chairman of a study of high schools, says that "the largest private school system in the nation is suburbia." Esty agrees that social class distinctions and property values determine to a large extent the school population, the quality of education, and the degree of cultural and ethnic diversity of a community.

Should you send your gifted child to a private school? A general guideline might be this: if your child's public school offers what are listed above as private school advantages, or if the characteristics of the public school satisfy the main reasons cited for choosing a private school, your child's public school may be quite adequate. In fact, there is some evidence suggesting that a public school's ethnic heterogeneity more accurately reflects a microcosm of the "real world" than does that of private schools.

However, if the positive characteristics of private schools are not present in your child's public school, and if you can afford an alternative, you might give serious consideration to joining the independent school movement. Each school, public as well as private, must be evaluated on its own merit, of course; but the decision will be made on how well a particular institution motivates, challenges, and develops your child's exceptional abilities.

Schoolwork and the Gifted Child

THOUGH THE question of whether or not the gifted and non-gifted children learn in different ways has been controversial, studies have shown that general differences in learning *styles* do exist. Research using the *Learning Styles Inventory* developed by Joseph Renzulli and Linda Smith at the University of Connecticut to discover learning-style preferences of the gifted, found that these children tend to choose educational games, independent study, and discussion over six other learning and teaching techniques. Both gifted and nongifted students like drill and recitation least of all. According to the research, gifted students showed less preference or tolerance for lectures and projects than nongifted students did.

It was also discovered that learning style preferences are not static, that they change and are "a function of sex, grade level, favorite subject, IQ level and whether the student's locus of control is perceived as internal or external."

What about the "back-to-basics" trend? The National Assessment of Educational Progress, a project of the Education Commission of the States in Denver, Colorado, has reported that the "back-to-basics" movement, which greatly influences education in the early grades, often focuses on lower-level skills, "perhaps at the expense of a challenge for more able learners." It explained that basic skills are not necessarily the fundamentals needed for acquiring higher-order cognitive skills. Nor are the teaching skills used for the basics the same as those for higher-order skills. Approaches to teaching fundamentals to gifted children need to be imaginative — always including inquiry, problem solving, critical thinking, and, if possible, a creation or product of some kind.

Parents of gifted children should be acutely aware that, as bright as their children may be, if the children are not sufficiently challenged in appropriate ways, there is a real danger of their becoming underachievers, either from boredom or insecurity. Parents should be aware, too, that whatever learning style the gifted child prefers, simply adding more and more work is not the best way to help this child use his or her intellectual gifts. Accelerating the course of a child's study does not develop the higher learning skills with which the gifted child needs to be challenged and fulfilled.

UNDERACHIEVEMENT

Underachievement is fueled by pushing the child incessantly to do more, forcing him to take risks, and establishing a pattern of inappropriate praise. According to James Delisle of the Kent State University, writing in the *Roeper Review,* gifted children suffer if they know that they are disappointing their parents and teachers, and come to assess themselves in relation to their "failures" rather than their successes. The discrepancy between what a child accomplishes (or fails to) and what others expect of him, Delisle points out, can be defined as "perceived" underachievement. He emphasizes that it is important for parents and teachers to examine their own attitudes and behavior to lessen the child's conflicts, lest his or her feelings of self-worth become totally eroded and exceptional abilities neutralized.

Among the possible conflicts are:

• *Pushing vs. Pulling:* The underachieving gifted child who is pushed is given the explicit or subtle message: "You should be doing more." Guilt and a lowered self-concept are the obvious and debilitating effects of such pressure. If the child knows he is failing to measure up, why should he try? The result is apathy.

The "pull" side of this duality, according to Delisle, is an internal, self-initiated pursuit of excellence that allows a gifted child to acknowledge shortcomings and personal dissatisfaction without a detrimental effect on his or her own image. Here's an example: insisting on perfect spelling papers — when the child's marks are consistently in the 90's — is pushing that can have detrimental effects. Pulling means giving the child credit for good work, but also conveying gently, "I know you yourself want to do better. Perhaps you're being a bit careless or need to review the rules for tricky words."

• *Risk Taking vs. Risk Making:* The source of risk taking, Delisle states, is once again an agent outside the child: parent or teacher. Perceived by the child as another kind of pushing, and coupled with the fear of failure (attaining less than perfection), risk taking can result in inertia.

In contrast is risk making, which Delisle says deemphasizes the central role of parents and teachers — except for "cursory guidance but blatant encouragement" — and allows the child to pursue an untried activity solely under the motivation of his own genuine interest. Take music lessons, for example. "John, I think you're capable of studying a difficult instrument like the violin. Let's have you take lessons." This is forcing the child to become involved in something that may be very risky to the tranquility of his or her world. In contrast, children should be encouraged to pick their own activities to try. "John, you mentioned you'd like to take music lessons. Have you given any thought to what instrument you'd like to study?"

• *Praise vs. Encouragement:* Praising a child is closely related to rewarding only the child's best work. Less than the best is not worthy of praise. Delisle says, "Praise connotes expectations for more of the same." Encouragement, on the other hand, represents sequential and ongoing approval, which "imbues the child with a sense of purpose." Praising a child's successful execution of an elementary movement on a balance beam, for example, may deter the child from trying harder moves. In contrast, one might say, "Very good cartwheel, Sally. You've really improved. Are you ready to try a backflip?"

Mary Compton, president of the National Middle School Association, discusses in the *Roeper Review* various reasons for underachievement in gifted students in relation to the physiological and biochemical changes taking place during adolescence. For example:

• *Uneven Rates of Brain Growth:* One interesting theory of intellectual development, though it is yet to be proved, speculates that the human brain has periods when little growth occurs. Middle school youngsters may reach a lull or plateau in their brain growth, rendering expectations of advanced academic work inappropriate.

• *Nutrition:* While there may or may not be a growth spurt for the human brain in the adolescent age bracket, there most definitely is an increased demand on the child's storehouse of nutrients as the nutritional level needed for physical growth increases. Compton suggests that perhaps this physical growth spurt drains the energy required for sustained intellectual acuity. A balanced diet and vitamin supplements at the discretion of a pediatrician should ease this problem.

• *Peer Influence:* The group that the youngster chooses to identify with can have a significant impact on his behavior at adolescence. When the chosen companions are average or below-average students, the gifted student may be inclined to turn in substandard work in order to receive positive reinforcement from the peer group. For gifted adolescent girls, the problem may be even more traumatic, because they may be rejected by the dominant, nonacademically oriented majority.

• *Burnout:* Some gifted youngsters may be faced with some degree of burnout during the middle school years as they tire of extra work and the discomfort that comes from being different. With fluctuations in basal metabolism occurring as puberty begins, these children may find it difficult to maintain a high energy level, Compton notes.

According to Compton, some parents may not provide enough support for their children's academic strengths — hoping that they will just develop into *average* children. Others have expectations that are too high, believing that their children should excel in all subjects and pushing them in areas in which they have no talent or interest.

Concludes Delisle, preventing underachievement in gifted children requires sensitivity and "the recognition of behavioral dualities that may precede low performance." Although there is no panacea, he notes, parents need to focus on their children's strengths, accept their limitations, and provide encouragement and appropriate opportunities for self-discovery and growth. These include materials, lessons, extracurricular activities by which children can experiment and come to learn what's meaningful to them. Life at school is happier when teachers base some of the curriculum on a gifted child's interests and delete areas that the student has already mastered.

READING

"Not my child!" you say. "He gets straight A's in reading. *My* child doesn't have a reading problem."

Maybe not. But do you really know what school officials mean when they say your child is doing "exceptionally well" in reading? Do you know how they measure success? Do you know what your child actually does every day during his so-called reading period? If you don't know, you should. You may find that "a waste of time" is the best that can be said about some, if not all, of what's going on.

The efficacy of school reading instruction has long been a matter of public debate. And school officials, in an effort to overcome declining scores and go "back to basics," have allowed the subject to be reduced to a list of skills and subskills.

Highly articulated skills programs now dominate school reading instruction. Until they leave sixth grade, most children spend an hour or more each day occupied with paper-and-pencil drill work — in a period called "reading" — no matter how well they can read. Some of the period they actually spend reading. The rest they spend doing worksheet exercises that can range from identifying phonetic characteristics of words to drawing inferences from isolated groups of sentences. The whole process seems very systematic and important. But for children who already know how to read, it is often a waste of time — or worse, powerful evidence that reading is a relentless bore.

To avoid boredom and consequent underachievement, parents must find out what's going on at school. Begin by asking the teacher to explain exactly what your child is doing during the reading period. Parents' acceptance of letter grades and reading-level designations as substitutes for real dialogue about what children are doing only exacerbates a destructive situation. You know how to read. You also know whether your child knows how to read. By reading with him or her from time to time and paying some attention to what he or she reads, you can tell whether or not his interest and comprehension are expanding and maturing. Therefore since you don't need to depend on the school to assess your child's reading ability, you can inquire instead into the value of classroom "reading" activities.

You may learn that your child is "practicing skills" the point of which you do not understand. If you are told that the practice is intended to teach your child a skill that will make him a better reader, then the teacher should be able to explain to you how the activity will do that. If the point is simply to make him a participant in a reading lesson, then the teacher ought to be able to explain why your child continues to be taught what he already knows.

How the teacher reacts to your questions will depend on the teacher, on local school politics, and on your diplomacy. If your district is using an elaborately designed reading-skills program, then you may assume that any teacher who substitutes her own good sense and judgment for the demands of the program risks being labeled a troublemaker. Some school watchers — educational journalists, poll takers, etc. — estimate that as many as a third of the nation's teachers are in fact taking that risk to varying degrees. Those teachers may well be delighted to find you an ally as they attempt to make reading instruction meaningful for all their kids.

And what of the other teachers? Some rigidly administer the program because they believe in it. The rest do it because their bosses have told them to. In either case, you will be asking them to consider changing practices that have administrative support. It will take time to carry your questions to the principal, district administrators, and school board, but if you are truly concerned, then by all means do so. To become familiar with the kinds of arguments you may encounter, take a look at *Reading without Nonsense* by Frank Smith, a psycholinguist at the Ontario Institute for Studies in Education in Toronto. Among other things, the book should persuade you that what you are asking for is not something that favors the gifted to the detriment of other children — an accusation that is almost certain to be made.

Critical and Creative Reading

For some insight into the value of your efforts at home, regardless of what is happening at school, you might look at *GNYS AT WRK: A Child Learns to Write and Read* by Glenda Bissex. At five, Bissex's son Paul began to write, using his own invented spellings.

The book documents his growth in reading and writing over the next five years and contains some interesting comparisons of his work at home and his work at school. Although she has not written an antischool tirade, Bissex does suggest that the diversity of reading matter available to Paul at home may have played a more important role in his reading development than did the more carefully controlled materials he used in school. And she is very clear about the importance of the parental role.

Paula Boothby, a fourth-grade teacher in the Malcom Price Laboratory School at the University of Northern Iowa and an expert on teaching strategies for gifted children, offers the following suggestions for helping to make your child a critical reader, not merely a rote reader:

• Encourage your child to think about what she is reading by asking her to anticipate the outcome of a story, then to seek information confirming her prediction. Predictions can be based on the title, on several paragraphs, on several pages of reading — or on anything but the conclusion of the story. Ask your child such questions as "What do you think is going to happen? Why? What part of the story proves you were right?"

• Use the same stories to stimulate creative reading by having your child rewrite the climax of the material, add her own epilogue, dramatize the story, set it to music, or interpret it through visual arts. These activities help children develop a deep understanding of plot and characters; the possible variations are limited only by time, space, and available materials.

• Develop vocabulary by discussing connotations and figurative language. What does the word *bookworm* connote, for example, beyond its explicit meaning? Do not assume that your child knows what a word means because she can pronounce it. Reading poetry and prose out loud to your child provides opportunities to talk about meanings of words and phrases. Descriptions in advertisements — promoting a "spiced peach" shade of lipstick, for ex ample — supply many examples of figurative language and how it is used to evoke feelings.

• Encourage your child to read widely on a topic and to see how different authors (including poets) treat the same theme. You can also encourage your child to question why and how newspaper accounts of the same event differ. You may pick the same major news story, for example, and read and observe how the event is described differently in a politically conservative and a politically liberal publication. These kinds of encouragement will help her develop the reading skills that will enable her to absorb more material and use language more effectively and persuasively.

Ellin Greene of the University of Chicago suggests another related avenue to developing creative thoughts, or "magical thinking," as she dubs it: returning to the art of storytelling. Greene is the coauthor of a book called *Storytelling: Art and Technique*.

"I would urge parents to begin [telling stories] right away, during the child's infancy" she says. "Singing lullabies is one way; and as soon as the infant can comfortably sit in a lap, the parent can direct the child's attention to colorful picture books or magazines and simply describe what's shown." Beginning with these unstructured moments, Greene suggests that parents and teachers can use storytelling rather than reading aloud to kindle the imagination.

For example, young children "like to hear about themselves," especially how a family prepared for their births. Children aged three to five "like tales with simple direct plots, little dialogue, and lots of action that ends quickly and happily. Children six to eight are most interested in traditional folktales," Greene notes. And preadolescents enjoy stories of romance and heroes and more sophisticated folktales.

Greene tells her education students that to be an effective storyteller one must "know the story by heart, be able to visualize the setting, and not be afraid of pauses and periods of silence."

Greene does not advocate neglecting reading to the child, but she thinks storytelling allows for greater variety of interaction and helps nurture a faculty all too often neglected: a flexible and vivid imagination.

One final note of caution about reading: not all gifted kids read early. Many people believe that early and proficient reading is a natural outgrowth of giftedness. In fact, your child may be required to demonstrate her reading ability before being admitted to a primary grade program for gifted youngsters. However, research has shown that reading should not necessarily be one of the criteria for selecting young children for gifted programs.

At least two researchers have challenged the assumption that superior intelligence is demonstrated by early reading skills. Jack

Cassidy, who teaches reading and gifted education at Millersville State College in Pennsylvania, and Carol Vukelich, who teaches reading courses at the University of Delaware in Newark, studied readers and nonreaders enrolled in a special instructional program for gifted prekindergartners. Among the 58 children being observed, about 20 percent of the four- and five-year-olds were reading. The mean IQ of this group was 158. The mean IQ of the 80 percent who were not reading was about 3 points lower.

The children who had been able to read when they entered the program made great gains in reading while in the program, but those who had come in as nonreaders went out as nonreaders, even though reading activities were a major part of the program. "A very surprising finding of this study is that young gifted children, even though they seem to possess the measurable readiness skills and have high intelligence, do not necessarily learn to read quickly, even when given instruction," concluded Cassidy and Vukelich.

Parents confronting educators using reading proficiency as the criterion for admitting children to programs for the gifted should point out that this prerequisite may be excluding a significant majority of gifted youngsters.

WRITING

By and large, the schools are doing a bad job of teaching children to express themselves in writing. Generally, instead of helping children with the difficult task of learning to write clearly, thoughtfully, and persuasively, schools have provided uninspiring drills in grammar and punctuation. Moreover, common assignment and grading practices have actually inhibited student writing growth by placing the emphasis on turning in a superficially "correct" product, rather than on acquiring more understanding of the writing process. Imagine the difficulty that physically handicapped children have — and even left-handers — when emphasis is on the technical skills, such as handwriting, at the expense of creativity and insight.

The plight of the gifted youngster learning to write is especially ironic. Because most gifted children are good memorizers, they do well on the grammar exercises and tests. And because most are achievement-oriented, they are eager for their papers to meet the mechanical standards being used to measure their work. Thus, they labor diligently at their assigned tasks, believing that they are learning how to be better writers — and they get the grades to "prove" that they are. In fact, though, unless they are fortunate enough to be with an exceptional teacher who has the courage and resourcefulness to go against common practice, *they receive no real writing instruction at all.*

Four assistant professors of English at the University of North Carolina at Wilmington have reviewed and summarized the last decade's research regarding writing instruction. The conclusions they drew from numerous studies can be given in two deceptively simple statements: (1) children learn to write by writing, and (2) teachers must interact with children as editors, not judges.

The professors found substantial evidence that studying grammatical theory (word and sentence classification, diagramming, etc.), completing workbook exercises, and memorizing rules of usage all result in negligible improvement in students' working grammar. Linguistic research, they say, shows that we learn language rules indirectly — through exposure and practice. Therefore, the primary concern of teachers marking papers should be dealing with content and organization; *mechanical errors should receive secondary attention.*

Their use of the word *secondary* is especially important. No one is arguing that children should not be taught to punctuate and spell correctly. Final drafts should be mechanically correct as well as expressive, thoughtful, and accurate. Too often, however, the only "revising" children are asked to do involves correcting spelling and punctuation errors. The message to students is clear: we are not much interested in what you say, or even in whether it's what you wanted to say. We care only about mechanical correctness.

If children are to write well, they must be taught specific ways to get started, to generate ideas, to shape, refocus, and edit their papers. They need to be encouraged to write tentative outlines and drafts. They need to be taught that revision is an essential, continuous part of the writing process, and they need comments and suggestions that will help them understand what and how to revise.

A look at your child's work can tell you what kind of instruction he or she is getting. Worksheets, grammar tests, single-draft pieces of writing that have been judged rather than responded to are all signs that students are getting poor writing instruction. Parents should also look at what happens to their children's finished work. In *The Enrichment Triad Model*, Joseph Renzulli persuasively argues that gifted children need opportunities to carry their interests through to the real world. Renzulli means that children's writing must routinely go beyond student-to-teacher communication. It calls for broader and more deliberately chosen audiences than those reached through the common practice of posting "good papers" on the bulletin board. Letters to the editor, editorials, feature articles for school and local newspapers, letters written to individuals and organizations on behalf of ideas a child believes in: these, as well as stories, poems, and essays represent publication opportunities that creative teachers of writing make available to their students. (See the resource list on pages 67–68 for names and addresses of publications that accept submissions from children.)

The sad fact is that you probably cannot do enough to reform the school system. Without a doubt, your children deserve good writing instruction each year they are in school. But most teachers received poor training in the skill themselves and therefore do not know where to begin or how to proceed. Moreover, knowledgeable teachers capable of conducting good writing programs often run up against school- and districtwide evaluation methods that work against them. Many teachers are being pressured to instruct students in skills — like grammar and punctuation — that can be evaluated by an electronic scanning device. Unfortunately, the machine that can evaluate the content of a student's writing has not yet been invented.

Joining with other parents to lobby for effective writing instruction won't reform the schools overnight. Your thoughtful remarks will help, though, and they will be a welcome contrast to the strident demands of back-to-basics advocates promoting a return to practices that did not work in the first place. You can communicate to the school superintendent, school board members, and to your children's teachers the desire that your children spend their time writing, not doing grammar exercises, and that their writing be responded to with suggestions for improvement, not judgments of "right" and "wrong."

Nurturing Writing Ability at Home

While working for improvements in writing programs at school —
or even during preschool years — parents can do a great deal to
help talented youngsters at home. Taking your child's writing —
or interest in writing — seriously is of major importance. Research
and experience demonstrate that not all gifted children have exceptional writing skills. However, it could be damaging to a youngster
who has great interest, but doesn't seem exceptionally talented,
to make a judgment too soon. A refined talent for writing, unlike
a talent for spelling or doing long division, depends on age and
experience for its nourishment. A passion for words themselves,
on the other hand, is a gift that may appear early in your child.
Although this passion — which could surface as writing talent
later — is a kind of giftedness that cannot be measured, it can
be nurtured at home.

In a film that features several diversely gifted young children,
the physicist of the group displayed a dazzling command of technical vocabulary; another child had organized numerous successful
social projects; the musician left little doubt as to who was the
best instrumentalist in the school band; and it was clear whose
drawing of a radiator looked most like a radiator. Each child's
gift, in other words, could be measured by a "product," something
of indisputably high quality.

The case of the young writer in the film was different. In the
several original poems that she read — and this criticism will
sound harsh — there was not one interesting line or sharp image
or anything that rose above the quality of greeting card verse.
Cliché compounded cliché: "To and fro" was rhymed with "high
and low"; "trees of gold" stood up "tall and bold." Conventional
ideas jogged along in harness with irrelevant forms of arbitrary
rhythms. Very little in the finished product suggested the time that
went into the writing of the poems; with the possible exception of
an ear for rhyme, an important element of poetry, nothing suggested
the genuineness of the child's talent.

Very little in the *product* revealed the child's giftedness. There
was, however, a great deal in the film, particularly the child's
persistence in thinking of herself as a writer, that illustrated the
gift. "I want to be a writer," she said. "I *have* to be a writer." The
large volume of work that she had turned out, and continued to

turn out; the hoarding of her poems in notebooks; her eagerness to be thought of as a writer, indeed her obsession with it; the joy she took in words, no matter how little fire her efforts sparked in others — these, not the poems themselves, were the signals of her giftedness.

As stated above, more than other skills, writing benefits from the writer's age and experience. Your young author, however, need not be thwarted by his youth. He may have a gift that reveals itself not as an astonishing achievement, but rather as a persistent passion, a rage to place order upon language, and he can be shown ways to make that order original and powerful.

For example, at the heart of good writing is surprise. The greatest literature will surprise forever. A large surprise, however, is not what the writer wants; large surprises leave the reader feeling cheated. For instance, nobody wants the problems of a story or poem to be solved by a tornado that kills off all the bad people. Small, persistent surprises, crafted by the writer because of the way he sees specific things, produce fresh writing. A careful description of a particular person or place, for example, will surprise the reader by causing him to remember, unexpectedly, a person or place like the one he is reading about.

Whatever you can do, then, to encourage your child to make detailed observations — free of gross generalities and clichés — will help the writing. *Tell him that writing is enriched by specifics and details.* Journals and diaries — some to be read by others and some to be kept private — are invaluable. One section of your young writer's journal might contain only descriptions of specific persons: friends, enemies, grandparents, and so on. These persons are known by what they say and by the sound of their voices; they are known by what they wear, how their breath smells, the tint of their face powder, and how their skin feels when you shake hands with them or give them their change at the cash register. Your young writer's careful descriptions of places, accounts of trips, and narrations of experiences will also clarify and sharpen his writing skills.

Your child's journal could also contain a faithful account of dreams. Dreams create new situations from the sights and sounds of our daily lives, in the same way that a poet will bend, extend, and otherwise transform ordinary images so that they reach beyond everyday life. Dreams can include daydreams and intentional distortions of reality, such as little lies that begin in the physical world and then creep imperceptibly into something rich and strange.

Diverse reading, diverse experience, detailed discussions of movies and television shows, word games, encouragement of the tendency to see things differently — for example, how the world would look from the point of view of a chair — honest examination of details, candor that is often impossible in conversation with parents and friends, and the willingness to write in the clearest language at his command: these are the things your young author requires if this gift is not to be wasted. There is no future for him in describing birds he has never seen or objects he has never looked at with a most careful eye.

The writer has to write and to keep writing. Writing about a thing in a general way, he may lose it forever, but conversely, by seeing its every blemish, as well as its every perfection, he may cause it to live forever.

"I want to be a writer. I *have* to be a writer." There is more poetry in these lines than in all the "trees of gold" that stand up "tall and bold" in all the world. The surprise that a child, at so young an age, knows what she has to do if she is to think well of herself, is the kind of honesty that surprises and is the beginning of good writing.

One excellent way for parents to encourage young writers is to expose them to the idea of writing for publication. A success at this is extremely motivating.

The following magazines accept contributions from children — subject to the limitations described. If your children are interested in sending material to one or more of them, suggest that they first study several representative issues from the library to get a feel for the kind of writing the editors are looking for. Also be sure they look for guidelines that describe the form in which the magazine wants contributions submitted.

Although these and other children's magazines offer young people perhaps the best chance for being published, your children should not hesitate to submit their writing to other publications as well.

• *Child Life*, P.O. Box 567B, Indianapolis, IN 46206. Publishes artwork, poetry, stories, and letters. (Ages 9–14.)

• *Cricket*, Cricket League, Box 100, LaSalle, IL 61301. Has monthly contest open to subscribers. Publishes story, poetry, and artwork winners. (Ages 5–12.)

• *Ebony, Jr!*, 820 S. Michigan Ave., Chicago, IL 60605. Publishes letters, riddles, jokes, games, artwork, poetry, short stories; "major works" appear as winners of annual writing contest. (Ages 6–12.)

• *The Electric Company Magazine*, Editor, Children's Television Workshop, 1 Lincoln Plaza, New York, NY 10023. Runs a monthly joke and cartoon page containing reader submissions. (Ages 7–11.)

• *Gifted Children Monthly*, P.O. Box 115, Sewell, NJ 08080. Publishes all forms of original work in monthly "Spin Off" section. (Ages 5–14.)

• *Highlights for Children*, 803 Church St., Honesdale, PA 18431. Publishes all forms of original work in "Our Own Page" section. (Ages 5–14.)

• *Jack and Jill*, P.O. Box 567B, Indianapolis, IN 46206. Publishes articles, letters, artwork, poetry, and stories. (Ages 8–12.)

• *Ranger Rick's Nature Magazine*, 1412 16th St., N.W., Washington, DC 20036. Publishes poetry, jokes, riddles, games, and letters, and occasionally requests submissions about a specific topic. (Ages 7–12.)

• *Sesame Street Magazine*, Art Editor, Children's Television Workshop, 1 Lincoln Plaza, New York, NY 10023. Publishes artwork. (Ages 3–6.)

• *Stone Soup*, Box 83, Santa Cruz, CA 95063. Contents entirely by children: fiction, poetry, artwork, and photography. (Ages up to 13.)

• *The Weewish Tree*, American Indian Historical Society, 1451 Masonic Ave., San Francisco, CA 94117. Publishes contributions from American Indians. (All ages.)

Other strategies to help parents help their young children to be good or better writers are contained in a multipoint program developed by the National Council of Teachers of English. If there is a general tenor to their suggestions, it is to start early, encourage patiently, and be a good model.

These are among the things the council suggests you can do at home:

• *Build an atmosphere of words*. Go places and see things with your children. Talk about your experiences in terms of all five senses. (What does the tree look like? How does the flower smell? What is the texture of sand?) The basis of good writing is good conversation.

• *Let your children see that you write often.* You must be both a role model and a teacher. Whether writing letters or stories or whatever, periodically read aloud to your children and ask their opinion of what you've written. Also, if they see you make changes, this assures them that revision is a natural part of writing.

• *Be helpful and resist being critical.* Talk about your children's ideas with them and help them discover what they want to say. (You mean you were "flabbergasted" by his appearance?) When they ask, supply help with spelling, punctuation, and usage.

• *Provide a quiet corner, if possible, for children to write.* Otherwise any flat surface with elbow room will do, along with a comfortable chair and a good light.

• *Give and encourage others to give your children gifts associated with writing* — such as pens, pencils, a desk lamp, stationery, a booklet for a diary or journal, a dictionary appropriate to their age, a typewriter maybe, and erasers or "white-out."

• *Encourage frequent writing, but don't demand it.* Be patient, as sometimes children are reluctant to write or have "nothing to say." This is an appropriate excuse; the desire to write is a "sometime" thing.

• *Praise your children's efforts at writing,* focusing on their successes and creativity. Resist the tendency to focus on errors and only the mechanical parts of writing.

• *Share letters from friends and relatives with your children.* Treat these as special events and urge family and friends to write to your children, no matter how briefly.

• *Be alert to occasions when your children can be involved in writing* — such as grocery lists, notes at the end of your letters, holiday and birthday cards, telephone messages.

• *Encourage your children to write away for information,* such as free samples, travel brochures, government pamphlets, menus, writers' guidelines.

MATHEMATICS

To provide parents and teachers with ways to recognize mathematical talents in their children or students, Carole Greenes, an associate professor of mathematics education at Boston University, has identified seven attributes characteristic of students gifted in the field. In *Arithmetic Teacher,* an official journal of the National Council of Teachers of Mathematics, Greenes discusses these attributes and the need for programs designed to develop them. In your youngster, look for:

• *The Spontaneous Formulation of Problems:* Given a mathematical situation, your child might ask additional questions and provide the answers, frequently using experimentation. For example, a fifth-grade student reading about the Statue of Liberty was interested by the stated width of the statue's mouth and became curious about the length of the statue's arm. Instead of looking up the information in a reference book, as her teacher suggested, she measured the width of her own mouth, reduced that to a fraction of the mouth on the statue, measured the length of her own arm, and used the fraction to calculate the length of the statue's arm.

• *Flexibility in Handling Data:* When presented with a problem that is customarily solved using a widely known formula or approach, your child might see a simpler or alternative strategy for finding a solution.

• *The Ability to Organize Data:* If random information in a problem can be broken down into sets, the gifted child will tend to organize the material into lists or tables to find patterns and relationships.

• *Mental Agility:* "Gifted children are able to think of divergent ideas and make unique associations," says Greenes. Sometimes doing this means that your child will delay in giving an answer because of seeing ambiguities in the problem or the possibility of multiple answers. For example, one gifted fifth grader did not immediately answer the question of how many kilometers Mrs. Johnson traveled each hour if she went 360 km in six hours. The youngster told the teacher that the problem was not clear because it did not state that the same number of kilometers was traveled each hour; the solution could be any set of six numbers that add up to 360, said the student, and "there is an infinite set of such sets."

• *Original Interpretations:* The gifted child, says Greenes, is able to leave the well-trod path — departing from the obvious to visualize things from different perspectives. Greenes gives the example of a second grader who made up the term "underneath number" for a negative number.

• *The Ability to Transfer Ideas:* Your gifted child may have a special aptitude in mathematics if he or she frequently applies to mathematical situations information learned in other contexts.

• *The Ability to Generalize:* The gifted young mathematician examines things thoroughly, observes relationships, and generalizes from those relationships.

Greenes has also found that children gifted in mathematics prefer oral rather than written communication, because it is faster, and that some find it difficult to explain their thought processes "because of their tendency to combine several mental operations in one step and leap to the solution."

Traits that indicate superior mathematical potential in preschoolers, according to H. Laurence Ridge and Joseph Renzulli, writing in the *Mathematical Education of Exceptional Children and Youth,* include the following: a passion for numbers and measuring; a "personal" relationship with numbers — including a like or dislike for certain numbers; a well-developed and abstract conception of numbers and how to use them; evidence of advanced mathematical reasoning; a good memory; persistence; concentration spans of three to four hours or more; IQ scores related to mathematical prowess of about 120; ease in school math; a tendency to do mathematics with pleasure and without compulsion; mastery at an early age of definite mathematical skills and habits.

You may suspect, from indications similar to those already mentioned, that your child is mathematically gifted. But how should parents identify giftedness in their elementary school child? What should they look for in the mathematical education of their gifted child? According to Martin L. Johnson, director of the Arithmetic Center at the University of Maryland, the standard identification and teaching approaches in math are too "heavily computational" — that is, children are required to do too much addition, subtraction, multiplication, and division.

What then? Writing in *Arithmetic Teacher,* Johnson says, "Mathematics knowledge consists also of the ability to perceive patterns and relationships, and to form concepts and generalizations about the perceived relationships. . . . In my opinion, the characteristic that separates a gifted from a nongifted child in mathematics is the quality of the child's thinking; that is, how does the child reason about mathematics."

Describing research by the Russian psychologist V. A. Krutetskii, Johnson describes mathematically capable children as having the abilities "to proceed quickly from a specific set of instances, to eliminate intermediate steps in the thinking process, and to switch from a 'direct' to a reverse order of operation."

These characteristics could be disclosed about children through "interview protocols" — following their efforts out loud on specially constructed problems that demonstrate thought processes. It's a question of *method:* for example, "How would you figure out the area of an odd-shaped table top?"

The next step is to design an instructional program that challenges these thought processes. One good approach is open-ended activities, where a minimum of clues is given to help a student solve a problem and a single solution is *not* preferred. "An open-ended activity allows the student to plan a method of problem attack, thereby providing opportunity for divergent thinking and for the student's creativity to be demonstrated," Johnson says. He suggests problems such as "How high does a ball bounce?" or "How fast does a bug run?"

The inadequacy of school math programs inflicts the greatest damage on gifted children by neglecting their potential and denying them the instruction, support, and encouragement they need to develop their mathematical talents, says a report from the National Council of Teachers of Mathematics. However, the report includes numerous suggestions and guidelines for upgrading math education in the schools. *An Agenda for Action: Recommendations for School Mathematics of the 1980s* is a major study based on years of comprehensive research and analysis. It not only describes the shortcomings in math education and points out remedies; it puts the responsibility for improvement on parents and other non-professionals as well as on teachers.

As a parent, you have a formidable ally in this professional organization for math teachers. The council's candid statements about females and some minorities being "underrepresented" in math courses, and its admonition to schools to encourage and help these groups, are ammunition in the fight for quality education. In its report, the council also urges colleges and schools to cooperate in devising "imaginative" programs for the mathematically gifted. Programs for the gifted, it states, should be based on a sequence of enrichment opportunities that focus on problem solving rather than on acceleration alone. And materials and resources with "sophistication and depth" should be developed for the gifted student.

To improve math instruction for all students, the report recommends that parents, teachers, and others concentrate on these priorities:

• School math at all levels should be organized around the development of problem-solving ability, rather than the current emphasis on computational skills that are divorced from their practical application.

• "Basic skills" must be broadened to include estimation, application of math to everyday situations, measurement, working with data, and use of tools such as calculators and computers. (Activities to enhance problem solving and "practical math" may be found in *Creative Problem Solving in School Mathematics*.)

• Because school math programs should make full use of calculators and computers at all grade levels, computer literacy should be a part of every student's education (and teachers should take the initiative to help parents develop guidelines for using computers in the home. This means recommending educational software that supplements what is taking place in the classroom).

• Obsolete material, such as computing with large numbers (a task that is more efficiently performed by calculators and one that doesn't reinforce basic understanding), should be eliminated.

• All high school graduates should have no fewer than three years of math in grades nine through twelve, with diverse programs meeting their various needs and abilities. Parents should keep an eye on this, making sure that their children are sufficiently challenged.

• There should be incentives to attract and retain competent math teachers.

Other specific suggestions for teaching the mathematically gifted elementary grade student come from Benny F. Tucker, assistant professor of mathematics at Illinois State University, writing in the *Roeper Review*. Parents should recommend and advocate the following kinds of activities to school personnel and provide as many of them at home as possible.

Tucker recommends these specific strategies:

• *Puzzles:* Puzzles are an excellent source of enrichment because they require flexible and analytical thinking, and they are readily available from many sources. However, some gifted students are not interested in puzzles, so parents and teachers should avoid relying too heavily on them.

• *Mental Arithmetic Games:* Mental computation and estimation provide a base for success at problem solving and the study of new mathematics content. Consequently, games that require children to practice computing and estimating quickly have an important place in programs for gifted math students and in the home.

• *Projects and Applications:* Since gifted children constitute our greatest pool of potential problem solvers, it is essential that they have opportunities to see the usefulness of mathematics. Providing experiences that allow them to solve the kinds of problems they are likely to encounter in the real world — determining a crop's yield or the amount of nuclear energy needed to run a city — is more difficult than gathering puzzles and games, but many parents and teachers have been successful at the task.

Thomas Gibney, director of the Curriculum and Instruction Division in the College of Education at the University of Toledo, focuses on problem solving. In stressing the need for gifted elementary students to learn all the mathematics that the average student learns, and *more*, he points out that the *more* should not be additional exercises involving skills at which the student is already proficient, but activities that develop the ability to solve practical problems in a broad context while applying higher levels of thinking.

As a source of appropriate problems for gifted children to solve, Gibney recommends two Ohio Department of Education booklets entitled *Problem Solving . . . A Basic Mathematics Goal, Becoming a Better Problem Solver* (*Book I*) and *A Resource for Problem Solving* (*Book II*). The booklets contain more than 200 problems suitable for use at home or in gifted curriculums. Grade levels are suggested, although adapting their use to the needs of individual students is recommended. Write Dale Seymour Publishing, P.O. Box 10888, Palo Alto, CA 94303.

Be a Plus in Your Child's Math!

Parents' interest and involvement are important elements in a child's mathematics education, says the National Council of Teachers of Mathematics. The council distributes special parent gift certificates redeemable for a free copy of *How to Be the PLUS in Your Child's Mathematics Education*. The brochure discusses such topics as using calculators to learn, converting your home into a learning center, how to use the newspaper as a math tool, and using the home computer to improve math skills.

At-Home Math Activities

Many parents have a fear of mathematics that is transmitted to their children (especially to females). If you make just a little effort to expose your children early to mathematics in everyday life, they will recognize its importance and see how it relates to nearly every aspect of their lives. Any parent, whether or not he or she is math-oriented, can do it.

You and your young child can have fun with mathematics, provided you approach it as fun and not a learning activity. Whet his or her appetite early enough, and your child will develop a "comfortableness" with mathematics that will encourage uninhibited growth and expansion as the complexity of the subject increases. It is of primary importance to do this with girls, who begin early to develop math and science blocks that will influence them in later years.

Imagine, if you can, a world without numbers. Have your child point out the absurdity of such a world. He or she will immediately begin to see the impact — addresses, phone numbers, money, time, speed, cooking, temperature, measurement. Point out, too, that mathematics is not strictly numbers, but that it incorporates as well ideas, methods, shapes, logic, reasoning, and a myriad of other facets.

Following are a few activity suggestions in several specific math areas. From these you'll be able to develop many others.

GEOMETRY The preschool child is ripe for an initial exposure to geometry. When the situation permits, point out geometric shapes like circles, squares, triangles, and rectangles in familiar, everyday objects — furniture, buildings, art work in picture books, for example. Take advantage of opportunities to broaden his or her mathematical vocabulary by introducing ovals (and their relationship to and difference from) circles, pentagons, octagons (stop signs!), and diamonds. Help your child distinguish between squares and other rectangles and name objects that are examples of each.

Develop creativity by challenging your child to make a variety of objects from the same basic shapes. For example, given a large triangle, a smaller triangle, a large circle, a smaller circle and a rectangle, your child may put together:

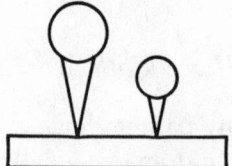

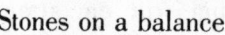

A bird on a branch

Two ice cream cones on a tray

Stones on a balance

A toy on a wagon

Almost everyone has at one time or another made "snowflakes" by folding paper and making cuts on the folds to create symmetrical designs. What you may not realize is that this simple activity is an excellent introduction to symmetry. Have your child try to visualize what the designs he or she cuts will look like when the paper is unfolded. Introduce the term *symmetry* to your child and explain the differences between line symmetry (as in a couch), rotational symmetry (as in a square), and mirror symmetry (as in a capital T). Together find examples of each type of symmetry in familar objects, furniture, clothing designs.

Another useful activity to make your child comfortable with geometry is visual estimation. Estimation of numbers, measurements, amounts, and so on, is becoming an increasingly essential skill as we rely more and more on computerization for the actual computation in order to judge the accuracy of the results. Make a game of it. Without peeking, estimate and draw *to scale* familiar shapes such as the triangle a can opener makes, the hole (or button) on the telephone dial, postage stamps, and so on. Take turns choosing the shape to draw and check your final drawings for accuracy. Be imaginative. Use coins, ice cream cones, et cetera, for both models and prizes!

MEASUREMENT   If your child enjoys estimation, try it with weights and measurements. Children don't get enough practice with measurement in school, and it's often taken for granted as a previously mastered skill. Especially useful is metric measurement. For the grade school child, don't try to relate metric to English. Conversion charts will always be available. Instead, decide upon a "standard" that is something familar (ex: mm = width of a pencil lead, cm = width of one of your child's fingers, and so on) so your child has an approximation of the proper sizes of the relative measurements. (Be sure to measure your standard to get a fairly accurate approximation.) Now look at an object — a pencil, for example — and try to guess how many millimeters or centimeters it is. Then measure to test your accuracy. How many decimeters long is your dog? How high is the swing set? You may want to get older children involved. Try converting recipes into metric and whipping up some tasty metric morsel. With practice you and your child will become "metric masters," and when the metric system is introduced in school, it won't seem ominous.

BACK TO BASICS   If your child has mastered addition, subtraction, multiplication, and division, nothing can be more boring or redundant than the repetitious exercises in a textbook. Develop fun and creative challenges to entertain your child while at the same time providing valuable practice in the basics. How many seconds in a day? How many years is a million days? (If you want to, remind your child of leap years.) If you have slept eight hours a day for (your child's age) years, how much of your life have you spent asleep? What is the percentage or ratio of sleeping hours to waking hours?

RATIO, PERCENT, AND PROBABILITY   Simple probability — the ratio of the number of possible chosen outcomes to the total number of possible outcomes — can be fun and educational. For example, the probability of tossing "heads" on a coin is one in two, or 1/2 or 50 percent. Start with coins or cards and work your way up to more complex probabilities. What is the probability of drawing a face card from a deck of cards? (12 in 52, or 3/13.) A black face card? A diamond face card? What if, as you draw, you don't replace the last card you drew? What happens to the probability? Try creating situations and determining the probability.

STATISTICS   Thought to be one of the drier aspects of mathematics, statistics can, however, be exciting if tailored to your child's interests. Suggest conducting polls among family members or friends to see what their favorite vegetable, TV show, or color is. Calculate percentages or tabulate results. Your child may even be interested in random surveying, like tabulating the number of people who walk by his window wearing hats versus the number without coats. Or the number of open shoes or sandals versus the number of sneakers or leather shoes. Let your child choose what interests him or her.

LOGIC AND PROBLEM SOLVING   Logic and reasoning are extremely important disciplines in any area of study. Spawned at an early age and nurtured, these abilities will grow and develop into natural responses by your child. High intelligence and common sense don't necessarily go hand in hand. Four fundamentals of logical reasoning and problem solving that are easily adapted to other areas are organization, pattern recognition, precise verbalization, and concentration.

From preschool through college, organization can be taught and practiced in activities ranging from planning for a picnic to writing research papers. To combine an exercise in organization and pattern recognition, present your child (aged seven to ten) with cards numbered 1 through 9. Ask him to figure out how to arrange them face-down in a pile so that as *every other* card is turned over, the numbers count sequentially from 1 to 9. Replace on the bottom of the deck the cards that have already been turned over. (This arrangement happens to be 1,6,2,7,3,8,4,9,5.) Depending on your child's age and skill, increase the difficulty of this game by changing the number of cards used, the frequency of the selected card (every third one, etc.), or whether or not the card is replaced at the bottom of the deck. (The same activity above done *without* replacing the cards, but stringing them out on a table, becomes 1,9,2,6,3,8,4,7,5.) Two or more children can challenge each other to see who can complete the specified arrangement first.

The benefits of precise verbalization are obvious, and the skill can be honed in a variety of ways. An enjoyable exercise for children of all ages is to have them draw or construct a simple design or pattern and have another person try to recreate it, unseen, through oral instructions from the creator. For example, if your child draws $\ominus$ and instructs the other person to draw a circle with a line through it, the possibilities are limitless, whereas if your child instructs the other person to draw a circle with a horizontal line through the center extending slightly beyond the perimeter of the circle, the drawing is sure to approximate more closely the original. Likewise, constructions with common objects such as pencils, cans, or cards can be used, and as the designs or constructions become more complex, your child's vocabulary will increase through necessity.

There are numerous variations on the game of "concentration," where players try to match numbers or objects selected from an array of cards face-down. Use the same technique, but instead stipulate a *sum* that must be obtained. For example, the cards selected must add up to exactly 10 for the player to keep the cards and win another turn, or *three* cards must be selected totaling a specified sum.

ON YOUR OWN   Create your own activities to develop your child's interest and ability in mathematics. Continue exposure, but don't bombard the child with these activities. Too much of a "good thing" — even for able children — can have the opposite results. Encourage, but don't push. Other activities you may wish to adapt include:

• A home or allowance "checking" account — perhaps overseen by an older brother or sister. Have your child balance the account periodically, and if the child is artistically inclined, have him or her design and make the "checks," deciding for himself what information is necessary.

• Research or reading about some of the fascinating people and discoveries in the field of mathematics. Check your local libraries for biographies.

• Puzzles, mazes, and so on, found in almost any activity book for children. Calculator Corner and Logically Speaking activities in *Gifted Children Monthly* are excellent examples.

• Suggested reading from which some of the above ideas were adapted are *Math for Smarty Pants* and *The I Hate Mathematics Book* by Marilyn Burns.

SCIENCE

Scientific exploration can help unlock the mysteries of the universe as well as solve critical social and environmental problems. This will depend, of course, on our most talented minds getting quality training in scientific thinking, yet many schools are still using "canned experiments" from laboratory workbooks to teach their gifted students scientific research. According to Robert Sternberg, an associate professor of psychology at Yale, this kind of research is "ascientific" and "mere mimicry of what one is told."

A better approach, says Sternberg, is to simulate a learning environment that is closely aligned with the way scientific research is actually conducted. Rather than following blindly the sequential steps of prescribed experiments, which often only proves that gifted students can follow instructions, budding young scientists need to learn how to think scientifically.

Sternberg says "scientific thinking" can be broken down into four complex thought processes: problem finding, problem solving, problem reevaluation, and reporting.

Problem Finding: This involves coming up with "significant" problems — those the solutions of which advance existing theories or create new ones, clarify current puzzles or inconsistencies, provide a breadth and depth of explanation, and have practical implications for the world we live in. Students should be taught to seek out and define their own problems, Sternberg contends, rather than depending on teachers to provide them. Parents can help here by "dinner time" discussions on current events and by listening to the child share what concerns him or her. These concerns might range from world hunger to pollution to nuclear war.

Problem Solving: Sternberg suggests, once a concrete problem is "found," a nine-element model, which involves problem identification, selecting means and strategies for solving the problem logically and expeditiously, allocating resources for the solution, monitoring results, gathering feedback, and implementing an action plan. With world hunger as an example, ask these questions: What is hunger (being hungry, malnutrition?) and how widespread is it? How can it be eliminated? (Shipping food? Helping countries harvest food?) Who will pay for the program? How will we know it's working? What human and material resources are needed to get started? Existing problem-solving programs are too abstract, he says, and should be applied to actual, real-life scientific investigations.

Problem Reevaluation: Here students need to know that in all scientific research the outcome of an investigation may be quite different from what is expected, meaning that the scientific contribution may be greater or lesser than anticipated. Asking students to consider what they have learned about a phenomenon, compared to what they expected to find, is a good way to teach analysis and interpretation of data, Sternberg advises.

Reporting: This is integral to the scientific process and, according to Sternberg, should be taught with the idea of avoiding a number of common student misconceptions about the scientific endeavor. Below is a partial list of those misconceptions. Parents and teachers will find them useful as a checklist for evaluating their children's paperwork.

• *Writing a scientific paper is the least creative aspect of the enterprise.* On the contrary, Sternberg says, writing usually helps scientists form and organize their thinking. Writing should be approached as part of the discovery process.

• *What is said is important, not how it is said.* Sloppy writing and sloppy thinking go hand in hand, Sternberg argues. It is no accident, he adds, that many of the best scientists in a field are also the best writers: "They are the scientists who have most successfully communicated their ideas."

• *The longer the paper the better.* Brevity is as important for the scientific writer as for any other. A general rule Sternberg offers is that the length of a paper should stand in direct proportion to its scientific contribution. An account of the historical development of ideas in the student's mind should *not* be included.

• *The main purpose of a scientific paper is the presentation of facts.* "Scientific papers should be guided by ideas," Sternberg states. "Facts are presented to help elucidate, support, or refute these ideas."

• *The purpose of scientific writing is to inform rather than persuade.* Successful scientific reports must inform *and* persuade, Sternberg says.

• *Refuting someone else's theory is a good way to gain acceptance for your own.* This is an "indirect method of proof," which tends to cardstack evidence against alternative theories. Sternberg says it is a "common ploy in poor scientific papers."

Nearly every parent has discovered the joy of turning an everyday experience or household object into a science lesson for a child. Homes and neighborhoods are rich with opportunities: an insect carrying out its life cycle and bread rising in a warm place are just two examples.

Bright, highly curious children can benefit from such shared experiences earlier and are more likely to be ready for hands-on activities not generally part of science curricula in early grades at school. In addition to making observations about the kinds of natural occurrences already mentioned, you can easily run actual experiments or demonstrations in your home. Below are just a few — representing a variety of scientific areas — to get you started.

These experiments are adaptable for a wide range of ages and ability levels, though younger children will, of course, require a great deal of supervision.

As you work with your child on the following projects, you can introduce the principles of the scientific method: observing and stating the problem or questions, forming a hypothesis or possible answer based on logical thinking, devising and conducting a set of procedures to test the hypothesis, interpreting what happens in the experiment and drawing conclusions, and revising the hypothesis. Depending on your child's level of ability, encourage her to record the observations and results of the experiment. Explain that good scientists record data neatly and always note unusual circumstances.

The idea of teaching the scientific method may seem a little too structured, but the steps can really take the form of a natural progression of questions and answers for very young children. Older children may enjoy learning the language of science. Whatever you do, keep the level of excitement and discovery high. Don't turn the experience into a lesson to the degree that it dampens enthusiasm and motivation.

Some Experiments

KITCHEN CHEMISTRY

Purpose: To expose children to a simple chemical separation technique (chromatography, used in medical and crime laboratories).

Materials: a glass jar, white paper towel strips 5 cm (2 inches) wide and 25 cm (10 inches) long, children's washable ink markers.

1 Fill jar with about 2.5 cm (1 inch) of water.

2. 4 cm (1½ inches) from the bottom of the paper towel strips, place a row of various colored inks. About four .3 cm (⅛ inch) dots will fit on each strip. Label each dot by color in pencil at the top of the strip.

3. Place the paper towel strips upright in the glass jar, with the ink dots near the top of, but not covered by, the water. The bottom of the strip will be submerged in the water.

4. Let the water rise up through the paper towel for about 15 minutes, checking periodically the progress of the inks.

5. Remove the strips and hang with clothespins on a string suspended over your sink. When the strips are dry, examine them and make observations.

Younger children love to watch the inks separate into different colored bands as they move up the strips. They can see what primary colors have been mixed to make the various secondary colors in the marker ink. Older children enjoy explanations of why some colors move up the strip faster than others, so be prepared to dig out your old chemistry book to look up capillary action and solubility.

Questions: What happens if you use a shorter or longer piece of paper toweling to do the chromatography? What results will you get if you combine two different-colored inks in one dot (for example, red plus blue)?

BACKYARD BIOLOGY

Purpose: To introduce children to plant anatomy and reproduction.
Materials: a flower with stem cut near the ground; a magnifying glass.

1. Using the magnifying glass, examine and point out the various parts of the flower, including the stem, sepals (which are usually small, green, leaflike structures under the flower petals), petals, pistil (the central, female organ of the flower), and stamens (the male reproductive organs surrounding the pistil).

2. Dissect the flower by splitting it in half lengthwise with a

single-edged razor blade. This exposes the ovary, which houses the embryo in a seed until the ovary itself becomes a fully ripened fruit, at which time the seed can be released and grow into a new plant.

3. Explain how pollination can occur by bees, animals, wind, and sometimes purposefully by human beings. This is a wonderful opportunity to explain fertilization and the growth of the plant embryo.

Questions: What do you suppose would happen if you tried to self-pollinate an amaryllis plant? What differences do you see in the number, size, and shape of flower structures from various species?

AMATEUR MICROBIOLOGY

Purpose: To provide children with a method of culturing micro-organisms.

Materials: meat broth left over from a meal (be sure to cool the broth overnight and skim off any fat), five clean baby-food jars, aluminum foil, pressure cooker (you could use a boiling water bath, but you'd have to boil at least an hour), masking tape.

1. Pour 60 ml (about ¼ cup) portions of the broth into each baby-food jar.

2. Cover the jars with 10-cm (4-inch) squares of aluminum foil, pressing the foil securely down around the top edges of the jars.

3. Place the jars upright in water in the pressure cooker. Follow manufacturer's directions for amount of water and proper operation of the cooker. Process the broth at 15 pounds of pressure for 25 minutes. Then let the pressure drop normally by leaving the cooker covered and exposed to air. (Do not cool under a faucet.)

4. When the cooker has depressurized to a safe but warm temperature, remove the jars carefully.

5. Place a piece of masking tape on each jar and number it. Save one jar as a control. In a notebook, keep a record of what is going to be placed in each jar. Good choices are soil, saliva, a sterile cotton gauze square, and simple exposure to air.

6. Leave the foil on the control jar. Remove the foil on the others and inoculate each with one substance you have chosen.

7. Replace the foil and incubate the cultures in the jars (including the control) by putting them on top of your refrigerator or

in another warm place until bacterial growth occurs in the numbered jars.

8. Record observations in your notebook.

9. After completing your observations, resterilize the jars as in steps 3 and 4. Then dispose of them.

Questions: Were you careful with your sterile cotton gauze? (Think about it — your fingers have microorganisms on them, too.) How could you keep the gauze sterile? Did any growth occur in the control jar? Why or why not?

HATCHING BRINE SHRIMP

Purpose: To introduce children to the joys of marine biology.

Materials: a small vial of brine shimp eggs, obtainable from an aquarium store or pet shop for around $1.50. (Be sure to buy eggs sold for hatching. A vial contains enough eggs to run numerous experiments. Many shops offer special hatching solutions and apparatus, but you can do well using things found in your own kitchen.) Salt, bicarbonate of (baking) soda, a 1½-quart clear, shallow glass dish, a gooseneck or study lamp.

1. Make a salt and bicarbonate of soda solution according to directions on the brine shrimp package.

2. Pour this solution to a depth of about 3 cm (1¼ inches) in the dish.

3. The temperature of the water should be kept at approximately 27° C (80° F), which is slightly warmer than room temperature. The lamp will keep the solution warm, as well as provide light, which encourages hatching.

4. Sprinkle some eggs into the solution and stir them. Leave the light on and let the eggs incubate for 24 to 48 hours. With the naked eye, the shrimp can be seen swimming in the solution after they have hatched, but they can be observed even better with a magnifying glass or microscope.

5. Adventurous young scientists will think of many experiments to do with brine shrimp. They can vary the temperature, light intensity, nutrients, and other factors. If you want to count the shrimp, use a piece of paper toweling or a coffee filter inserted into a funnel and pour the solution in it to filter the shrimp out.

Questions: Do most of the brine shrimp tend to prefer the lighter or darker side of the bowl? What contribution do brine shrimp make to the ecosystem of an ocean?

MAKING AN ELECTROMAGNET

Purpose: To help a child to build a solenoid and discover its uses. *Materials:* thin insulated wire; a 6-volt lantern battery; an iron nail (not galvanized).

1. Wrap a long piece of wire evenly many times around a pencil. Slip the coiled wire off and attach the ends to the battery.
2. Insert the iron nail inside the coil. The electromagnet thus created will pick up iron filings and pins. Your child can experiment with other metal objects found around the house.

Questions: What effect does the number of coils of wire have on the strength of the electromagnet? How could you quantify the strength?

SOCIAL STUDIES

Inquiry and simulation are also appropriate approaches for teaching social studies and history to gifted students. For example, students might be asked, "Do you think you could ever go back to a 'state of nature' — a simpler life in the wilderness away from society and civilization, as Jean-Jacques Rousseau recommended?" This question would make adults ponder. But in a history classroom for gifted students — or in a discussion of your child's homework, for example — it could open up a whole world of personal growth. It is one of the examples given by Fredrick Letzter, a teacher of gifted and talented students in Nyack, New York, High School. In an article from *Social Education,* on teaching world history to gifted children, Letzter encourages teachers not only to ask high-level and thought-provoking questions — which can be objective and highly structured — but to expand beyond these with approaches that allow students to express themselves personally. Emphasize the "you," he says, not just the "what" or the "why."

Teachers of world history, too, should ask questions that call for more than one possible answer, Letzter states. (The same goes for parents who want to stimulate high-level thinking in their children.) In discussing the explanation of an historical event, ask, "The absence of which factor would significantly alter the course of events?" For example, "Would the nature of the French Revolution have been significantly different without the Enlightenment?"

Generally Letzter recommends that gifted students be encouraged to study history through an open search for alternatives. Primary and secondary materials should be selected to reflect a range of alternative interpretations of the same historical event or individual. Such strategies "could encourage students to analyze, conceptualize, make comparisons and, in general, think at higher levels," he says.

Letzter also suggests that teachers (parents could do this at home) use an "inquiry pattern" of classroom discourse whereby a teacher "redirects" a student's question in a challenging and probing fashion. He provides an example from his own classroom. In a world history lesson on the Protestant Reformation, a curious gifted student asked: "What is a 'cult'? Were the Protestant groups at that time 'cults'?" Letzter suggested that he search in the library for different current magazine articles and books on cults, taking note of their general features. The student was then encouraged to analyze the behavior of such Reformation groups as the Anabaptists for the degree to which they reflected the general characteristics of cults. Taking the child's interests and questions as the starting point, parents can encourage similar research. (See Chapter 4 for how to develop research skills.)

The study of history can develop intuitive thinking as well. Letzter says that "the formation of bold guesses can be a rich source of possible solutions to a problem." Teachers are cautioned, however, to help students "learn to separate a possible guess from an impossible and/or bizarre guess." (The parent, too, should remember this advice.)

Family History

Daily our grandparents are moving out of our lives. . . When they're gone, magnificent . . . and haunting stories . . . go with them, and what a loss. . . . the logical researchers are the grand-

children. . . . In the process these grandchildren gain an invaluable knowledge about their own roots, heritage, and culture.
— Eliot Wigginton, *The Foxfire Book*

Because it is especially important for gifted children to engage in projects that are not solely personal or self-indulgent, but relate to people and show caring for others, recording oral family histories and doing related cultural journalism are wonderful activities for gifted children and their parents alike.

Among the abilities both tapped and developed in such a project are communication and psycho-social skills, thinking and research skills, and creativity. In the process, gifted children will discover their own heritage, gain an appreciation for a broader cultural and historical milieu, and produce invaluable mementos to share with their families for years to come.

Once your child shows an interest in finding out about his family or a member of it, a pursuit that may be sparked by your encouragement, help him to think of and plan ways to share what he will learn.

For example, on the basis of interviews with grandparents or other family members, he can produce a tape for a family tape library, a book or booklet recounting what he was told, or a set of drawings depicting interesting events. Something as simple as a birthday card with a drawing and quotation based on the recipient's stories can become a family treasure and a source of pride.

An older child may want to go beyond the family interview and find out more about the times her grandparent lived through, in a way that relates to that relative specifically. If a child interviews a grandparent who is or was a fireman, for example, she may go on to talk with other older firemen at the local firehouse and do library research on the types of equipment and problems involved with firefighting at that time. Finally, she can make a book including the interview as well as the additional information. Such a personal link with a subject will make studying it much more meaningful than it would be if the child had merely read about it in books.

Since most of the items your child will create from the study of her family are based on personal interviews, it is important that she have a firm idea of how to conduct one. This may seem easy, and it is if the interviewer is prepared. It's also easy, unfortunately, to conduct a really unproductive interview. However, people who seem at first to have little to say can be the most interesting if they are given the right questions. Have your child keep the following tips in mind in getting ready to interview:

- *Prepare questions in advance.*
- *Have many questions ready.*
- *Prepare the interviewee in advance.*
- *Be a good listener.*
- *Ask for details based on what you hear.*
- *Don't let the interview run too long.*

(An excellent source of questions to start with can be found in William Zimmerman's handy paperbound book, *How to Tape Instant Oral Biographies*. As well as the questions, the book includes interviewing techniques, pages to record family facts and dates, and a guide for parent or teacher.)

HOW TO RECORD THE INTERVIEW   The easiest way to preserve a family history interview is to use a tape recorder. A simple, inexpensive recorder is easy for children to use and, of course, takes down everything exactly as it is said. If your child isn't adept with a tape recorder, be sure he practices before doing the interview. If there is confusion about the tape, the interview won't go as well. Recorders with built-in microphones work best, because the person being interviewed isn't inhibited by having to speak into a mike.

If the interview is taped and the child wants it written out, you may have to transcribe it for him or help him with the transcription. Some children (especially detail-oriented, gifted ones with long attention spans) enjoy the painstaking process of transcription. Some younger children can't handle it physically; others are too impatient.

AFTER THE INTERVIEW   Once the interview is written out, your child can begin to put it into book or other form and combine it with drawings or additional research material. Be sure the tape is carefully labeled with the date and subject if it is going to be saved or kept as part of a family tape library.

You and your child may also want to go beyond the interview and search out family photos and documents to include in an album with a series of interviews. A terrific extension of this activity is for you to become involved yourself and do an interview with your child, asking what *his* first memories and impressions were. Kids love listening to these tapes over and over again — especially as the years go by.

Most important, don't forget to bring out the family history tapes and albums and books often and share them with the interviewees and other family members. They are wonderful additions to family reunions. They may even inspire one. The questions and comments that come out of listening to and looking at these materials will lead to more stories, more tapes, and more sharing and learning.

FOR MORE INFORMATION   Other excellent sources of information for the young cultural journalist are the "If You . . . " series of books by Ann McGovern, as well as the Foxfire publications and Fund. McGovern's books, which include *If You Grew Up with Abraham Lincoln,* . . . *Lived in Colonial Times,* . . . *Sailed on the Mayflower,* . . . *Lived with the Circus,* are arranged in an informative question-and-answer format that will give younger children lots of ideas for asking questions.

Foxfire, begun in 1966 by Eliot Wigginton, a teacher in Rabun Gap, Georgia, as a class project for unmotivated students, was to be a single magazine based on student interviews with older citizens of the community about their lives and skills. The students did everything, including selling ads for the magazine. The outcome was so successful that the magazine continues today and has spawned seven best-selling book compilations and numerous other cultural journalism projects and magazines — including a number of elementary school and junior high publications. To receive a free packet of information write: "Hands-On Newsletter," Foxfire Fund, Inc., Rabun Gap, GA 30568. Be sure to specify whether you are interested in the elementary or junior high age level and that you would like examples of children's work. Though the interviews in these magazines are primarily community-, not family-based, your child will undoubtedly be interested in seeing similar recording and writing done by other children of the same age.

For supplementary reading if your child wants to pursue the interest still further, *Black Theater in America, When I Was Young in the Mountains, Life in a Medieval Village, Folktales from Southern China, Kids in Court,* and *You Shouldn't Have to Say Good-Bye* are a few of the many 1982 books selected for students in primary school through eighth grade by a joint committee of the National Council for the Social Studies and the Children's Book Council. The list is entitled "Notable Children's Trade Books in the Field of Social Studies."

Single copies of the list are available free from the Children's Book Council, 67 Irving Place, New York, NY 10003.

STUDY-SKILL SECRETS FOR SCHOOL SUCCESS

Gifted children do well in school, so they must know how to study. Right? Not true. However, being gifted doesn't mean that everything in school — or in life — will come easily. In fact, there are special pitfalls for gifted youngsters, who often sail through in the early grades. They don't seem to need study skills in the beginning, and then, when they hit the first rough spot in junior high, high school, or college, they often come up short.

Following are some basic study techniques for parents to share with their gifted children about homework, reading to remember, memory methods, and note taking. Many of the ideas presented here are really strategies the child will use all his or her life in school, and it's never too early to acquire them. Teachers rarely teach students how to study; somehow, it seems, kids are supposed to absorb these techniques by osmosis. Gifted kids are particularly receptive to shortcuts and plans. They'll be interested, and you'll do them a tremendous service by showing them the ropes.

Homework Hints

Encourage your children to think about the order in which they do their homework subjects and to do the hardest subjects first. Getting the hardest subject out of the way is a great help. Your child's energy level will go down while tackling it, but as he or she starts to do the easier subjects, he or she will begin to pick up. As the child finishes with the subjects he or she likes best, interest and energy will be high. For example, if your child has thirty minutes of science, his hardest subject, to do and he saves it until last, it will probably take forty to fifty or even sixty minutes. And he'll leave the session feeling grouchy and irritable. When he finishes with a subject he likes, he'll end feeling powerful and good about himself.

Another important technique to share with your children about homework is the idea of taking breaks. As they plan their homework schedules, have them plan to stop now and then. In a nationwide test on concentration, it was found that an average junior in high school can concentrate on homework for about twenty to twenty-five minutes. The gifted child may be able to concentrate for hours on end on what he or she likes, but all homework isn't going to fall into that category. After a certain amount of time the brain needs a relief from concentration. Breaks are also needed to allow the subject to move from short-term memory into long-term memory.

By a break I mean a little one. Five minutes of stretching, getting a drink or snack after twenty minutes of study can do wonders. But warn your children of the trap of starting to watch TV or play with a game or puzzle — anything that will keep them from coming back to homework.

Reading to Remember

Most gifted students don't have much difficulty with their textbooks in the lower grades, but at some time in the future, they may. Either the arrangement within the book is poor or the material itself is complicated. So give them this insight early: you do not read a textbook the same way you read a novel or newspaper. When you read a novel you want surprises. When you go to a movie you want surprises. But when you read a textbook you don't want any surprises. The key to textbook reading is to *preview* before you do the reading. You'll get more interested in the subject of the textbook and get more out of it if you know about it in advance.

To preview a whole chapter have the child read the introduction, conclusion, questions at the end, and then skim each page, reading everything printed "differently" — the boldface print, italics, captions, charts, graphs, and so on. Give him or her this advice: read the introduction and you'll know what is important to come. *Do not read the chapter* — yet. Read the conclusion and you'll know what *was* important in the chapter. *Still do not read the chapter.* Read the questions at the end and see how many answers you have already found from the introduction and conclusion. *Even now, do not read the chapter*. Take about a minute to skim each page by reading anything printed differently. These items will be important points and will answer many of the remaining questions.

This preview process (once it becomes a habit) will take about fifteen minutes for a forty-page chapter. But now the child knows what is important, interest is raised, and study will not be as boring, and if the textbook is well presented, sometimes *all* the child has to do is to skim it by this method.

Now it's time to read the chapter. The trick in reading the material is to *read in small chunks* and then ask, "What have I just read?" If a child can read three pages and remember what's in them, or even one page and remember it, his or her memory is better than average. Start the child with about a paragraph. When the child has finished the paragraph he or she *must* answer the question "What have I just read?" This will take the material from the short-term memory and force it into long-term memory.

If the method of previewing and reading in small chunks becomes a habit, your child will see that textbook reading isn't nearly as difficult — or boring — as it sometimes seems.

Mnemonic Devices

We've all heard of the absentminded professor. He knows all there is to know about physics, for example, but forgets to stop at the supermarket on the way home. Even the gifted child cannot be expected to remember everything; no one can. Memory is very selective in what it wants to remember. Emotions and feelings are easily remembered, while specific intellectual items are sometimes lost.

One very simple way for a child to improve memory — and test scores — is to write things out. You should never give your child a spelling test, for example, and have him or her answer it orally. The teacher isn't going to do it that way. The students are going to have to write the words. It doesn't matter how correctly they think or how much they say, if they can't write the answers, they can't prove to the teacher that they know the material. Never read them science, social studies, or English questions and have them answer orally, either. Have them write the answers to prove they know them.

On a higher level, did you ever anticipate an essay question on a test? Surely you have! Encourage your child to write out the answer, instead of just thinking it through. When the question appears on the test, the answer will just flow from the pen. The process of writing it to prove you know it will take about five to ten minutes, and through following this practice, students will also discover that they don't know everything. They can look up what they don't know and then they *will* know everything.

Another excellent memory method uses index cards. When most students study for a test, they don't know what they don't know! If they did, they'd look it up, and they would know it. Many students who may study sixty minutes for a science test, for example, will spend forty-five of those minutes studying what they already know. What a waste of study time! Why don't they study what they *don't* know?

Well, how can they find out what they don't know? It really isn't hard to do. As a matter of fact, it takes only about two minutes a night for each subject and avoids the ever-present danger of falling behind and having too much to do at the last minute.

Aren't the *new words* in each subject the important things? Have your child write each new word on one side of an index card, and on the other side — where it can't be seen — will go its definition; the person/what he did; the date/what happened; the English word/ the foreign word; the chemistry symbol/what it stands for; the math formula/when and how it's used; and on and on.

Now, the night before the test the child *looks* at fifteen pages of notes but *studies* all the index cards. Because the teacher will mix the questions from the chapter, the child will shuffle the index cards. As he or she goes through the cards, the information he or she knows is put on one side and the cards to study on the other. Following this method, the child has found out what he or she doesn't know and can concentrate study time accordingly.

What do you do with your index cards when the text is read to the end? Throw them away? No! Save them for exams. *Look over* 150 pages of notes, but *study* ten chapters of index cards. What do you do with them at the end of the year? Throw them away? No! You can give them to a younger brother or sister or to a friend. You could even sell them.

Another trick that children enjoy is to speak their notes and index-card information into a tape recorder to play back anytime they wish. A good time is in the morning while getting dressed. An extension of this idea may seem a bit exotic, but many students have stated that it works. Plug the tape recorder into a twenty-four-hour automatic timer and set it to play at about 2 A.M. At this hour, one is in a deep sleep pattern and the information goes into one's subconscious mind.

Review strategy can also make a big difference in remembering information successfully. If youngsters realize that they'll forget 80 percent of what they learned that day, they'll see how important the following advice can be: Review the notes, or chapter, three times — the night of the class, two nights later, and the night before the test.

The first night, review by going over the material and making up index cards. Two nights later (within 48 hours) review the cards again. For example, on Tuesday night make up the index cards from Tuesday's classes. On Wednesday night make up index cards from Wednesday's classes and review Monday's cards, and so on. Once the student falls into this pattern, the review becomes easy, and when he or she studies the cards before the test, it is truly a review. Your children will find that if they can trace a memory path three times over a period of days they will find it almost impossible to forget the material.

Finally, don't forget association tricks and other mnemonic devices. These are fun and extremely effective. Have you ever heard of this sentence — using the first letters of the words — for learning the spelling of *arithmetic:* "A Rat in Tom's House Might Eat Tom's Ice Cream"? Or this idea for remembering the nine planets in order of increasing size?

Mercury	Men
Pluto	Plan
Mars	Many
Venus	Venus
Earth	E
Neptune	N
Uranus	U
Saturn	S
Jupiter	Jumps

Note Taking

As children advance in school, they'll gradually begin to need good note-taking skills, and the very bright child can use these effectively early. Here is a basic, extremely helpful tip to give your child about note taking: *Do not hold the pen* when taking notes. Do not hold the pen when the teacher writes notes on the board, when the teacher lectures, or while reading the textbook. Sound crazy? Maybe, but what does the student do when the pen is in his or her hand? Play with it? Chew on it? Fill in the dots? Doodle? These are all distractions. But, worst of all, one tends to write things, without even knowing what one is writing. Tell your child to listen and write only when he or she understands. The child will take fewer, but better, notes.

Now that your child has the pen out of his or her hand, here is a simple form to use for taking better notes. If your children use standard spiral notebooks, have them write only on the right-hand pages and save the left-hand pages (drawing a line to divide the pages in half vertically works well, too). On the right will go whatever the teacher says, whatever is copied from the board, or whatever ideas come from the textbook. On the left will go two kinds of items — your child's own ideas and the teacher's questions.

Has your child ever thought of an idea over and above what the teacher was discussing? If he or she writes these ideas on the left side. they'll be easily accessible and not forgotten when it's time to write essays and term papers. These original thoughts are the ideas teachers are always hoping to see. Too many students just regurgitate exactly what the teacher said in class. Boring!

Besides putting their own ideas on the left, encourage your children to put the teacher's questions there, too. Ask your gifted children if they have noticed that teachers often ask questions during class. Even if the teacher answers them on the spot, the children should write them down, because if a teacher asked a question once, he or she is very likely to ask it again — on a test.

How do teachers construct tests? They automatically go back to the same questions that they asked in class. If the only notes your child takes are the teacher's questions, and he or she looks up the answers, the child will have perfect notes. If two or three students use the technique and compare questions and answers before the test, they'll see that they have studied almost every question on the test.

Get your youngsters started on effective study skills early, and they'll benefit all through their school years.

Critical Thinking and Research Skills

CRITICAL THINKING

T HE HIGHER-LEVEL thinking skills, or critical thinking, that gifted children are capable of need to be encouraged through specific strategies in every area of the curriculum. The content for all areas — reading, math, science, and so on — should be modified according to the student's interests and he should be involved in planning and evaluation. The emphasis should be on the learning *process* — rather than on merely remembering content — and on flexibility, inquiry, discovery, investigation, and creativity. Critical thinking skills developed through such an approach will involve analysis, synthesis, and evaluation of information.

Parents of gifted children should be aware that activities that are enriching and intellectually stimulating for their children include application and association of learning across subjects, not accumulation and regurgitation of information about just one area; learning conceptualization and generalization, not merely memorization of "facts"; complex thinking, not just harder and harder work; extension or replacement of traditional learning experiences, not simply more work; and visualization of probabilities and possibilities, not only actualities.

Critical thinking encompasses both the so-called cognitive (intellectual) and affective (emotion-involved) aspects of thinking. Emotion-related thinking involves how one approaches the world. Both approaches require problem identification and solution, perceptual judgments, analysis, synthesis, evaluation, and decision making. A curriculum built around solving problems merges cognitive and creative thinking (see the diagram of the basic elements of thinking and where critical thinking fits in).

THE CHEMISTRY OF THINKING:
SOME BASIC ELEMENTS

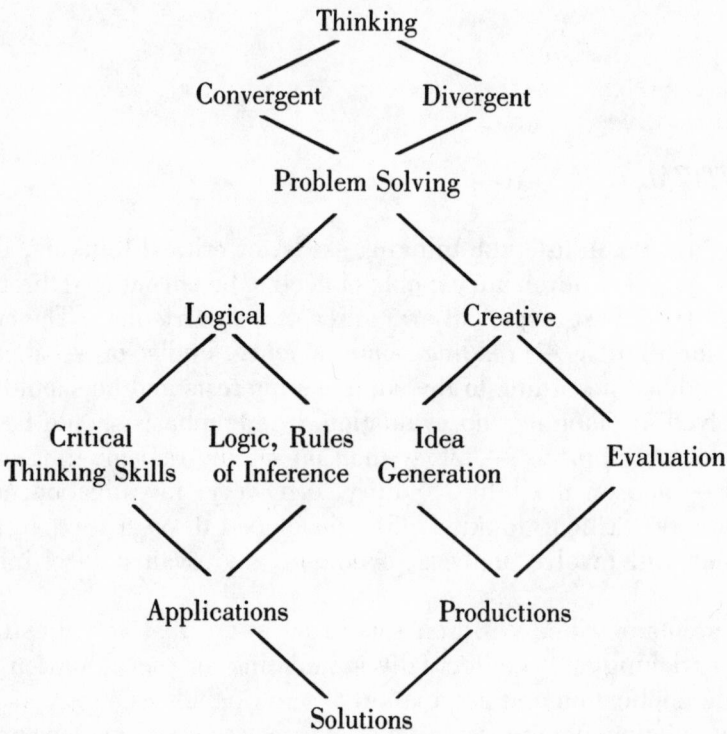

What is a critical thinker? According to the developers of the Cornell University critical thinking tests, a critical thinker using intellectual skills is characterized by proficiency in making certain kinds of assessments. This thinker can tell when a statement follows from the premises; knows if something is an assumption; can determine if an observation statement is reliable; can assess whether an alleged authority is reliable; can determine if a simple generalization, hypothesis, or theory is warranted; can tell when an argument depends on an ambiguity or if a statement is overvague or overspecific; knows if a reason is relevant.

In addition, a critical thinker using instincts (affective processes) has been defined by Anita Harnadek for Midwest Publications as doing the following: is open-minded about new ideas; doesn't argue about something when she knows nothing about it; knows when he needs more information about something; knows the difference between a conclusion that *might* be true and one that *must* be true; knows that people have different ideas about the meaning of words; tries to avoid common mistakes in her own reasoning; questions everything that doesn't make sense to her; tries to separate emotional thinking from logical thinking; and tries to build up his vocabulary so he can understand what other people are saying and can make his own ideas clear to other people.

Steve Allen offers similar suggestions in a record album for children called *How to Think*, in which nine rules for logical thinking are presented amid original songs and stories that exemplify the rules. They follow.

1. Control the emotions.
2. Understand the difference between *fact* and *opinion*.
3. Look for the evidence before making up your mind.
4. Don't kid yourself: *tell the truth* to yourself as well as to others.
5. Understand the difference between the *concrete* and the *abstract*.
6. Use words carefully.
7. Remember that no two things are ever the same.
8. Don't be afraid to change your mind.
9. Remember that much truth is *relative*.

A definition of critical thinking may be summarized as follows: *critical thinking is a cognitive, affective, and creative mental activity that reflects analytical and open-minded reflection applied to all kinds of assertions and situations.*

Parents can help enhance their children's critical thinking skills and point their children toward independent, logical, and ethical thinking by encouraging *philosophical thinking*. Philosophical thinking is the effort to penetrate beneath the surface of things — language and behavior — to find out what they're based on. Through philosophical thinking children can discover alternatives for look-ing at things, impartiality, consistency, the feasibility of giving reasons for beliefs, the need for comprehensiveness, the influence of particular situations, and what whole-part relationships mean.

You foster philosophical thinking by asking your kids questions. The questions below were developed by the Institute for the Ad-vancement of Philosophy for Children (IAPC) as part of a program now used in several thousand classrooms across the country. De-veloped in 1974 by Matthew Lipman, a philosophy professor at Montclair State College, it is very rare in that it teaches philosophy per se to children. It is based on a series of children's novels. Any parent or teacher may ask these types of questions to elicit responses that require thought and analysis. As children become better at discussing a subject philosophically, they are likely to answer many of the questions before they are even asked.

In asking the questions, it is best to make an effort to appear wondering and curious yourself and to respond positively to your children's remarks. Relate the subject matter to the children's own experiences, as you coax them to move the dialogue gradually to a more general or universal level. Make every effort to avoid manipulating the situation to foster your own point of view, and encourage them to clarify their own points of view. These questions can be applied to any subject matter and will give you a sense of the form a philosophical dialogue may take. Of course, every question doesn't fit into every discussion. Following each question is a brief explanation of what the question is trying to elicit in a child's response.

1. *Why?* Requests an explanation for the basis of a child's response.

2. *If that is so, what follows?* Asks children to elaborate, ex-trapolate, draw a valid inference — hypothetical or casual.

3. *Aren't you assuming that . . . ?* Asks for an explanation of premises upon which a statement or argument might be based.

4. *How do you know that?* Calls for more information, a source of information, or for a child to explain his line of reasoning.

5. *Is the point you are making that . . . ?* Requests confir-mation of the parent's (or teacher's) clarification, focusing on the main point of a child's response.

6. *Can I summarize your point as . . . ?* Asks for the child's

confirmation of the adult's restatement or condensation of her statement.

7. *Is what you mean to say that . . . ?* A rephrasing that requires children to interpret their statements and be certain of their meaning.

8. *What is your reason for saying that?* A request for a rationale that offers criteria for making a certain judgment, as well as a justification of that rationale.

9. *Doesn't what you say presuppose that . . . ?* The parent or teacher points out assumptions that might be hidden in a child's argument or point, requiring her to explain the validity of her assumptions.

10. *What do you mean when you use this word?* A request for precise meaning and contextual usage.

11. *Is it possible that . . . ?* The parent or teacher offers other possibilities and points out possible contradictions and inconsistencies in the child's argument.

12. *Are there other ways of looking at it?* A call for alternative perspectives, connections. A check on objectivity and impartiality.

13. *How else could we view this matter?* Gives children a chance to be creative. Stresses flexibility and open-endedness.

An Exercise in Critical Thinking

DID X SHOOT THE CANDIDATE?   Here is a critical thinking activity for gifted children to do with the help of parents or teachers. Older children will require less assistance than younger ones will. A statement is given describing a set of circumstances, and discussion follows.

Statement. A political candidate was shot and wounded while speaking in favor of an unpopular alliance between radical leftists and right-wing extremists. X, a suspicious-looking character, was arrested at the scene of the shooting. A witness present at the scene alleged that she saw X "just snooping around" prior to the shooting. The police interrogated X and learned that X had actively campaigned against the candidate leader in the last national election. No weapon was found, but the casing of a .32 caliber bullet was worn on a chain around X's neck. This was the same caliber as the weapon used to shoot the political leader. X denied all involvement; however, a polygraph (lie-detector) test administered by police showed that X was lying. On the basis of this evidence, a preliminary hearing was set to determine if X should be bound over to the grand jury for indictment.

Analysis and Evaluation. The above statement describes a set of circumstances and a chain of events in which a person has been linked to a crime. Using some of the thinking techniques mentioned in this chapter, have your children develop a series of questions in assessing whether the presiding judge should turn the suspect over to the grand jury. For younger children, sample discussion questions follow.

Sample Questions
1. What constitutes a "suspicious-looking character"?
2. Should suspicion be based on a person's looks?
3. What does "just snooping around" mean?
4. Is this adequate as a *probable cause* for arrest?
5. Did the police read the suspect his/her rights before the interrogation?
6. What did the suspect do when "actively campaigning against" the candidate?
7. Is shooting someone a necessary consequence of what the candidate had done earlier?
8. Is the caliber of the bullet conclusive evidence linking the suspect to the crime? If so, how so?
9. What factors influence the outcome of a lie-detector test?

Sample Questions Based on Components of the Cornell University Definition of Critical Thinking
1. Which "facts" in the Statement are "uncontroverted" (established and indisputable)?
2. What "facts" are implied and which are inferred?
3. Is the observation made by the witness reliable?
4. Is the witness reliable?
5. Where do ambiguities exist in the account of the incident?

Creative Synthesis. Taking as a basis information given in the Statement and what can be deduced or derived from sample questions, analysis, and evaluation, have your children assume the role of investigative reporter and "piece together" a different story of the incident by pursuing various "leads" discovered in the previous discussion.

RESEARCH SKILLS

As noted, the gifted need to approach all curricular areas with critical thinking, and research skills are eventually integral to these thinking skills. Experts think that gifted youngsters as young as eight are ready to learn research skills.

It might be helpful to check with your child's teacher to determine when and how research skills are taught at school. In this way, any research project conducted at home can be structured to reinforce the school's approach. When your child "learns" the skills at school, he or she will not have to spend as much time on the mechanics of note taking, and so on.

Jack Cassidy, a specialist in gifted education at Millersville State College in Pennsylvania, writing in *The Reading Teacher*, presents a research method he calls "inquiry reading." He says the technique allows gifted children to research an area of particular interest to them — with little help from a parent or teacher. Cassidy has developed a four-week program.

During the *first week*, help your child define and understand the word *inquiry* as it appears in the dictionary. Then proceed to determine the topic your child wants to explore. Of course, it can be on anything of interest to him, with the agreement that he will spend four weeks on it and that at the end of this period he will communicate the results of his research to others. This may take the form, for example, of a cassette tape, a skit, a clay model, a research paper. Let's say your child wants to do an oral history project on a family consisting of three generations of firemen. Built into this activity can be an agreed-upon reward for your child at the completion of the project.

After discussing her interests and deciding on a project (which she may alter as her research proceeds), have your child develop three questions to be answered through her research. For example: How did the family first become interested or involved in firefighting? Did the second and third generations serve an apprenticeship with the earlier generations? How have firefighting techniques changed in the last century? Together list the references that are available for finding the answers. In addition to the standard research tools — encyclopedias, library reference books — include such things as magazines, maps, travel brochures, newspapers, filmstrips — anything pertaining to the topic selected. One interview should supplement the research: a professional in the community, a teacher, a relative, or anyone with advanced knowledge in the child's area of interest.

Cassidy says that during the *second and third weeks* the child should spend most of his time working independently. Suggest to her that notes be taken in a notebook or on small cards. At the top of each card or paper, your child should record the source of information and the page number. All of these notes can be kept in some type of pocket folder. Experience has shown that some students may be distracted from their original questions once they begin their investigation, Cassidy says. The outside of the folder should list the three questions as a reminder for your child where to direct her energies. During the latter part of the third week, she should begin constructing the project.

The *last week* is for "wrap-up" activities, putting on the final touches. Then your child will share her project with family members and friends.

If you're feeling uncertain about whether you can provide useful assistance and guidance on this activity, don't worry. Cassidy claims that for the "inquiry reading" project to work, one has to "guard against providing too much initial information." For example, to use the library a child doesn't have to know everything about its contents and operation. Nor does a child have to know everything about conducting an interview before proceeding. The "inquiry reading" method is a way of "learning by doing" — and that includes inevitable mistakes. After the first week your main role will be to keep your child on schedule and to celebrate her effort and accomplishment.

One common problem relating to research is what teachers often call the "copy-it-out-of-the-*World-Book*-syndrome." That's when students copy the first couple of paragraphs from an encyclopedia and let those stand as their "research report." At Gaithersburg Junior High School in Maryland, gifted and talented students enrolled in the SEARCH program can't get away with "token" research.

The six-step SEARCH project has been incorporated into seventh-grade science and ninth-grade English classes for the gifted. Students are given a SEARCH information packet which guides them through the research process step-by-step: *S*elect a topic; *E*xplore; *A*sk questions; *R*esearch reference books; *C*ompile information; *H*ow to share what you have learned. SEARCH helps students to read and take notes only on what they need, although they learn to consult a variety of sources looking for facts to support an original idea.

The advice under "Selecting a Topic" is an example. The seventh-grade science packet says: "The topic ANIMALS is too broad because there are thousands of animals. Even SNAKES is too broad a topic; there are thousands of snakes. CORAL SNAKES would be an acceptable topic for your research paper." The first thing a parent can do is help his or her child further refine and narrow down the topic. What region of the country or world will be investigated for coral snakes? Will you concentrate on poisonous or nonpoisonous varieties, or both? How to present the research findings is another area for parental consultation. Help your child see options and their feasibility: will it be a paper, slide show, or exhibit of snakeskins?

For ninth-grade English, Gaithersburg students are asked to write about a person, but not just a biographical sketch. They must choose a person who has made a significant contribution to society and explain some aspect of that person's life, providing a "thesis" statement and supporting their opinion with research. Project staff members say this approach puts life and originality into students' writing.

SETTING UP A HOME REFERENCE LIBRARY

A child's own reference library can be as much of an investment as a blue-chip stock portfolio. Initial cost is comparatively minimal, the gleanings continually increase, and the benefits grow more lucrative over time.

The obvious reason for developing a home reference collection for children is the advantage of having books available when the children are completing homework assignments, but there are other assets as well. Questions that surface can prompt the look-it-up habit, with the whole family joining in. Reference books are natural springboards to deeper investigations, especially for gifted children, who often develop intense interests in a specific field. Also, children's fields of concentration tend to be narrow, and having books about a variety of subjects will promote general interest and perhaps stimulate exploration.

Below is a two-part bibliography of reference selections suitable for beginning a home reference library for your child — both general titles published as reference books and more specialized titles. The order is that chosen by Barbara Elleman of the American Library Association. Selections will, of course, vary with individual needs and tastes.

1. General Works

The Concise Columbia Encyclopedia. Columbia University Press, 1983.

This one-volume reference work, containing 15,000 entries in a single alphabetical order, covers a broad range of historical and contemporary topics. A center section features colored political and topographical maps of the world.

The National Geographic Atlas of the World. National Geographic Society, 1981.

More than 60 political maps, grouped by continent and almost always double-paged, are extremely legible. Some 155,000 place names are indexed in this comprehensive work.

Webster's New Geographical Dictionary. Merriam, 1972.

The 47,000 entries give basic information on the world's countries, regions, cities, and natural features in concise alphabetical order. Excellent for quick reference.

Webster's Biographical Dictionary. Merriam, 1980.

An alphabetical arrangement of 30,000 entries capsulizes the lives and achievements of men and women throughout history.

The New Roget's Thesaurus in Dictionary Form. Putnam, 1968.

A mandatory guide for any kind of writing, this alphabetically lists words and their synonyms and gives useful cross-references to other words with similar meanings.

Bartlett's Familiar Quotations. 15th and 125th anniversary ed. Little, Brown, 1980.

A classic reference, with sources, to prose passages, phrases, proverbs, and poetry, from ancient to modern literature.

Benét, William Rose. *The Reader's Encyclopedia*, Crowell, 1965.

An excellent, standard source for locating information about plot summaries, authors, titles, characters, settings, and other areas pertinent to readers of literature.

World Almanac and Book of Facts. Newspaper Enterprises Association, Annual.

Annual facts, dates, and statistics on everything from sports to theater and elections to weather is listed in this handy guide.

Concise Dictionary of American History. Scribner, 1983.

Designed to give quick access to all American history (pre-Columbian to 1982), this helpful index is arranged in dictionary format.

II. Specialized Titles

The Prentice-Hall Encyclopedia of Mathematics. Prentice-Hall, 1982.

Helpful explanations of every topic of interest — from calculating a circle's circumference to understanding a computer — are presented along with intriguing puzzles and practical applications that will aid and delight math buffs.

The Oxford Junior Companion to Music. Oxford University Press, 1979.

A wealth of reference material about the world of music including the people, instruments, great works, and other areas associated with it. Lavish illustrations make this a special delight.

Janson, H. W. *History of Art for Young People*. 2nd ed. Abrams, 1982.

A comprehensive overview of the history of artistic endeavors from cave to popular art. Reproductions of many famous pieces illustrate the works of the great masters through the centuries.

National Geographic Book of Mammals. National Geographic Society, 1981.

This two-volume work, which contains striking illustrations, presents a general introduction to the world's mammals and gives the vital statistics and behavior for each of the entries.

Reader's Digest ABC's of Nature. Reader's Digest, 1984.

Thoughtful answers about the physical world, its plants and animals, and their adaptations and interactions in various environments are provided along with full-color maps and pictures.

Scarry, Huck. *Our Earth*. Julian Messner, 1984.

Young readers are guided across time and space in a heavily illustrated presentation that depicts atoms and galaxies, dinosaurs and the first people, civilizations of the past, geographical discoveries, and the worlds of today and tomorrow.

Canaday, John. *What Is Art?* Knopf, 1980.

A complete course in understanding and appreciating art in all its major forms — painting, sculpture, architecture — is provided in this richly produced volume.

Sagan, Carl. *Cosmos*. Random House, 1980.

Based on Sagan's extremely popular 13-part television series, this book treats science in the broadest of human contexts. More than 250 full-color photographs from the show are included.

Fisher, Margery. *Who's Who in Children's Books*. Holt, Rinehart and Winston, 1975.

Children will enjoy meeting familiar characters in this treasury from childhood reading as it catalogues Alice, Pooh, Tom Sawyer, Paddington, Gulliver, Mowgli, Robin Hood, Ramona, Peter Pan, and many more.

Outstanding Science Trade Books for Children

Acid Rain, cars, catnip, computers, lasers, dinosaurs, viruses, and volcanoes are among the subjects of the top 1983 science books for children. Selected by a National Science Teachers Association committee in cooperation with the Children's Book Council, the books — aimed primarily at grades K–8 — are judged for accuracy, readability, and pleasing format.

For a free copy of the 75-book list (which weighs 2 ounces), send a stamped self-addressed #10 envelope to the Children's Book Council, Inc., 67 Irving Place, New York, NY 10003. If you are interested in obtaining more than one copy for a parent or other group, multiple-copy price information is available.

Another good resource is *The Best Science Books for Children*, available for $15.95 from Association for the Advancement of

Science, Tenth Floor, 1101 Vermont Ave., N.W., Washington, DC 20005. It includes 1,200 science books for kids aged 5 to 12.

Choosing the Right Dictionary

You can contribute to your gifted child's mental growth by providing appropriate intellectual tools. Bringing a good children's dictionary into your home is an excellent way to begin. Often a young child will ask for the spelling or meaning of a word and parents can take the opportunity to suggest: "Let's look it up together." In so doing, you can also point out the elements of a dictionary — including some of the more esoteric information such as primary and secondary meanings, preferred and permissible pronunciations.

The first requirement of a good children's dictionary is that it include words that your child is likely to encounter both in speech and in writing. For the beginning reader, information about correct word usage and pronunciation must be given. For more advanced readers, shades of meaning should be explained, synonyms and antonyms provided, and etymologies included.

As you examine the selection in your local bookstore, remember that children's dictionaries are products in a highly competitive business. Publishers are constantly on the lookout for gimmicks to make their entries more marketable. In some cases, too much attention is paid to the form and not enough to the substance.

All of the following dictionaries have worthwhile features. The thumbnail reviews should help you judge which is most likely to stimulate your child's interest and imagination. (While age and grade-level guidelines are included, it is best to clarify this with the retailer or publisher before making your purchase. Keep in mind, too, that individual children will differ. Ultimately, your judgment as to the suitability and usefulness of a specific text for your child should prevail.)

FOR BEGINNING READERS

500 Words to Grow On, illustrated by Harry McNaught. Random House, 1973.

This paperback wordbook does more than simply name objects. It puts them into categories — such as animal words, house words, toy words, tool words. Within these categories, it differentiates between objects — mittens and gloves, a screw and a nail, a mop and a broom, a tricycle and a bicycle — that young children frequently confuse.

The pictures are exceptionally clear, detailed, and accurate, and their arrangement on the page is interesting. Although the words in the body of the book are not in alphabetical order, a list of A-to-Z words — with appropriate illustrations — is included at the back.

Richard Scarry's Best Word Book Ever. Golden Press, 1963.

Every page of this entertaining book is bustling with activity. Filled with the familiar and much-loved characters who populate Richard Scarry's world, it contains over 1,400 common objects and the words that describe them.

Scarry has divided the book into sections — "Mealtime," "Boats and Ships," "In the City," "In the Kitchen," and so on — and has provided each section with an introductory paragraph that invites the child to participate. "At the Supermarket," for instance, begins: "Mrs. Pig is buying groceries for her family. What would you like to buy the next time you go to the market? Would you like to buy a pickle?"

FOR MORE ADVANCED READERS

"The Cat Himself and P. D. Eastman." *The Cat in the Hat Beginner Dictionary.* Random House, 1964.

This dictionary, which contains a basic elementary vocabulary of 1,350 words, has all the action, humor, and visual interest usually associated with the many books inspired by Dr. Seuss. This dictionary is suitable for preschoolers, kindergartners, and first graders who are already reading.

Abstract words are handled particularly well. *Above,* for example, is illustrated by Aaron the alligator flying an airplane above the clouds. Different meanings of the same word are also cleverly and clearly explained. *Horn,* for instance, is illustrated by a picture of a goat with two horns on his head, blowing a third and different kind of horn with his mouth. The caption reads, "A goat with three *horns.*"

Charles M. Schulz. *The Charlie Brown Dictionary.* Random House, 1973; paperback edition by Scholastic.

Based on Wendell Wright's classic, *The Rainbow Dictionary,* it contains 2,400 basic vocabulary entries and definitions. The dictionary is suitable for first and second graders. Charles Schulz's inimitable drawings and characterizations, plus explanatory sentences using the Peanuts gang, are incentive enough to engage young readers. The Peanuts characters are amusing and particularly apt for expressing emotions and states of mind that are difficult to explain in words. Who, after all, can better portray rudeness than Lucy?

E. L. Thorndike and Clarence L. Barnhart. *Scott, Foresman Beginning Dictionary*. Doubleday, 1976.

Kenneth Kister, author of the respected *Dictionary Buying Guide* (R. R. Bowker, 1977), calls this full-scale basic dictionary "the most authoritative, up-to-date and best-illustrated elementary school dictionary available." It includes many of the features of an adult dictionary but presents them in a form children aged eight to eleven can understand. Each of the more than 700 pages includes guide words, and there are numerous pronunciation keys throughout the book. Entry words are accurately defined. Example sentences are vivid and interesting and clearly show the various forms and meanings of the words.

Illustrations are outstanding and include a variety of forms, from etchings to collages. Photographs, in color and in black-and-white, are used extensively. Subject matter includes movie stills, famous paintings, animals, and athletes. The illustrations portray a culturally diverse world in which men and women participate in a wide range of occupations and activities. They also show a keen understanding of what interests a child. *Stethoscope,* for instance, is illustrated by a color photograph of a veterinarian (a woman) listening to the heartbeat of a puppy.

A 40-page section at the front of the book tells the child — through a series of interesting, gamelike "teach yourself" exercises — how to use a dictionary.

FOR OLDER READERS

The Macmillan Dictionary for Children. Macmillan, 1977.

Although the Macmillan dictionary is not as imaginative as the Scott, Foresman book in its use of graphics, it is an attractive book illustrated with appealing full-color drawings.

There are nearly 30,000 entries, and both definitions and word choice are good. A clearly written introductory section tells the 9- to 12-year-old child how to use the dictionary. Such things as alphabetical order, pronunciation keys, syllabication, and parts of speech are explained simply and concisely.

"The Story of English," a well-written and nicely illustrated chapter about the history of the language, is an additional feature. It starts with the origin of language and goes on through the growth of English, its incorporation of many French words, and its eventual acceptance as a global tongue.

Children's Dictionary. Houghton Mifflin, 1979.

This attractive volume has approximately the same number of entries (30,000) as *The Macmillan Dictionary for Children.* Its reading level, however, is lower. It is designed for grades 3–6.

Accuracy and clarity of definition, as well as word choice, are excellent. Difficult-to-define words are frequently illustrated by photographs. The meaning of *agile,* for instance, is effectively conveyed by both the written definition and a photo of a slim young gymnast at work.

The book is well designed, with wide margins and ample use of illustrations. All of the attractive artwork is done by one person — George Ulrich — which gives the book a satisfying feeling of unity and contributes to its considerable visual appeal.

Webster's New Elementary Dictionary. Merriam, 1975.

Compared to the above books, this one appears staid and conventional. It contains over 32,000 entries and is designed for use in grades 4–7. Definitions are clear, however, and the *New Elementary* has two striking advantages over its flashier competitors: it is less expensive and smaller. It fits easily into a bookbag or a student's desk, where it will be close at hand, ready to perform the fundamental task of any dictionary — simple word definition.

Choosing the Right Encyclopedias

Few home resources offer your gifted child more starting points for research and exploration than a good set of encyclopedias. Unfortunately, finding the *right* set is no easy matter. The intelligent shopper has available little clear-headed advice to balance flashy supermarket promotions, glib television commercials, and slick magazine ads. It is possible, however, to come up with a sensible plan for making an informed decision, and if the entire family is involved, the selection process itself can be a significant learning exercise for everyone.

Reading publishers' promotional materials is one possible place to start, but checking unbiased reports (see the resource list on page 115) and setting critical standards are essential. Here are seven criteria to consider in selecting an encyclopedia set.

1. *Reliability:* Accurate information on a wide range of subjects is an obvious top priority. With today's information explosion and the multitude of subjects children encounter in school and on television, it is no longer a luxury to have on hand a reliable source for identifying people, locating places, and substantiating facts. Sets such as the *World Book Encyclopedia* and *Compton's Encyclopedia* continuously update material to ensure reliability. However, keep in mind that *all* encyclopedias, regardless of reputation or publication date, contain erroneous statistics, deceptive biographical material, and inaccurate dates. Children, who are inclined to take print as truth, need to know this.

Checking data in an encyclopedia against another standard source (such as the *Information Please Almanac*) or against one's own knowledge is a worthwhile exercise. Have each family member read about and make notes on several favorite topics covered in different encyclopedias. Then have them make comparisons with other sources to determine the accuracy of the material.

2. *Objectivity and timeliness:* Politics, religion, anthropology, and a host of other such areas are open to prejudicial treatment; people or topics related to these fields may be included or excluded at the whim of the writers. You should also be aware that the word *revised* on an encyclopedia does not necessarily mean that *all* the data have been updated. *Encyclopedia Americana,* for instance, has not been completely updated since 1972, although various sections are revised each year. Always check to see whether and when the entire encyclopedia has been updated. Again, spot-checking in areas of expertise or against another reliable source will shed light on areas of misinformation. The biographical dates of a recently deceased, well-known person, new rules in a sporting event, or an explanation of a recent scientific discovery are good data to check.

3. *Accessibility:* The organization of the material is an important

consideration because, regardless of accuracy or updating, children will not use the information if it is difficult to find. The alphabetic arrangement in *Compton's*, for example, tends to be less cumbersome than the *Lincoln Library*'s thematic organization. In addition to a set's general arrangement, cross-references and indexes that guide the reader to related information should be tested. Check specific topics in the index to see whether the information can be located easily (this also tests the scope of topics included). Then open a volume at random, select one item, and check to see if it has been listed in the index.

4. *Readability:* The age of children who will be using the set is another factor that will influence your purchasing decision. Although something can be said for selecting an encyclopedia children can grow into, the reading level of the work should be within the children's reach; otherwise, the set's value as a supplement to school texts and library books will be minimized. You should be aware of editorial policies regarding this factor. *World Book*, for example, accommodates a wide range of young readers by constructing its articles to read from simple to complex; *Britannica 3*, on the other hand, is clearly designed for adults.

5. *Style:* Lively, stimulating writing encourages independent study and motivates further exploration. Precise language, straightforward definitions, lucid explanations, and simple, direct presentations are the elements of good style. Read several passages yourself; then have your child read a few on unfamiliar topics to test whether the material is understandable and whether it encourages further exploration and inquiry.

6. *Design and format.* Don't let glossy photographs, intricate artwork, and appealing drawings distract you from making a thorough physical inspection of the set. Durable bindings, easy-to-read typography, and attractive spacing are the ingredients of a well-designed set. Look for print that does not show through on the reverse page — a sign of poor-quality paper — and for matte or semigloss paper, which alleviates glare. Check for use of letters and numbers on the spines as well as for guide words on the tops of pages. These may seem incidental at first, but lack of them can cause real frustration when one is trying to locate information. Diagrams, maps, and photographs can be colorful and attractive additions, but they must be integral to the main text; the adage that a picture is worth a thousand words is not necessarily mean-

ingful for conducting research. To be most effective, they should be carefully reproduced, well placed, up-to-date and pertinent to the subject, and they should include concisely worded captions that identify and explain their subject.

7. *Supplementary materials.* Encyclopedia companies often tout extra features. Examine the bibliographies following articles (noting publishing dates), the indexes, and the glossaries. Inquire about accompanying dictionaries, atlases, study guides, additional reference services, and availability of yearbooks. Evaluate these carefully; find out if extra costs are involved, and weigh the materials' future use against today's appeal.

With these criteria in mind, visit your local library, where several sets can be appraised simultaneously. Compare similar material in different sets and determine which set is best for your child's needs. If the library does not have a particular encyclopedia that you're considering, be sure to make other arrangements to examine it. Friends who own sets might be consulted, but keep in mind that individual needs and situations vary.

Once this evaluation procedure is completed, it is time for the family to discuss cost (and any special cost-cutting measures available) and shipping arrangements with a sales representative. If possible, arrange for a home trial period. When your encyclopedia set arrives, you can be sure your evaluation efforts have resulted in an intelligent selection that the entire family can use for years.

RESOURCES

Kenneth Kister, ed. *Encyclopedia Buying Guide: A Consumer Guide to General Encyclopedias in Print.* Bowker, 1978

Christine L. Wynar. *Guide to Reference Books for School Media Centers.* Libraries Unlimited, 1973

American Library Association. *Purchasing an Encyclopedia: 12 Points to Consider.* 1979

Carolyn S. Peterson. *Reference Books for Elementary and Junior High School Libraries.* Scarecrow Press, 1975

Creativity:
Development and Applications

O VER THE PAST thirty-five years, study of the creative process
and creative people has revealed that being or becoming
creative is not an either-or, all-or-nothing phenomenon.
Like intelligence, creativity is found to exist in some measure
among all people. Creative behaviors generally abound untamed
in young children. However, as children get older and become
adults, except for a very few, creativity tends to get smothered
and lost through the usual experiences associated with schooling
and "growing up."

A major concern for parents of gifted young children — for whom
development of creativity is an essential step to realizing their full
potential — should be to sustain that which is *natural,* that creative
tendency most children seem to be born with. Extensive research
indicates the necessity for continuous attempts made both at home
and in school to enhance this creativity. Even though creative traits
are complex, a multitude of evidence suggests that creativity can be
defined, developed, learned, taught, and measured.

The following essay by the brilliant, multitalented Steve Allen
shows how dreams and the "twilight periods" between sleep and
waking can open the door to creativity.

CREATIVITY AND DREAMS:
AN ESSAY BY STEVE ALLEN

The primary, and perhaps the original, example of human creativity
is the dream. I do not mean this in a loose poetic sense, but in the most
factual sense possible.

If anyone were to present us with a written story, we would certainly consider the account an instance of creativity. Let us assume that the story had a cast of characters, that the persons described perform certain actions, have certain adventures, say certain things to each other or to themselves. The point is that this is precisely what occurs in dreams. We are unfortunately denied access to the overwhelming majority of details of dream-stories, simply because of a weakness of recollection. But, from time to time, a particular dream does impress itself on our consciousness. The wealth of detail is invariably remarkable. Not only do separate characters people our dreams, but we might say of them the same that we say of characters in theatrical, film or television dramas.

Now in the case of a play or film we may be impressed by the contributions of a producer, a director, a playwright, several actors and actresses, a lighting expert, a scenic artist, and a costume designer. But in the case of dreams, the individual dreamer functions as a particularly dramatic example of creative versatility. Each of us, every night of our lives, functions as producer, director, playwright, actor, etc.

And the creative "supervision," as it were, extends to the minutest details. It is we who "decide" the colors of costumes; the size, strength, speed, ferocity or gentleness of animals; the condition of the weather; the content of conversations. That we would extemporize our own remarks in dreams is perhaps no more remarkable than that we are able to do so in the waking state. Although what is involved in both cases is remarkable, we simply fail to perceive the wonder of it because it is part of our daily experience. But in dreams we have not the slightest difficulty or hesitancy in creating dialogue for the other characters as well. Even more magically, in dreams we *become* those other characters.

More recently this has come to be called "lucid dreaming," a state in which the dreamer is both conscious of dreaming during the act and can direct what goes on at the same time.

There is even a separate plane of creativity in dreams because we are no longer bound by physical laws, no longer even necessarily limited to acting in time and space as they exist in the real world. In dreams we are able to fly, to exist under water, to walk through walls, to move from one place to another quite distant in a moment of time. Indeed, the time factor of dreams is one of the most mysterious of all. Not only are we creating the equivalent of a motion picture, but we may be projecting that motion picture scene in just a few seconds, whereas in real time and space a given scene might take twenty minutes to transpire.

From this, then, I conclude that creativity is not something with which only rare individuals are blessed. It is rather, on the most fundamental level, an identifying characteristic of the human species. And yet, what a crushing tragedy it is that most humans are unable, or at least unlikely, to function creatively in the conscious state. It is certainly the case, after all, that artistic individuals constitute a small minority. Not many of us are novelists, poets, playwrights, painters, sculptors, composers of music. But the reasons for this may be largely environmental. Thousands of individuals in their early years may never hear their native languages spoken with grace or style, may never be exposed to the literature of their individual cultures, either because they are illiterate or, if they do learn to read, are never educated to the point where they develop an appetite for reading.

But creativity itself is by no means limited to the formal arts and their professional or amateur practitioners. Proficiency at problem solving is, beyond question, an exercise of creativity. Some undoubtedly have greater genetic potential for it than do others. But I assume that most of us have some innate degree of potential for such thought, just as we can all draw some sort of picture, create some sort of story, or hum some sort of melody.

I recall once reading that Bertrand Russell, when wrestling with a particularly knotty problem — which in his case might involve mathematical, political or philosophical concepts — would simply cram himself with as much input material as possible and then retire for a good night's sleep. The solution to a problem, he discovered, was often present in his mind, sometimes quite fully developed, when he awakened in the morning. I assume that one thing that happens in the act of sleeping — remaining unconscious for long hours at a time — is that we get out of our own way, so to speak, and let one portion of the mind roam wherever it will, without being inhibited by the conscience or other ego-affecting faculties.

From time to time I write jokes in my sleep and also songs. Oddly enough my most successful song, "This Could Be the Start of Something Big," was written in a dream. Thank goodness it occurred to me just before awakening one morning since we remember most clearly the dreams we experience at those moments. I jotted down the first few lines of the lyric, which enabled me later to consciously recall the music, and the job was done.

Also, I have learned to pay close attention to my brain in those brief twilight or dawn periods when it is drifting off to sleep or awakening. It is during those moments that the brain will sometimes produce either the resolution to a problem or drop into the slot, as it were, a fairly important factor, one requiring prompt attention, but which had been overlooked in the rush of business and personal concerns of the preceding few days. Since I would be surprised to learn that my brain is the least bit unusual in this regard, I suggest to others that they pay the same attention to their internal computers when dropping into or rising up out of sleep.

Since there is apparently no way of predicting when a worthwhile idea will occur to the conscious mind, it seems to me most unwise to be habitually unprepared to capture those fleeting ideas that do present themselves. Which is to say, one ought to go about armed with pencil and paper — I prefer a small hand-held tape recorder — to make an immediate record of thoughts worth remembering that come to mind. I make an immediate impression of ideas for jokes, poems, songs, plays, short stories, novels, inventions — indeed almost any sort of idea except those that are obviously trivial and of no evident practical use.

It is no accident, in my view, that many remarkable theories and discoveries in the area of mathematics and physics have been made by persons in their late teens or early twenties. Galileo was still a teenager when he made one of his important scientific observations. This is not to say that creativity must necessarily decline in later years; but rather that a young and therefore relatively uncluttered brain may, in some strange sense, have more room to swing ideas about and may be less encumbered by cynical, negative prejudices of the sort that inhibit our own freedoms in creative and other areas. Actually, the process by which I, or any other second-rate thinker, conceive of a fresh idea is probably the same as that by which the truly great minds turn the trick.

As it happens, there's no question but that I am indebted to my mother and her entire family for nurturing such a tendency to humor and ideation as my genetic equipment might have allowed. I guess they taught me the importance of placing an emphasis on spontaneity, discovery, laughter, and in providing an environment for children that is creatively nurturing.

It seems to me that we should encourage children to take their dreams seriously as a rich source of creative material and for problem solving as well.

TWENTY-THREE SIGNALS OF CREATIVITY: A CHECKLIST FOR PARENTS

Creativity is a key component in most definitions of giftedness. Below are twenty-three characteristics that signal creativity in children and some sample statements by children that reflect those traits. The list was developed by E. Paul Torrance, Distinguished Professor of Educational Psychology at the University of Georgia. While few children will display all of the characteristics, several of them in combination indicate creative promise in your child that should be nurtured at home and school.

1. Intense absorption in listening, observing or doing: "But I didn't hear you call me for dinner."

2. Intense animation and physical involvement: "But I can't sit still — I'm thinking."

3. Use of analogies in speech: "I feel like a caterpillar waiting to become a butterfly."

4. Tendency to challenge ideas of authority: "Why do I have to go to school until I am sixteen?"

5. Habit of checking many sources: "Mom, I looked at all the books and watched a TV special and asked my teacher, and I still cannot figure out where God lives."

6. Taking a close look at things: "Hey, this centipede only has ninety-nine legs!"

7. Eagerness to tell others about discoveries: "Guess what! Guess what! Guess what!"

8. Continuing in creative activities after scheduled time for quitting: "I did my art work right through recess!"

9. Showing relationship among apparently unrelated ideas: "Hey, Mom, your new hat looks just like a flying saucer!"

10. Following through an idea set in motion: "Tomorrow I'm going to dig for gold in our backyard."

11. Various manifestations of curiosity and wanting to know: "I just wanted to know what the yard looked like from the top of the roof."

12. Spontaneous use of discovery or experimental approval: "I thought flour and water would make bread, but all I got was white goo."

13. Excitement in voice about discoveries: "Flour and water make paste!"

14. Habit of guessing and testing outcomes: "I put detergent in the birdbath, but no birds came to clean up. Can I try some bubble bath today?"

15. Honesty and intense search for truth: "Mom, I hope this won't upset you, but I don't think there is a tooth fairy."

16. Independent action: "There are no good books on racing cars, Dad. I am going to write my own."

17. Boldness of new ideas: "But I think that children should be allowed to vote."

18. Low distractibility: "I cannot come out to play. I'm waiting for my chemicals to dissolve."

19. Manipulations of ideas and objects to obtain new combinations: "I'm going to take this string and this pencil and make a compass."

20. Penetrating observations and questions: "When the snow melts, where does the white go?"

21. Tendency to seek alternatives and explore new possibilities: "This old shoe would make a great flowerpot."

22. Self-initiated learning: "Yesterday I went to the library and checked out all the books on dinosaurs."

23. Willingness to consider or toy with new ideas: "What if dogs were masters and people were pets?"

NURTURING YOUR CHILD'S CREATIVITY

Creative behaviors begin at birth and increase to about the ages of six or seven. These are the crucial years during which children are eager to take initiative to be original and discover on their own. If this behavior is suppressed or ridiculed during this time, the joy of creative activity is likely to be replaced by apathy or guilt.

Questions continue to plague parents and teachers about how to educate youngsters who abound in energy, thrive on risk, and exude inquisitiveness, without killing their capacity for creative images, insight and fantasy on the nonverbal levels. All behaviors highly related to creativity must be linked together in some learning pattern unique to each child. The following strategies for elementary-school-age children will serve to channel this vital human potential both at home and in school.

• *Establish a responsive and expressive climate* loaded with materials and a diversity of opportunities for exploring. The materials need not be expensive, but there should be plenty of them. Include lots of old magazines, books, newspapers, games, old clothes, and gadgets. By giving children "space" to peruse and explore such things on their own, you'll be creating an environment that stimulates, challenges, and supports ideas, movements, discoveries, questions. Creativity requires freedom to just "mess around."

How can you make sure the environment is sufficiently ripe? Make a list of the things in the child's room at home or in the classroom. Better yet, have your child make his own inventory. Look at the list together and categorize it to see how many different types of activities there are that may stimulate him to creative action. Variety is the key here. In additon to the above, you may want to include art supplies, posters to cut up, old decks of cards, etc. Your imagination is the limit!

• *Provide encouragement for self-reliance.* Demand and expect children to do something and produce on their own, so that they experience feelings of self-esteem and of being responsible to and for themselves. Responsibility is an essential ingredient for maturity and creative self-direction. It is well recognized that children are significantly more productive in divergent ways as their *self-sufficiency* increases.

How can you keep track of responsibility and resourcefulness? One way is to keep a "production roster." The parent, teacher, or child should list all the things the child has accomplished, regardless of quality, over a specific period of time. This list will reflect the child's *fluency*, a sheer count of attempts to be productive. Look for and identify periods of high productivity and the conditions under which they took place so you can duplicate them. Look for growth and changes in production over time.

• *Recognize, respect, and give emotional support for questions, mental manipulations, or unusual thinking.* Watch for times when your child puts things together in some unique, clever way. To show that you care, listen very carefully to your child's ideas and thoughts. Be constantly alert to the uniqueness of his behavior. It is important to show interest and approval, but sometimes silence can be the best form of emotional approval.

To stay aware of your child's originality and to be sure you are giving enough support, keep a "listening roster" for yourself. Check how many times each week you have listened without being judgmental. As your listening record increases, you will be showing that you really do respect your child.

• *Expect and allow for comfortable regression in growth patterns* of your child, even though she is gifted. You will help your child prepare for occasional anxiety and failure by teaching her to accept mistakes, to laugh at them, but to capitalize upon them and learn from them. Allow time for contemplation, daydreaming, and use of the imagination, or just for being quiet or doing nothing. Be particularly receptive and alert to plateaus in growth, when no apparent progress is being made, and creativity may even decline. Sometimes children will appear lethargic or complain of boredom during these periods. This is natural, unless the condition extends for weeks on end. *Do not expect your child always to act logically and be productive.* Give her space to come to terms with her limitations as well as her abilities. Always be ready to discuss such things with your child; during low times in particular, give your child opportunities to work things out alone.

One way to allow your child the needed space for regression and contemplation is to provide an unused "pigeon loft," "think tank," "office," or "quiet place" somewhere in the home. It can be a closet, a cupboard, underneath a bed, or an unfrequented corner. This place will serve as a psychologically safe haven where she can go to fantasize or just to sit and wonder. It should be accepted as *her* place and not interpreted as a "hiding" place. Be sure she knows that while she's there she is not expected to be practical or productive. Allow time for escape to the "special place" at least once a day. Many creative thoughts follow such incubation periods separated from action and progress — in privacy with one's self.

• *Allow and provide some balance between interpersonal and solitary experiences.* Certainly socialization is important for your child, but so is time alone for inner exploration. If children are hostile at times because they are unable to face themselves, they are certainly not willing or ready to face you or others. Building personal self-worth and self-respect must take priority over a forced togetherness. If children are to be free to be creative, they must be secure in separating from you or the group without guilt or rejection. *Do not be suspicious of your child's time alone or constantly monitor it.* With such freedom, children are more prone to work out their hostilities quietly, and hostility can be a major roadblock to creative productivity.

Anyway, most socialization will take place in school or through school-related activities. Children should know they are expected to participate in family get-togethers also — such as visits to their grandparents. But in other cases, your child can be the judge — whether or not she wants to call or see a friend, for example.

• *Establish well-defined standards of discipline and conduct.* Your child should have no doubts about what you regard as right and wrong. What rules there are (and rules should be few, as they are generally conformist in nature and stifling to creativity) must be enforced consistently with fully predictable consequences. At times children should be expected to be "on task" practicing music, taking out the garbage — such times and tasks decided on and regulated by the parent or teacher. But there should also be free times for children to be involved with their own tasks determined by their own interests. In either case, creativity and high productivity require *discipline*.

How can you help your child achieve discipline? Agree with her on a clear-cut set of rules, write them out in list form, and post the list in a prominent place. Make sure that there are incentives, reinforcements, and rewards for following the rules, and consequences for infringement. Keep a log of good as well as bad behavior so that both you and your child know what is going right and wrong. In an accompanying "task" log, record weekly the times and tasks you have assigned your child and the times and tasks he has assigned himself. Be sure these are well balanced. This doesn't mean there has to be an equal number of each, but only that there are both. In the final analysis, the more tasks a child assigns himself, the better — as long as there is still some time reserved to do what you ask him to do. Review and discuss the entries together each week. The log is as much a monitor and incentive for you as it is for the child.

• *Exhibit an attitude of basic trust* that your child will do what is reasonable in a responsible way. Trust is absolutely necessary for children to feel comfortable taking *risks*, a basic element of creativity. Parents and teachers must not become distressed by the many anxieties and stresses of today's growing child. Trust can best be built by noticing the positive ways children operate in spite of all the obstacles they face: their willingness and desire, for example, to please, to do what's right, and to meet their responsibilities at home and at school. Giving them positive recognition for what they do is vital. "I realize you've had a very stressful day, and I appreciate your cleaning up around here as you promised."

Keep track of the times you allow your child to seek alternatives and make choices. Guard against always dictating to your child what needs doing and how to do it. "Brainstorm" with him, asking how many different ways something can be done. Allow him to make a choice and act on it — whether this involves cutting the lawn in an orthodox pattern or design or deciding which illustration best accompanies an original story. Supporting your child by trusting him to make choices is the best way to help build a good self-concept. The child who feels good about himself will then risk the unknowns in attempting to pursue creative paths.

APPLYING CREATIVITY

Family Problems

Apply creativity to difficulties arising from family interaction and, with the right kinds of practice, you can achieve wonderful results. When your gifted children learn the following techniques of "creative problem solving" along with you, they will be intrigued, and tensions among family members often vanish as all work together to find solutions.

Creative problem solving is like the scientific method. It first involves recognizing that you have a problem. Then you start analyzing the problem and all of the difficulties involved. After gathering as many "facts" about the situation as possible, you make "guesses" about possible solutions, evaluate these, modify them, and put the best possible solution into effect.

A family may have been aware of a problem for some time. For example, toys may always be scattered about the house, creating hazards to safety. The usual reprimands, punishments, and cautions have failed. Suddenly the parent, or the parent and child, thinks of the idea of setting up a toy library, where toys must be checked out just as books are checked out of a library. Then there is the job of evaluating the idea: how much time will it take? Is there space for the toy library? Will it solve the problem? Finally, of course, there is the task of putting the solution into effect and testing how well it does solve the problem.

There are many variations of the creative problem-solving process, but here is one that is widely used all over the world.

STEP 1. RECOGNIZING PROBLEMS   The *first big step* in the creative problem-solving process is *recognizing and admitting* that there is a problem. A person will not be motivated to think of possible solutions for a problem and then to carry out a solution until he or she recognizes that a problem exists and accepts responsibility for meeting the challenge. If the family is involved, all members must recognize that the problem exists and accept responsibility for doing something about it. Conflicts in families about the use of space and equipment, respecting one another's property, waiting turns, and so on are examples of the kinds of problems that affect all members of a family and which need to be recognized and accepted as family problems.

STEP 2. FIGURING OUT WHAT THE "REAL" PROBLEM IS   The *second step* in the creative problem-solving process is figuring out what the *real* problem is. As a family searches for information about a problem and looks at the difficulties involved in it, a "mess" of data will accumulate. However, it is very important to keep an open mind and postpone judgment until there has been a thorough job of fact finding and problem definition. Finally, you must determine what specific problem, if solved, would clear up or eliminate "the mess." It is usually a good idea to state this problem in the form of a question that, if satisfactorily answered, will remove all or most of the difficulties. It is very helpful to begin this statement with "In what ways might this family . . . ?" or "How might our family keep the floors clear of toys and games?"

At times, *defining* a problem correctly may actually solve it. For example, in one family, the children were always mixing various foodstuffs together. It made the mother fly into a rage, and everybody suffered as a consequence. As the family began discussing and analyzing the problem together, everyone came to realize that the children did many things out of curiosity and not for the sake of doing something naughty or making the mother fly into a rage. The mother then made a chart with columns headed: *Rage, Screaming, Counting 10,* and *New Solutions to the Problem*. She checked and logged her behavior every time one of the children had an accident or did something naughty. She found that by counting to ten first, she usually thought of some solution to the problem without flying into a rage. Counting to ten became the way of solving *her* problem before she could contribute to solving the other one.

STEP 3. PRODUCING ALTERNATIVE SOLUTIONS The *third step* in the creative problem-solving process is to *produce many alternative solutions*. During this step, it is important to postpone judgment and remove the usual blocks to creative thinking — habits, conventions, and conformity. The following four rules developed by the creativity researcher Alex F. Osborn many years ago are still useful in doing this:

• *Rule out criticism*, at least while you try to think of possible solutions.

• *Welcome wild ideas*. Even offbeat, impractical, silly ideas may trigger a practical "breakthrough" idea that might not otherwise occur.

• *The more ideas the better*. The more ideas produced, the better the chances of finding useful, new ideas.

• *Seek combination and improvement of ideas*. Encourage group or family members to "hitchhike" on one another's ideas: for example, combine two or more suggestions into a single solution.

STEP 4. EVALUATING IDEAS When the members of a family defer judgment, all kinds of ideas occur. Their evaluation of these ideas becomes the next major task. To select the best, develop criteria — concrete standards for judging the possible solutions. These may include such things as cost, time required, usefulness, social acceptability, and other considerations. The application of criteria helps to identify the most promising solution. In some cases, even when the ideas for solutions are sorted out, it still may be possible to combine two or more solutions to create a better one.

STEP 5. DEVELOPING A PLAN OF ACTION After the most promising solution has been determined, there is the challenge to make it workable. In implementing the solution, further changes and additional possibilities may occur. It is necessary to think of the possible consequences of the application of the solution, as well as the possible obstacles to its implementation. All of these considerations should result in a successful plan of action. Getting back to our toy library, for example, the family discovered that the solution worked best when the children took turns — on a weekly basis — sharing the role of "librarian," seeing to it that each day the toys were put away on their proper shelves.

WHAT MIGHT COME FROM CREATIVE PROBLEM-SOLVING IN A FAMILY? If families master, practice, and use creative problem solving consistently in coping with new experiences, the following outcomes are likely:

1. It will create the conditions that encourage curiosity, exploration, experimentation, and the development of the talents of family members.

2. It will provide opportunities for developing skills of creative expression, problem solving, and success in coping with change and stress.

3. It will prepare family members for new experiences and help them develop creative ways of coping with these experiences.

4. It will provide a means whereby destructive energies can be transformed into productive behavior.

5. It will provide creative ways of resolving conflicts among family members.

6. It will challenge and make use of the creative contributions of each family member.

7. It will give the family purpose, commitment, energy, and zest for the future.

Inventing

If you want to help your gifted child develop thinking skills and spend time together engaged in a fascinating activity, try inventing. People tend to think that inventors have some magical key that opens closed doors, but the art of invention need not be cloaked in mystery. Parents and children can learn it together using a step-by-step technique.

Learning the process of inventing is especially valuable for gifted youngsters because it develops their problem-solving abilities and creativity in the broadest sense. They learn to think systematically by correlating ideas rapidly. They learn to recognize a specific problem and solve it. The outcome is practical, and the process is exciting.

Once gifted students grasp the concepts involved with inventing, they easily create novel and useful products. For example, a first grader devised the idea of a blackboard that has an automatic eraser bar which moves from one side to the other by means of a motor mechanism, which also extends the height of the board. A seventh grader invented a baby's spoon with a colored temperature gauge so that the parent can readily see whether the food is at the right temperature.

Don't begin with complex ideas or complex mechanical devices. Children can improve such things as a pencil, comb, blackboard, chalk, eraser, hammer, or screwdriver. A complex laboratory isn't necessary. If a child actually wants to manufacture his invention, this can often be done with simple materials and can start with a rough sketch. The main purpose of instruction is to see that children learn the thought process that underlies step-by-step inventing. It doesn't really matter whether the invention is something that has already been invented; it is novel to them.

A practical course on invention includes six main divisions: Introduction, Identification, Foundation, Data, Imagination, and Limitations. These consist of a number of steps that should be applied to any problem in order to arrive at a usable invention that will solve it.

INTRODUCTION   Begin your introduction by developing a definition of invention with your child. You may start by looking up *invention* in the dictionary. One first grader in an inventing class said, "It is making something that has never been made before." This is an astute definition. Although breakthroughs (X-ray, atomic energy, the laser) do occur, most inventions are based on the improvement of existing conditions, developments, devices, or technology.

The introduction will also include a general history of the development of invention, which will show how a specific need for an invention may arise. Start by discussing that there are *eight areas of invention:* shelter, food, clothing, communication, transportation, health, weapons, and culture. For example, see if your child can think, in a general way, of how invention has affected the development of clothing from primitive times to the present — for example, sewing, weaving, iron needles, cotton gin, sewing machine, washing machine, synthetic fabrics. Once children are led to try this kind of thinking, they quickly get the idea.

IDENTIFICATION   This simply means becoming aware of the three ways to recognize problems that can be solved by invention. These include listening for complaints, looking for difficult and inconvenient situations, and being aware of breakdowns and injuries to persons or things. By keeping in mind these three methods of finding problems, your child will soon have a long list of problems to solve and will be able to select an area in which to work. One seventh grader recognized that when sawing it was necessary to stop periodically to blow away sawdust. Thinking this interruption inefficient, he invented a saw with a bulb in the handle connected to a small tube directed downward to the edge of the saw blade. When the bulb is squeezed, it causes air to blow the sawdust away.

FOUNDATION   To help your child gain a foundation of knowledge for the particular area in which he wants to invent, have him develop a general history of an item he may want to improve. Let's say it is a simple spoon. He can trace the spoon's development from the crude ladles used by primitive societies, to small spoons such as teaspoons, and then to large "spoons" such as steam shovels.

Your child may enjoy doing research on the areas she is particularly interested in. Encyclopedias may be used for starters. There are also excellent books at all reading levels about inventions and inventors. Any library will have several. An excellent resource, which is fascinating to children, is *The Story of the U. S. Patent and Trademark Office*. It lists inventors, briefly describes their inventions, and gives the dates when these were patented. You can obtain a copy by writing to the Superintendent of Documents, U.S. Government Printing Office, Washington, DC 20402.

DATA   This category is designed to teach the young inventor to correlate information. She learns to obtain data and reach solutions by asking the right questions. Teach your child to ask many detailed and specific questions about a problem area in which she would like to invent. First: "*What* is it?" For instance, if you were trying to solve a problem about a matchbook to produce a better result, you would break down the major physical components of the book: the cover, striker, match, and fastener. What are they made of? What about appearance? Weight? A change in weight can lead to a new invention. If the weight of a blackboard eraser is reduced by hollowing the upper handgrip, a sliding cover can be added to provide a receptacle for holding chalk.

The next question in data gathering is "*Why* does it exist?" Once the young inventor understands what need an invention serves, she can anticipate and create improvements. Be sure she doesn't take anything for granted and that she describes the device in detail. How does each part function? Under what conditions? Realizing say, that trying to light matches in the wind is difficult, the inventor might consider constructing a matchbook with a wind guard. Recognizing the limitations of a device produces the rationale for an addition or improvement: the "why" of the new invention.

IMAGINATION   Once your child has collected relevant information by asking and answering the questions, he is ready to use his imagination to develop solutions to problems. A good way to begin thinking imaginatively is to create alternate images of, or change the words used for, a tool or problem area. Considering synonyms for blackboard eraser — eradicator, wiper, scrubber — can lead to the generation of new ideas that might enable the young inventor to think of changing the structure of the eraser to incorporate a liquid, a chemical compound, or an electronic device for removing the writing from the blackboard. He realizes that he cannot focus on only one aspect of the problem.

Approaches leading to a new invention can include combination of two or more inventions, substitution of one part for another, the rearrangement of parts, or the addition or deletion of parts. For example, a wind guard on a pack of matches would replace the standard cover (deletion, substitution), and at the same time function as a cover also (combination).

LIMITATIONS   Once your child has decided to pursue the development of a specific invention, it is important that he consider any limitations that might be imposed by law, material, time, space, or use, in order to create the most efficient device for the intended purpose. Would the wind guard be too costly to make or cause the pack of matches to be too cumbersome to carry in a shirt pocket, for example?

For detailed assistance on the process of inventing, you may wish to obtain a copy of *The Art of Successful Inventing* available from FIA publications.

Bookmaking

Making books or booklets at home is an ideal activity for gifted children of all ages and their parents and offers unlimited opportunities for family togetherness. And creating a product gives the gifted child a necessary outlet for self-expression. Younger children are highly motivated to read and reread anything they've helped put together; older elementary-school-age children relish the chance to brainstorm and develop original ideas. If your child is too young to write complete sentences or paragraphs, simply jot down what she says. The important experience gained from most of the book topics to be discussed is that of *generating ideas*, not the physical act of writing.

SIZE AND FORMAT   The size and format your child decides to use will directly affect the bookmaking process itself. In fact, it is a very aesthetic process, which requires (and can develop) a sense of proportion and some understanding of the relationship between the whole, its parts, and the book's function. For example, a tiny booklet made of several 3- by 5-inch slips of paper folded over and stapled lends itself to a sentence per page with perhaps a simple drawing per thought. An 8½- by 11-inch page gives space for much more: one or more paragraphs or several detailed illustrations. An even larger size is a scrapbooklike creation, with photos or cutouts glued in as the art.

The book covers themselves can be works of art. Artistically gifted children may enjoy designing the outsides more than composing the contents. For younger children you can provide a wallpaper sample book from which to choose appropriate patterns for book covers, or use colored construction paper, adhesive contact paper, or Sunday comics for pasting on cardboard. The idea of creating collage covers will intrigue the budding author-illustrator. Pieces of magazine photos and ads can be cut and pasted to form an interesting pattern that relates in some way to the subject of the book. Big letters from ads can be cut out for a variety of book titles.

Once provided with some choices, gifted children often know exactly how they would like to pursue a project. They might prefer to write the book on separate sheets of paper until the ideas run out or the subject seems adequately covered — then staple the pages together (or sew them, punch holes and use paper fasteners, or design some original way of putting the material together). Or sometimes it may work to prepare the mechanics of the book first, then write it — you know it's done when the pages are used up.

The range of bookmaking options is vast. Many of the following suggestions for topics are humorous, since gifted youngsters delight in giving their unique and advanced sense of humor free rein. Let your gifted child's interest determine what type of books he or she undertakes.

ALPHABET BOOKS   These need minimal explanation and can be created by children ages two to ten. Simply write "A" on page one and the child seeks appropriate examples of "A" words. Pages may be filled with magazine cutouts, handmade drawings, lists of "new" or uncommon words compiled from a dictionary, things that end in the chosen letter, whole sentences with every word an A. A beautiful example of this type of book is *Hosie's Alphabet*.

WEIRD QUESTIONS   This book is made up of unanswerable, open-ended, and mind-boggling questions — one per page with a sketch of either the question or a possible (even outrageous) answer. Both you and your child can take turns generating these questions and answers. Example: "How many grains of sand are there on the beach?" The picture could show someone with a handful of sand, with a caption or cartoon-style balloon saying "Four quintillion and three, four quintillion and four . . ."

WHAT WOULD HAPPEN IF . . . ?   This is a similar concept, yet it opens new possibilities for challenging and original thinking. You can share with your child the task of devising open-ended, "what-if" questions. They can be nonsensical, and the answers can be as illogical as the child wishes. "What would happen if . . . kites were made of lead . . . horses were invisible . . . ice cream trucks played Beethoven . . ." Or they can be more or less realistic, such as "What would happen if oil were discovered in Brooklyn?"

DROODLES   A copy of Roger Price's *Droodles* will be most instructive for this type of book. Full (and funny) directions for Droodle-making are included. A Droodle is basically an odd bit of drawing which derives its sense entirely from its title. Thus, one of the simplest in Price's book, a straight line, is entitled "Used All-Day Sucker" or, alternately, "Postcard, Side View."

Price helpfully includes a selection of basic shapes that can be used to form Droodles. But, of course, the talented child will soon catch on and invent her own shapes, Droodles, and catchy titles.

BELIEVE IT OR NOTS   There are at least two choices in making up this type of book: your child can stick to reality and obtain from an encyclopedia or other reference books bits of information that are true but somewhat hard to believe. The research is half the fun (and more than half the learning). For example, "Pandas have an extra thumb growing out of their wrists." Or totally make up statements such as "Three-year-old Melissa James attains speeds of over forty miles per hour on a playground slide." Ripley's *Believe It or Not* books can be a useful guide to this type of bookmaking and can help your child make up her own amazing "facts."

TV GUIDE TAKE-OFFS   The world of television offers several interesting prospects for bookmaking. Some gifted children may like to fill pages with "incredible stunts," "you-asked-for-its" (the abominable snowman with a crewcut), and "What's My Lines" (odd occupations like putting the rubber caps on metal chair legs). Or they can make up a phony TV program guide altogether — complete with fake listings, funny program descriptions, illustrations, and advertisements for upcoming specials. "Coming soon on channel 93: the debut of 'Linen Closet' — the first prime-time soap opera disaster miniseries performed entirely by nude bath towels and floor mops!" Indeed, such listings can form the basis of more detailed "scripts" in which family members can star in their very own sit-coms.

BOOK OF LISTS   This book topic is based on the bestsellers of the same name. Here the young author makes lists of all sorts of divergent things. Examples: "Six reasons for not finishing my homework on time," "Four colors that look awful with purple," "My five favorite dreams." Pictures and drawings are optional.

BOOK OF RECORDS   This is a personalized book of the Guinness type, one "record" per page. The entries may be genuine milestones, or simply made up for the fun of it. As a "benchmark barometer," this book will chronicle your gifted child's accomplishments in and out of school. It's also a good technique for building your son's or daughter's self-esteem. "On January 17, I read a whole 342-page book." "On March 3, I set up a domino layout consisting of 500 dominoes which tumbled down in 18 seconds." On a less momentous note: "On April 12, I brushed my teeth after all three meals and also after two snacks."

HOW-TO BOOKS   Many gifted children have skill or knowledge in an area that most other children may not have. Another great self-concept builder is to have your child design and write a book explaining how to do something she knows a lot about or likes to do. This could be of a hobby, a variation on a famous chess defense, how to perform the perfect forward roll — anything. The book should include step-by-step explanations and illustrations where they could help clarify the subject.

Whether for fun, enrichment, or publication, bookmaking can be a rewarding learning experience for your gifted child and you.

Getting Work Published

Many children's magazines solicit and welcome contributions from children. If your child is interested in this possibility, a complete listing of such magazines is contained in the annual *Writer's Market*, along with specific suggestions and guidelines for submissions.

However, help your child to realize that rejection is not necessarily a reflection on the quality of the piece. Many fine pieces of writing or artwork do not get published because of the volume of submissions a publication receives, or because something similar was published a couple of months before, or because the piece did not quite fit the needs of the publication.

The Visual and Performing Arts

WHILE MUCH emphasis has been placed on identifying academically gifted children in recent years, the federal guidelines for gifted and talented include artistically gifted children as well. These youngsters excel in the visual and performing arts — including painting and sculpture, music, drama, dance, and related media — and require special programs to develop their gifts.

A GIFTED PROGRAM IN THE ARTS

Writing in the *NJEA Review,* the official publication of the New Jersey Education Association, Albert Dorhout, a state consultant for gifted education, defines a gifted program in the arts as one that includes a comprehensive procedure for assessing aptitude, achievement, and attitude; activities commensurate with the needs of the artistically gifted child; and an in-service program for arts teachers.

Criteria for identification may be formal and may require auditions or the review of writing and art portfolios. Another effective approach is to offer elective programs so that children may select courses based on their interest in a specific area of the arts. When teachers or parents discover that a child displays an exceptional aptitude or achievement level in an artistic discipline, they can encourage the child's involvement in that particular art form. Sometimes, Dorhout notes, it is necessary to stimulate the child to develop his artistic potential, particularly if he or she has a negative attitude about it.

Attitude may be measured through an "inventory of feelings," an informal questionnaire completed by the child showing his likes and dislikes for the arts and interest in arts activities. Dorhout insists that attitude should be given "equal weight" with aptitude and achievement when selecting children for an arts experience. "Without a positive attitude," he says, "the aptitude and achievement levels may be irrelevant."

An essential component of planning programs for the artistically gifted is in-service teacher training, to make sure that faculty members working with students have opportunities to review the latest research on gifted education. For example, teachers of the arts should investigate the latest methods designed for identification of students. Dorhout also suggests alternative and flexible programs for artistically gifted students so that a child of multiple abilities may work in more than one artistic area at a time. For example, a child who is gifted in music and dance could combine his talents to compose a musical arrangement that he or she then choreographs.

By contrast, a study by Benjamin S. Bloom, professor of Education at Northwestern University and the University of Chicago, shows that schools are probably *not* the best places to develop exceptional talent. Bloom's "Development of Talent Research Project" described the results of interviews with more than 120 people who excelled in an artistic area before the age of thirty-five. The purpose of the study was to determine the factors that were significant in developing their talents — specifically, how the home and school contributed to a "world class" level of accomplishment by individuals in three areas: the artistic (concert pianists and sculptors); the psychomotor (Olympic swimmers and tennis players); and the cognitive (research mathematicians and neurologists).

In the majority of cases, Bloom reports, the subject's family members had a personal interest in his or her field of interest and gave him or her strong support as well as encouragement and rewards for developing the talent. In fact, the family usually took it for granted that the child would develop the talent. This family atmosphere was especially important between the ages of three and seven.

Most of the other environmental and educational ingredients

Bloom found to be essential to the development of a specific talent were the *opposite* of characteristics of most school experiences as a rule. For example, the general approach to learning in the home is informal and varied. The instruction that the talented individuals in Bloom's study received at home was usually given on a one-to-one basis — from parents, siblings, and teachers in the particular field of talent. Consequently it was individualized and personalized. Classroom learning, on the other hand, is like an "assembly line," states Bloom, and emphasizes group learning of the same tasks.

Also, such public arenas as recitals, contests, and concerts, which do not exist to the same degree in academic areas, spur children on by providing "significant rewards and approval," Bloom says. They are the benchmarks of a child's progress and a context in which a group of individuals who share a special interest can form a community.

"The major point," Bloom says, "is that in the talent field the individual becomes fully engaged. . . . The school does not encourage or permit many students to become fully involved in any one part of the curriculum. . . . We report very few instances in which talent development and schooling function to enhance each other."

Since appreciation for the performing and visual arts is so haphazardly taught in most schools, it is up to you, the parent, to introduce them to your gifted children. Artistic awareness aids in the development of taste and sensibility and adds an essential dimension to your child's existence. An appreciation of classic forms helps combat the low standards of popular entertainment. Good and exciting art involves stretching the rules, experimenting, and risk-taking — behaviors we want to encourage in our bright children. The broader part of art appreciation is learning to look closer, listen better, increase awareness in everyday experience, and add a depth of perception beyond the practical.

STAGES OF DEVELOPMENT

Up to the age of eight or so, the child will benefit most from continuing to make his or her own art, to express his imagination by dabbling in painting, clay, singing, and dancing. It is important for parents to allow freedom of self-expression and minimize deadening criticism. Younger children are learning to distinguish fantasy from reality, and it is your job to help them retain their imaginations.

From about nine to eleven, children think things have to be and look just so; they are beginning to make judgments, and you can teach them to compare and contrast. They begin to be hard on themselves and self-conscious. You'll especially want to encourage inventiveness and a sense of humor during this factual age. When your child is observant, perhaps critical, of the shape of an unusual vase or the appearance of a statue or the melody of a song, try to help him or her define why. Children will begin to see that there is more to taste than mere liking; that sensitive people agree on certain, but not all, objective standards.

For youngsters of about twelve and up, the arts provide a way of reflecting on themselves and their personal points of view. They are sensitive to artistic messages and styles, and you can explore together a wealth of artistic varieties. You can discuss "what it means," and your child can comprehend.

Use your child's interests as a springboard to fitting art appreciation into the everyday life of your family. In every form of art there is abundant choice; the child who is technologically tuned and the one who is people-oriented will each find styles to which to respond.

Take your own interests into account, too. Since you will probably not feel equally knowledgeable in all areas of the arts, choose forms that you particularly enjoy and that relate to your own experience.

Consider subscribing to an arts channel on cable TV. And don't neglect your educational channel.

AN EYE FOR ARTISTIC TALENT

The visual arts are all around us. Everywhere you and your gifted child look, you'll find exampes of form, line, color, and design used in particular ways to achieve specific effects. Even the least visually attuned among us can learn to be more aware, to see with more clarity, and to share our visual discoveries with our children.

Though the language we are most familiar with — the one emphasized in school — is the written and spoken language, the expressive language of signs, symbols, and shapes is the one in which the visual arts communicate. Systematic training in visual perception increases the power of the right hemisphere of the brain, frees the imagination, and even gives the analytical side of us something to think about and to say.

Included among the visual arts are painting, drawing, sculpture, ceramics, crafts, photography, graphic arts, and architecture. These arts have much in common. Your gifted child can learn some general principles that apply to all and will learn much by direct experimentation in several areas.

Artistically talented children are often overlooked in school because many of the current identification procedures are "clumsy and inadequate." This is the conclusion of Gilbert Clark and Enid Zimmerman, art educators at Indiana University at Bloomington, in an issue of *School Arts* magazine. They particularly regret that many students "who do not take art classes in their later public school years are seldom screened for artistic talent."

The authors surveyed identification procedures of more than fifty art programs for the gifted and talented and present the following list of these criteria in order of popularity.

1. Self-nomination
2. Portfolio review
3. Classroom teacher nomination
4. Interview
5. Creativity test
6. Informal art test
7. Art teacher nomination
8. Achievement test scores
9. Structured nomination
10. Peer nomination
11. Parent nomination

Here is a summary of the authors' comments on some of these in terms of their own expertise and knowledge of research. You'll note that the most popular techniques are by no means the best. What system does your child's school use? Is it adequate? Or is your child an unnoticed artistic talent? Check with your child's school to determine how artistically talented children are identified and what provisions exist for developing their talents.

• *Self-Nomination:* The authors think that self-nomination and peer nomination (low on the popularity list) are the most valuable means of identification. Artistically talented students are usually highly critical of their own work, and other students know about the skills and strengths of their classmates in and out of class.

• *Portfolio Reviews:* Though the advantages are obvious, the technique does have some drawbacks, say Clark and Zimmerman. It eliminates identification of *potential* talent, and the more prior art classes students have taken, the bigger their advantage.

• *Classroom Teacher Nomination:* This, according to the authors, yields "very poor results." They say, however, that "structured nomination forms (very low in popularity) and in-service nomination training greatly improve teacher nomination." There are nationally available checklists such as the *Visually/Artistically Talented Student Profile* (from "Project Art Band: A Program for Visually Gifted Children," DeCordova Museum, Lincoln, Mass., 1982); however, teachers must be trained to interpret them.

• *Interview:* This is worthwhile with other techniques, the authors say, but interviews are costly and time-consuming.

• *Creativity Tests:* Though these are commonly used, questions have been raised about their value. Some researchers say that students who score well on such tests may not necessarily be artistically gifted or talented because the tests do not measure skills used in art tasks.

• *Informal Art Tests:* The authors believe such tests "lead to very subjective assessments of talent." They would like to see objective tests standardized for all parts of the country.

Biographical and student interest inventories and observation are two strategies not on the list that the authors believe are particularly useful. Inventories, if developed with the goals of the program in mind, they say, can provide information that other school procedures might not reveal. And they believe that "a student's persistent interest in art is probably the most salient identification indicator." Also observing student behavior, they say, though it's costly and requires training, "yields information unavailable from any other source." A student who draws and doodles constantly does have a desire to create images.

Learning by Doing

Children start out as "naive" artists, drawing according to their own inner vision. Later they turn imitative. And, in striving for adult perfection, may lose confidence in their ability to draw at all. You can encourage your child to be true to his instinctive artistic sense by allowing lots of time for work on paintings and drawings (no coloring books!); by providing a safe, uncritical environment; by encouraging the addition of details to artwork; and by exposing him to a variety of museums. There is more than one "right" way to draw a thing, as is obvious when the child becomes familiar with the style of such artists as Picasso and Chagall. Also, introduce your child to surrealists such as Dali, to show that art can have a sense of humor. Always keep a supply of art materials on hand. Consider taking your child to an artist's supply store to examine the variety of items available. You might give the child a gift certificate to one of these stores as a birthday or holiday present. Thousands of activity ideas are available in the magazines and books listed in the resource section.

Learning to See

An increased sensitivity to the obvious is one of the goals you and your youngster will both achieve when you embark on an informal arts appreciation course together. For example, soon you'll be noticing the subtle shadings in a tree branch, order in the design of a leaf, and many other details and differentiations.

Visiting small art galleries provides a glimpse of the disparate visions of artists working currently. Using art books and museum trips, expose your child to the art of other times and other nations. Compare volumes of reproductions of European paintings, for example, and discuss the differences from period to period and from artist to artist. This brings history alive, and the variety of styles gives your child insight into the particulars of artistic genius.

When possible, compare paintings with photographs of the same subjects, and observe the differences. Purchase art postcards at museums and miniature reproductions of interesting artworks. Your child can hang these in her room, or collect them in a book.

Try to develop the following as you work on training your child's visual sense: the ability to discriminate among varying uses of color, line of shape, space, and texture; the ability to recall and describe what has been observed; use of a variety of subject matter and media in personal expression; learning to value originality; use of the vocabulary of art as the child's aesthetic judgment evolves. The child will be able to compare and describe works of art with respect to meaning, sensory qualities, style, materials, and processes used to create them. The youngster will also begin to recognize how the quality of design affects the function of products and of the environment.

COLOR   Colors provoke strong emotional responses, varying with the particular context. Red can imply excitement, love or danger. As recent scientific research has shown, colors affect mood. Encourage your child to notice colors used on packages at the market and to become aware of gradations of color: for example, the shades of green when you're out walking. You might have your young child point to all objects in a room that are of a single color and notice how light affects color, as in stained glass. Van Gogh wrote in a letter about his painting *The Night Café* (see *Just Imagine: Ideas in Painting*): "I have tried to express the terrible passions of humanity by means of red and green."

Allow your young artist to experiment freely with mixing colors. Some are complementary — they clash: red and green, yellow and purple, blue and orange. Others blend: red and orange, yellow and green, blue and purple, blue and green. Help the child observe the colors of sunlight and of shadows, and how you cannot always tell exactly where one ends and the other begins. Some artists — Monet, for example — made use of this indistinctness of light and color.

LINE   Talk with your child about how the eye follows lines, and that lines lead to the center of interest in paintings, sculpture, and architecture. The width, smoothness, and intensity of line conveys a range of attitudes and emotions. You could have your child draw line-words: different lines which express the words *scared, loving, nervous, daring, quiet, friendly*. A line is the path of a moving dot; it's an edge, and it can be used as decoration (in Persian rugs, Turkish mosques, art nouveau lamps, and so on).

SHAPE, SPACE, TEXTURE   Shape can be two- or three-dimensional; some two-dimensional artworks *seem* to have depth. Show the child how the work of Escher uses tricks to create an illusion of depth. Some of the words used to identify shape are *square, cube, cone, man-made shape, biomorphic* (lifelike, like an amoeba), and *free-*

form. You can point out how positive and negative space is utilized in walls, windows, and puzzles.

Space in an artwork can be narrow, wide, open, sweeping, cluttered, empty. To increase awareness of space, have your child try unusual viewpoints, such as seeing the room from under a table, or looking down from a ladder.

Textures of paintings and other artworks vary, and roughness and smoothness are only part of the story. Sometimes the thickness of the paint stands for high energy. Your child can make rubbings to become more aware of texture, or she may try to draw a textured model, such as a pet, someone's hair, a shoe.

DESIGN AND COMPOSITION   Go through an art book or visit a museum with your child and observe the repeated patterns and rhythms in the paintings. Unity is the way a design or work of art is joined together to make a whole piece. Integrated colors, similar lines, and recurring patterns contribute to unity.

Balance is achieved in different ways. Two small objects can balance a large one, dark can balance light, the upstretched arm of a statue can balance a leg on the ground. Some art is purposely asymmetrical.

MEANING   In all the arts, particular objects and animals commonly symbolize ideas. A lighted candle represents the brevity of life; an egg stands for creation or rebirth; a dog symbolizes fidelity or melancholy or the sense of smell; a bear often means gluttony.

Make your children aware that art can be interpreted in various ways. You and they can take turns guessing at the meanings intended by artists in their paintings and sculpture. For hundreds of years, the world's greatest painters used mythology as a central theme. Sometimes knowing the historical background of a piece will make a big difference in how it's interpreted; for this, some basic art history is helpful. Read biographies of artists. Become familiar with the Bible to understand religious art better.

To increase his or her awareness of symbols and meaning in art, your child can create a personal logo, incorporating shapes, images, and objects that reflect his or her interests and personality. Another activity might be to design a message using graphic designs and symbols to be carried aboard a spaceship to inform other intelligent beings about our lifestyles, homes, and work.

Discovering Art through Picture Books

Introducing children — particularly talented youngsters, who are often especially sensitive to visual nuances — to art at an early age can shape the development of their powers of imagination and discrimination.

The exciting world of picture books is an ideal vehicle for making children aware of good art and exposing them to it on a regular basis. Though parents sometimes think of them within the context of literature, picture books offer true art through illustrations especially designed to be meaningful to children. They are illustrated by fine artists — representing a variety of artistic schools and employing a wide range of styles, palettes, and approaches — and are readily available from libraries and bookstores. Most important, the books can be shared often in the coziness of the home. Children can hold them themselves and examine the illustrations at close range

Developing an artistic awareness through picture books can begin with very young preschoolers. As children grow older, gain experience, and grow in their perceptions, parents can introduce more complex and sophisticated concepts. And older children can also benefit from exploring the art in the picture books intended for younger ones.

SHAPES, DETAILS, COLORS Enjoyment of the story should come first, but at the close of a read-aloud session, you can encourage even the youngest children to look at the pictures and notice shapes, details, and colors. Counting and alphabet books are particularly good for getting started. Molly Bang's *Ten, Nine, Eight* (uniquely presented from ten backward to one) uses, for example, shoes, usually thought of in pairs, as the unlikely object for number seven. Sharp-eyed youngsters will find the "missing blue sneaker," being chewed on by a cat, on the number "five's" page.

Youngsters allowed to take time to look and look again will delight in these innovative touches, and it will help them be aware that pictures contain all kinds of surprises. Years later they will be ready for the detail of Brueghel and the idiosyncrasies of Bosch. Both Frank Asch's *Happy Birthday, Moon* and Mirra Ginsburg and Nancy Tafuri's *Across the Stream* are stories that use clear colors and simple shapes against sparse backgrounds, letting their images stand clear and unobstructed, perhaps paving the way for the austerity of Vermeer or Hopper.

Somewhat older children will enjoy discovering nuances in a story's characters. The parent can help them to see how they can know if a character is sad or happy, scared or silly, from clues in facial expressions and body stances that illustrators have carefully included. Rachel Isadora's *Max,* about a boy's visit to his sister's ballet class, Steven Kellogg's *Ralph's Secret Weapon,* concerning a boy's hilarious attempt to charm a sea monster, and Rosemary Wells's *Timothy Goes to School,* about a rabbit-child's problems in first grade, are particularly noteworthy.

Setting is often given an added dimension by the graphics. Illustrations can suggest a place that is only hinted at or perhaps not described at all in the text. Pictures of famous landmarks, styles of architecture, geological formations, and peculiarities of weather come alive under a talented artist's brush. Lead children into observing how Robert McCloskey builds his storm in *Time of Wonder,* how Uri Shulevitz gradually enlarges his pictures to parallel the coming of dawn in his book *Dawn,* or how Parisian scenes in Ludwig Bemelmans's *Madeleine* add an authentic air.

As They Become More Sophisticated

As children grow in their artistic understanding, discussions of the art in picture books can be broadened to include other aspects such as the way color influences mood (mentioned above), and the rudiments of line work, composition, and perspective. How artists create a mood is a fascinating study for children. Sometimes it's through color: the dark, brooding atmosphere that Elisabeth Zwerger projects in *Hansel and Gretel;* the whimsical patterns and misty sea shades that Irene Haas fashions in *The Maggie B;* the jelly-bean colors that evoke the jolliness in Karen Gundersheimer's *Happy Winter;* or the combination of deep blacks and bright yellows that heightens suspense in Dennis Panek's *Detective Whoo.* You can talk about how, on the other hand, Maurice Sendak creates mood through expansion of action as the monsters begin their rumpus in *Where the Wild Things Are.*

Comparing and contrasting several books by one artist can also be challenging. For instance, Tomie de Paola's use of subtle watercolor in his impressionistic *When Everyone Is Fast Asleep* is very different from the bold colors and primitive style of his *Night before Christmas,* and the dramatic and somber realism he employs in *The Legend of the Bluebonnet* varies again from the playful scrawl and cheerful colors he brings out in *The Knight and the Dragon.* Children enjoy being able to identify illustrator's work, and practice in finding similarities and differences will sharpen their artistic acumen.

ACCENT ON COLOR   We, as well as children, are attracted to books featuring multishaded pastels and joyfully combined bright colors; however, books executed in black and white can be equally effective. Just pursue Chris Van Allsburg's *Jumanji,* David Macaulay's *Castle,* or Rachel Isadora's *Ben's Trumpet* or *City Seen from A to Z.* Children will appreciate the intricate line work and its created effects if you inspect the work closely together and bring this aspect to their attention. Stephen Gammell brings the art of pencil shading to new dramatic highs in Olaf Baker's *Where the Buffaloes Begin,* and Diane Diamond's meticulous pencil work could be mistaken for photographs in books such as *Swan Lake* and *Rumpelstiltskin.*

Or, encourage a child to discover the effect of line and color working together. Many illustrators use the combination to add depth and texture to their pictures. One without the other wouldn't be nearly as effective. William Steig employs this technique most effectively in *Doctor De Soto* and *The Amazing Bone,* where color adds emphasis and line supplies humor. Peter Spier uses more vivid watercolors punctuated with scraggly, expressive lines in *Noah's Ark* and *Rain,* while Trina Schart Hyman's calligraphic lines flow across her pictures, fluidly shaping images in *Sleeping Beauty* and *Snow White.*

Detail also stimulates the eye. Steven Kellogg is a master of detail, and the signs, labels, characters, and happenings he creates in his book are electrifying because of it. Notice with your children how his stories often begin on the endpapers and end on the back cover, making the book a total experience, or how he includes an extra story in the background, as in *The Mystery of the Stolen Blue Paint.* These kinds of "secrets" are fun for children to discover on their own. Hilary Knight includes the antics of a curious raccoon in *The Twelve Days of Christmas*; a monkey craftily sets a tea table in de Paola's *The Quicksand Book*; and a cat can be found on every page of Hyman's *Little Red Riding Hood*. Nancy Burkert creates a beautiful medieval atmosphere in her *Snow White* as an example of a different kind of detail.

Another interesting facet of art for children to consider is the perspective from which the artist creates the scene. In Linda Heller's *Lilly at the Table*, a young girl has been reduced to food size, and her excursions down a slab of cheese and tightroping a strand of spaghetti are an interesting study in proportion. Eric Ingraham provides astonishing views of the ground from a hot-air balloon in Mary Calhoun's *Hot-Air Henry*.

KEEP QUALITY HIGH   Making these kinds of discoveries in picture books does not, of course, lend any immediate insights into the great works of art. What it does do is make children more aware of what they are seeing, of how artists work, how they obtain their effects, and how these extend the flavor of the story. At this point in children's artistic growth, it is especially important that they be given high-quality examples. When ready, they will be intrigued to learn about these different schools of art and will delight in pointing them out.

Fine books for children directly on the subject of art and art appreciation do exist and will help them understand the great masters. Two of the best of these art books scaled to children's understanding are by Richard Cumming: *Just Look — A Book About Paintings*, and *Just Imagine — Ideas in Paintings*. A series called *Looking at Art (Faces, People at Work, People at Home)* and Brian Holmes's *Enchanted World* and *Creatures of Paradise* are also helpful. Children's books have so much of that delight and wonder that Conrad spoke of, and to rediscover it together with your children can be a truly satisfying experience.

TIPS ON SHARING ART THROUGH PICTURE BOOKS   It is important that you and your child have a positive experience when you share the marvelous art and illustrative techniques in outstanding children's picture books.

1. Be sure that excursions into artistic appreciation in picture books do not interfere with the enjoyment of the story. Make your discussions about the art casual. Don't let them become lessons that may turn children away from books and art.

2. Don't spend too much time at one sitting or insist on dissecting every picture. Rather, look at the book together and let your child decide when to stop.

3. Allow quiet time for just looking; then, let your child make some of the discoveries and contribute ideas.

4. Make sure your child realizes that you, too, are involved in the process, so that it *is* a sharing experience. You'll be surprised at their insights and perceptions; undoubtedly they will notice things you missed, but you will both be richer for it.

MUSIC

A variety of experiences — singing, listening, moving to music, playing instruments — is necessary to provide the background your child needs for understanding music. Provide these as early and as often as possible.

Contact the public relations department of your local orchestra to find out about weekend youth programs and to obtain advance program notes for events you plan to attend. Posters or illustrations of the orchestra seating arrangements may be available. Take a tour of the concert hall if possible.

When you know the selections to be performed, obtain records (perhaps borrow them from the library) and play them at home. Point out key parts to your child. Read the record jackets for information about the music and composer. A trip to the library will provide books about instruments, musical vocabulary, and the lives of composers, too.

Take children to a variety of performances, from summer bandshell concerts to formal events. Get on the mailing lists of local colleges and check local papers; some events will be free. Discuss concert etiquette beforehand, especially the need for quietness. Explain how to tell when the piece is over. After the concert, play some of the selections again. Buy some of your child's favorites.

When listening to music with your child, talk about the setting of the particular work and whether it was based on another work. Point out variations in pitch, duration, and intensity. Discuss melody, rhythms, and accent. Explain what harmony is, and tempo. Share your knowledge of common musical terms (or look them up together).

Musical judgment and sensitivity grow by exposure to many

kinds of music. See that your child hears Indian music, choir music, children's classics, art songs (poetry set to music), chamber music, folk music, blues, light classics, instrumental solos of all types. Stories and related musical works that your child may enjoy include the fairy tale "Nutcracker King," with Tschaikovsky's *Nutcracker* Suite; *Mother Goose*, with the *Mother Goose* Suite by Ravel; *The Story of Peer Gynt*, with the *Peer Gynt* Suite by Grieg; and "Cinderella," with *Cinderella* by Prokofiev.

Stop at a music store and let your youngster see various instruments up close. If possible, have her take lessons. Pursuing an instrument for even a limited time will help a child gain an appreciation of the self-discipline required. Consult with a music teacher to help decide on an appropriate instrument for your child. And remember, sometimes it takes several tries before the "right" instrument is found. Initially, it is best to rent an instrument for a trial period.

Play two records of varying quality of the same piece and talk about where the differences are (an advanced skill). Choose one instrument at a time to concentrate on. Play various records, having your child try to pick out that instrument. Choose a form, such as march music, and listen to contrasting recordings.

Express interest in your child's taste. Even with rock music, it's a matter of really learning to hear. Point out patterns, time signatures, particular instruments and techniques. Rock videos may develop into an art form. Watch these with your child and discuss them — their similarity to TV ads, the relationship of the movement to the song, the use of repetition, and so on.

Musical Prodigies

According to David Henry Feldman, a developmental psychologist at Tufts University, "prodigies are children performing at or near the level of an adult practitioner in a given field." After studying prodigies for four years, he describes them as having been "pretuned" in certain ways to develop faster than other children in specific areas, usually music, math, or chess. Howard Gardner, an education researcher at Harvard University, explains that these are the disciplines in which one finds prodigies because they are fields characterized by complex rule structures not dependent on a good deal of worldly experience.

Music is probably the most common form of performing arts talent, and almost all schools provide some form of beginning opportunities to develop musical talent, through choruses and instrumental programs. A close look at how musically talented children adjust and function should be generally instructive and also may give insights into other artistic fields — such as the theater (see page 159).

What would five gifted teenage musicians say if questioned about such things as their commitment, practice, drive, personality, schoolwork, and social life? A young musician interviewed five fellow students, ages sixteen and seventeen, who are highly involved with and intensely dedicated to their music. What they say about themselves should help others gain some understanding of how creatively gifted teens adjust to their talents, personally and socially. Andy is a tuba and bass guitar player, Meg, a trumpet player; Eric, a clarinetist; Michelle, a French horn player; and Jennifer, a pianist.

EARLY EXPOSURE AND COMMITMENT   Experienced parents know that a primary reason why children get involved in a particular activity is because "everyone else is doing it." That is, in fact, the way most of these young musicians became interested in the field. Michelle, for instance, was surrounded by music from an early age. "Music," she says, "was always in the house." Everyone in Jennifer's family played "a little bit of something."

That "little bit of something" for these kids has become, by their own choice, a major commitment. The time such a competitive field as music takes from the child's day is immense. The five interviewees spend from one to five hours a day on practice alone. In addition, they perform on weekends and play at ensemble rehearsals. While nonmusicians may see practicing as "just sitting there playing for a long time," most instrumentalists agree that a musician usually emerges from the practice room "absolutely exhausted."

PRACTICE SETS A DAILY MOOD   For many, the practice session determines the attitude of the day. Meg summarizes that "a good practice equals a good mood." The need to play often nags at the student's conscience, making him moody or uptight until that need can be satisfied. Jennifer says, "As long as I've gotten practicing out of the way, then nothing can bother me."

Intense concentration is almost always required to achieve the barely perceptible progress possible at each practice session. In a solitary room, focusing so entirely on an abstract concept called "musicianship," the students admit to losing track of time and becoming disoriented when suddenly interrupted. Andy, who often uses free periods at school to play, says, "Sometimes I hear the bell to go to class and keep on practicing." However, hours put in without scrupulous attention to musical detail are more frustrating than fruitful. As Michelle puts it, "It's not how much you practice; it's how much you get done."

TAKING THE DRUDGERY OUT OF PRACTICE   Parents of a musically talented young child know how puzzling it is when the child's enthusiasm for music rapidly diminishes after the first few weeks of lessons. Parents may even conclude that an unwillingness to practice is directly related to a lack of musical talent, but today's virtuosi are quick to admit that thoughtful encouragement from parents and music teachers helped them to develop the self-discipline that is essential in the study of music.

Most children do need to be encouraged to practice — not nagged or ordered, but firmly encouraged. Lorraine Gorrell, a professional musician and assistant professor of music at a South Carolina college, offers four helpful steps for encouraging your musical child to practice:

• *First, you and your child will have to set a definite time of day that is most conducive for practice.* Once an agreeable time is established, it must become a regular part of the daily schedule. This prevents prolonged arguments and lessens the chance that bedtime, homework, or other activities will make practice impossible.

• *Second, parents need to become directly involved in their gifted children's lessons and practice.* Children seven or eight years old will show much more progress in music study if their parents are able to attend lessons and help establish good practice habits. This is an investment of the parents' "precious time" and is a good way of demonstrating to the child what is important to the parent. A willingness to practice with your child, or to be nearby in case assistance is needed, effectively demonstrates the importance you attach to musical study. If you cannot spend time each day at practice, then it is best to do it the first few days after a new lesson is introduced, when there are unfamiliar techniques.

As children develop a musical foundation and gain independence, you may gradually step back and allow them to take more responsibility for their practice sessions.

• *Third, take the drudgery out of practice.* Although daily study requires a serious approach, include fun activities in the practice session. Small children enjoy making tiny music books with colorful construction paper covers and simple musical questions inside. Ask questions about materials they are learning. This helps them learn to read music more readily by repeating and reinforcing what the teacher has gone over. During practice time, play question-answer games using these books. Children often decorate these books with smiley faces, stickers, or original drawings. Sample questions for beginners can include: How do you draw a G-clef? How many quarter notes equal a whole note?

• *Fourth, children often enjoy presenting their musical skills for others to hear.* Music is a performing art and gives great satisfaction to the performer as well as the listener. In addition to the yearly recitals that many music teachers schedule for their pupils, children should be encouraged to play for grandparents, other relatives, and classmates. This will contribute to the child's developing self-esteem and sense of accomplishment. Appreciative audience response is, in fact, one of the most important rewards for the child's efforts.

WHAT KEEPS THEM GOING? Support for their intense pursuit of music comes from many sources, but after a certain degree of proficiency and maturity is attained, the prodigies rarely draw on their own family members for encouragement. Teachers are the students' main source of support, and a strong mentor relationship is essential for a positive self-image. Where personalities or goals conflict, a bad rapport can develop and often obstructs learning so entirely that the student must search for a more ideal learning situation, one based on a better rapport with a teacher. The students cite honesty and sincerity as major ingredients of that ideal situation. Andy describes his discussions with his tuba teacher:

"During lessons we talk about music, not as student and teacher, but as people."

An equally important source of encouragement comes from the drive of the student himself. Because music is such a competitive field, talented youngsters specialize at increasingly early ages. All of these interviewees knew before they were eleven years old that they were going to be professional musicians. Such an immediate focus distinguishes these children from the others at school, and peer support has to be earned. Andy finds that the other kids support his bass guitar playing because "it's something they can relate to." Jennifer says teens in her town are not so appreciative: "Other kids can't comprehend the hours of practice you put in or the frustration that goes along with it." Strength must often come from within the musician.

TENSION AND PERFECTION   The general stereotype of the classical performer is often one of emotionalism and moodiness and was supported by the interviewees. They say that they think they tend to be much more nervous than the ordinary person. While some get nervous even for lessons, others don't feel sweaty palms until they are getting ready to perform or audition. Each expresses a need for concentration. "I just want to be alone," says Michelle. "I have to have my space." Without it, Eric says he often becomes "tense and irritable." Once on stage, however, the musician is in control, and, as Jennifer puts it, "you try to make the energy work for you."

Each of these prodigies speaks of being highly sensitive emotionally and talks candidly of his or her low boiling point and frequent mood swings. Eric: "I have no patience with myself. I have no patience with other people. I have no patience, period." More precisely, as Andy says, "I'm not tolerant of anything that's not perfect." The need for perfection leads at times to misunderstanding by others. Michelle explains the predicament: "You're focused on music, but to the outside world you appear angry and withdrawn. People say, 'Why do you look so serious?' Your natural reaction is 'Leave me alone,' and you snap. It's not necessarily moodiness. It's the same kind of mental seclusion needed for practicing."

SCHOOLWORK VS. MUSIC WORK   The prodigies' commitment to music does have an effect on their views of academic performance in school. In a broader poll of teenagers participating in music, but not particularly talented, 63 percent were in accelerated academic classes. However, 83 percent of the prodigies were not. There seems to be an inverse relationship between the degree to which the student is talented and involved in music and that to which he is involved in his school, both scholastically and socially.

All the interviewees admit to daydreaming frequently. Their attitudes toward school range from bluntly negative to accepting. Jennifer confides that she sometimes asks herself, "Why am I sitting here in this class when I could be practicing or doing something useful?" Andy avoids boredom by daydreaming: "I get in trouble for it, too." But they all recognize the importance of education. Michelle, for instance, takes not only the courses required for graduation, but many music courses and others in which her personal level of interest is high. "I've made school work for me," she professes. Meg voices the resignation to the inevitable that is typical of the whole group: "I could benefit more from practicing, but I know that education is important. I wouldn't want to be an illiterate musician."

WHAT ABOUT A SOCIAL LIFE?   Socially, these musically gifted teens' involvement with their peers in school is slight, and they show little interest in becoming any more active outside their field. Meg affirms that the high school scene "doesn't affect me because basically I stay out of it." Andy is equally removed. "People like to play those little games in high school," he says disdainfully.

The parents of gifted musicians tend to view their offspring's limited socialization as "too narrow" and often nag the children to "go out more, meet kids other than musicians, and have some fun." Sometimes this attitude conflicts with and fails to support the need their children have to satisfy their drive for creative improvement and ultimate perfection. For the most part, parents can relax. It's not really a lack of socialization that is occurring, but a focused and potentially more fulfilling form of socialization.

The interviewees expressed a special affinity for musicians that extended to committed artists in other creative fields. In fact, they find it difficult to relate to peers who have not needed to be as dedicated to an activity as they have. Meg explains that she immediately feels "something in common with other people who know what they want out of life and are working towards it now."

The prodigies indicated a decided preference for a few close friends, rather than large clusters of them. Within a group situation or among friends, they almost always assume an authoritative role and emerge as the initiators and leaders of an activity. Their divergent styles of thinking can delay their being accepted in some circles of friends. Jennifer says, "I wasn't the kind of person who would let people step all over me just so I could hang around with them."

THE GOAL   Though each interviewee has created several original compositions, performing — rather than conducting or composing — is the single career they anticipate. Beyond undergraduate and graduate training at a conservatory, the students echoed one desire almost word for word: "My basic goal is to be happy with my playing."

HOW TO HELP   No one knows for sure just what makes one child a musical prodigy when his or her siblings can't even play "Chopsticks." It seems to depend largely on innate creativity and an intense inner drive. But it is no less evident that attention and rewards are necessary, and encouragement from family, friends, and teachers is crucial at every step of the way. With the prodigies interviewed, music is something they grew up with, and practice, so important for developing what talent a person starts with, became as natural as brushing one's teeth.

Besides this, central to the fulfillment of one's musical abilities is a teacher who can be a mentor in the true sense of the word — one whose insight, honesty, and sincerity can be helpful with related personal matters as well as technique.

Undoubtedly the most important attribute that the child needs from his parents is understanding. The lines between active involvement, support, pressure, and even indifference are often subtle. Parents need to recognize that the strong goal orientation of musical prodigies sometimes precludes having the "average" social life of adolescents. But the "true peers" for these people are really other musicians like themselves and those who have exceptional ability in other performing arts.

As for schoolwork, gifted musicians need to understand its importance, achieving up to their abilities, but parents shouldn't expect or insist that their children be excellent at everything. Shouldn't it be enough to be "master of one trade"?

Talent, hard work, dedication, and stamina are mandatory for musicians, and youngsters entering the field must deal with the knowledge that their profession is an extremely competitive one. Asked if they regret the sacrifices they constantly make in order to pursue music wholeheartedly, the interviewees answered unanimously "no." One or two did say they wish they had more time to engage in some "outside interests," but Meg speaks for the group when she says that "music is more important in the long run."

Music Lessons: What to Look For

Yehudi Menuhin made his concert debut when he was not quite ten years old. He was billed as being eight, however, to make his accomplishments seem all the more remarkable — and marketable. Were he starting today, he probably would not play publicly (except at student recitals) until his late teens. The philosophy that now keeps very young children out of the limelight can be largely attributed to the publication of *Forbidden Childhood* in 1958. This book, by Ruth Slenczynska, offered a shocking look at the exploitation of musically talented children.

Developing, rather than exploiting, their child's gift in music should be the goal of parents today. But the child, not the parent, should determine when — and perhaps if — special attention is to be given to making music. Only your child can supply the first and most essential element: personal desire — desire so intense that it drives the beginning musician beyond the squeaks, scratches, and aching muscles that accompany his first efforts. The time to begin formal instruction is when your child, not you, expresses such a desire and an interest in a musical instrument.

Your child, however, need not be a prodigy to make an investment in music lessons worth while. Most bright children are able to gain some musical fluency even without possessing unusual musical gifts, and many grow up to treasure their ability to play an instrument as a particularly satisfying hobby (Einstein and his violin come to mind as a notable example). Moreover, music lessons help develop the right side of the brain and a child's creativity.

When your child expresses an interest in music, don't go out and buy an instrument immediately. Some musical instruments require too much lip and lung power for the very young musician. It may be necessary for your child to begin learning music fundamentals on one instrument while waiting to develop the strength needed for his or her first choice. Moreover, music store sales clerks, realizing your naïveté, may try to sell you a nice-looking but poorly made instrument. You need the considered opinion of an experienced musician.

If your child's school has a music program that offers students the opportunity to try out a variety of instruments, talk to the music teacher, who can advise you about instrument manufacturers and where you can rent an instrument while you are deciding what to buy. If you prefer to enroll your child in private lessons, choose a teacher before you buy an instrument. Then buy from a store that will let you return the instrument if it doesn't meet with the teacher's approval.

Choosing a teacher is the most important step you'll take. The music teacher can either fan a child's excitement, instill a lifelong love of music, or can squash exuberance with tedious daily exercises. If your child shows enthusiasm and progresses rapidly in the music program at school, group lessons may soon become frustrating and then boring. Encourage your child to participate in school ensembles (they are fun and teach young musicians to play with others and follow a conductor), but ask the school instrumental teacher to recommend private teachers, who can pace lessons to meet your child's particular needs. Ask for recommendations from a local musician you respect. Take special notice of the talented student your child admires, and inquire about that student's teacher. Usually there is an excellent teacher behind each "talented" musician.

When you talk to a prospective teacher, listen for enthusiasm, self-confidence, and pride when the teacher speaks of her students. Find out how long it has been since the teacher has worked with a beginner. Does the teacher have a stable schedule, or will lessons be sporadic? (Consistency is *very* important for beginning students.) Does the teacher teach pieces — specific songs — not just technique? (A child, after all, studies an instrument so that she can play *music*. By the third or fourth lesson, a student should be able to play a tune, no matter how simple.) Does the teacher encourage students to play music with others? Does the teacher provide opportunities for students to perform in recitals?

If possible, attend a teacher's student recital. What you see and hear are good indications of the teacher's style and success with students. Are the performers rhythmic? Do they "sing" when they play, or do they sound stiff and mechanical? Do they seem to enjoy playing? Do you and your child like the pieces they play? Do they speak enthusiastically about the teacher and confidently about what they have learned? Do they think the teacher is patient?

Finally, enlist the help of a friend more knowledgeable in music who is willing to evaluate a teacher — or refer you to one — and your child's progress once lessons have begun.

As "valuable as private lessons are to the serious student," says Robert Bonnevie, French horn principal for the Seattle Symphony Orchestra, "important skills — such as playing in tune, learning to listen to and play with others, and phrasing with others — are best learned in chamber music."

School-sponsored chamber ensembles — some consisting entirely of students and others including professional musicians as group members — have replaced conventional programs in a number of school districts and are receiving rave reviews for their role in music education. Ensemble groupings can be changed after each concert to give the youngsters exposure to different professionals and performance techniques. Students note that playing with a professional adds "just enough pressure" to get them to practice more and play better than usual.

Parents and professional musicians have often taken the initiative in getting chamber music started in their school districts. To find out more about chamber music opportunities for your child or to gather material for starting a program of your own, write: Chamber Music America, 14th Floor, 1372 Broadway, New York, NY 10018. This group is an informational clearinghouse for all kinds of chamber music activities, particularly public school programs, and for a small cost will send you the *Directory of Chamber Music Workshops, Schools and Festivals*.

An additional resource is a series of nine videotapes, "Chamber Music: The String Quartet," which describes how to start a chamber ensemble at all levels of student proficiency. The tapes, featuring the Pro Arte String Quartet, are available for rental. A free catalogue can be obtained from: Agency for Instructional Television, Box A, Bloomington, IN 47402.

THEATER

Begin attending plays with your child in the preschool years. The ones with audience participation are attention-getters, as are puppet and mime shows. When the child is old enough to be blasé about kiddie theater, try the real thing. With enough discussion beforehand, even Shakespeare becomes comprehensible. A ten-year-old begged to see a production of *Macbeth* after his teacher had told the class the story, emphasizing the bloody action.

If possible, see more than a single version of the same play and compare productions. Compare the limitations of theater with what is possible on film. Discuss how sets often serve several purposes, how important the audience's imagination is, the lack of editing in a live performance. Talk briefly about the history of drama, how males used to play female roles. Try to obtain and read parts of a play or script before seeing the play.

Discuss kinds of stages — proscenium, open or platform, and theater-in-the-round — and resultant changes in the relationship between audience and actors. Talk about the specialists involved in a play — playwright, performers, director, scene designer, costumer, and lighting designer — and how they create special effects that contribute to the whole.

Alert your neophyte playgoer to the importance of the stage picture, the way the director manipulates the players so that important elements dominate. See if he or she can tell if the actors are pretending to feel or actually are feeling the emotions they're expressing.

Even the game of charades at home — or other forms of psychodrama in which family members act out roles or situations — helps the young playgoer (and perhaps future actor) appreciate the process and difficulty of conveying emotions and states of mind.

OPERA

Opera may be the most complex art form, incorporating acting, singing, orchestral music, costumes, scenery, and often dance. Choose your child's first opera carefully, perhaps one with child characters *(Hansel and Gretel)*, or one with humor and a relatively fast pace, preferably one in English. Rock operas *(Jesus Christ Superstar)* are an interesting offshoot. Musical comedies, which have lighter music and much more spoken dialogue, may be more accessible to youngsters. There are several good opera movies (certainly less expensive than the theatrical versions). Bergman's movie of Mozart's *The Magic Flute* is a delightful example.

Read the libretto (text) in advance, or at least a detailed summary of the action, so your child will have some mental guideposts while watching.

Factors to mention: occasional unreality of casting (adults playing young people); the acting less realistic because the singing is more important, communicating passion and excitement particularly; the "free-flowingness" of arias, unlike the singing we're used to; the dark make-up, deep colors, sweeping gestures. Talk about singing ranges (women: soprano, mezzo-soprano, alto; men: tenor, baritone, bass) and find examples on records.

Teach the child some opera terms, such as *aria* (an elaborate vocal solo); *ensemble* (several characters singing at one time); and *leitmotif* (a short musical passage that identifies certain ideas, places, and characters each time they appear).

Six Tips for Parents of Talented Young Singers

1. *Help them develop musicianship.* Teach them to read music and count, train the ear, and expose them to knowledge of musical theory. Piano lessons are basic for almost all musical training.

2. *Expose them to good vocal and choral music.* Listen at home to classical music to offset the poor quality of music commonly heard on AM radio and records of popular music.

3. *Teach them how to take care of the voice.* There is no need to "baby" the voice, but it should be used with moderation. Shouting or screaming can damage the vocal cords.

4. *See that they learn the rules of singing.* Seek out a private voice instructor — a respected teacher or someone who is a fine singer — by the junior or senior year in high school. It is important that an accomplished singer work with a talented young person privately on basic vocal technique — such as proper breathing and relaxation of the throat and jaw.

5. *Urge them to become involved in speech, drama, or dance.* These can help the musician gain poise and stage presence as well as body awareness and acting techniques. But don't overdo it. Too many involvements can lead to exhaustion and lack of focus.

6. *Pay attention to physical conditioning.* Most important, don't let the child start smoking. Also see that he or she exercises, eats wisely and moderately. Singing is hard work.

FILM

Making a home movie, complete with editing and titles, is one way for a young person to get a firsthand idea of the complexities of filmmaking. Unlike theater, film can show, not only tell, what's happening and what went before.

Read film reviews together, and choose movies that are not purely entertainment. But be willing to leave before the end occasionally rather than forcing a youngster to sit through something agonizingly uninteresting to him. Let your child's age, experience, and visible levels of interest or boredom gauge this. Relate the plot or style to something familiar, if possible. Once a child is comfortable with reading, you can introduce him to art films and foreign films with subtitles. Get on the mailing lists of revival theaters. Learn something about the film and director before going. Discuss the layers of meaning and symbolism in art films. Books of common symbols are available. For example, a sun rising means rebirth, a sunset means coldness, death.

Talk about what *you* like and don't like about a film, why some are box-office successes, and what that means relative to artistic merit. Read reviews *after* seeing a film; what does your child agree with, what did he or she miss?

DANCE

Before attending a dance performance, discuss some things to look for: the positions of the dancers' feet, hands, and bodies; periods of nonmovement; the patterns created by dancers' bodies; the interaction of groups of dancers; parallel movements of two dancers or two groups of dancers. Point out that the best seats are often above stage level so that the floor patterns can be seen. Read a dance review together and plan to observe what the reviewer saw.

Discuss the different kinds of dance: folk, Oriental (where facial expressions and hand gestures communicate the message of the dance), modern (which sometimes includes the use of acrobatics), and, of course, ballet (when dancers perform unnatural movements for the sake of the line of the body). Suggest that the child read about pioneers and famous dancers.

EARLY DECISIONS, HARD CHOICES

Gifted children are always a challenge. They must be nurtured in the rich soil of experience if they are to reach that elusive goal known as potential. For some, however, this flowering period is cut short by talents that demand to be fulfilled before maturity is reached. Children gifted in the performing arts are making tough career choices while not yet out of their teens.

Jessica — A Young Ballerina

Thirteen-year-old Jessica Evans of Medford, New Jersey, is already working toward her professional goal of being a ballerina. She attends ballet classes six days a week and rehearses with the Children's Ballet Theater, a new dance company that she auditioned for and joined this year. In her spare time she teaches ballet to her friends, or practices in her room.

Jessica's teacher, Barbara Sandonato, a former principal dancer with the Pennsylvania Ballet Company, understands the compulsion to dance. She started dancing when she was five or six, taking classes every day. At fourteen, she had a scholarship at the School of American Ballet and commuted from her home town of Harrison, New York, to Manhattan every day.

The commitment to a career in dance must be total — and it is essential to decide early. "You have to be really into the study end of it by the time you're twelve or fourteen," says Sandonato. "We must train the muscles. The foundation must be cemented in the early years."

But who actually makes that decision? Is it for the child to make at a notoriously emotional age? Should the parents, with their longer perspective of life, decide for the child? And what is the role of the teacher in all of this?

Edward Rosato, a Haddonfield, New Jersey, psychiatrist specializing in family therapy, says that sometimes a child is caught on one point of a triangle with the parents on another and the teacher on the third. Parents are often caught in conflict with each other as well, wanting to recognize the child as an individual and at the same time wanting to make the decision for needs of their own. The ultimate decision, Rosato stresses, must come from the child.

For Jessica, the decision was fairly easy. She knows she wants to dance. She also knows that there will be no time for piano or singing lessons or horseback riding, and that time with friends will be limited.

Jessica's parents know their daughter is talented, having been told so since she began taking dance lessons in kindergarten. They didn't take the comments too seriously at first, but began to believe it when they were told the same thing by a number of subsequent dancing schools. "We will support Jessica in whatever she wants to do as long as it is Jessica who wants to do it," says Jessica's mother.

Marjorie — A Piano Prodigy

Fourteen-year-old Marjorie Lee started taking piano lessons in kindergarten as a hobby. She says that she and her friends "were all about the same, playing in the same books." She didn't think she had any particular talent.

Her elementary school music teacher thought differently. She sent Marjorie to Anthony Casario, director of the Conservatory Without Walls in Haddonfield. He recognized her potential and urged her to study seriously to be a concert pianist. That recommendation put considerable pressure on Marjorie and her parents. At twelve years of age, when most girls are concerned with school, friends, and clothes, Marjorie Lee was considering what she would do with the rest of her life.

Marjorie's mother, June Lee, once played the piano herself, so she had some understanding of what it would mean to Marjorie if she pursued her talent. "It's tough to be a pianist," she said. A piano career would mean that Marjorie would have to practice at least six hours a day, have private tutors, and give up many of the activities she enjoys.

"Is it my decision?" the mother wondered. "That's bothering me." She worried that if she didn't encourage her daughter, Marjorie would regret it later and say, "Mom, why didn't you push me?" At the same time, she was looking to her daughter's future. "If she wants to be a lawyer or a doctor, she can have a married life as well as a professional life," she said.

"I feel certain that she can be concert material," said Casario. He said that she has all the right combinations to succeed —

intelligence, ability to perform, talent. He tried to "gently coerce" Marjorie into that decision.

Casario's confidence in Marjorie's ability seemed justified recently when Marjorie participated in the conservatory's first piano student recital. While all the performances were applauded, Marjorie's drew appreciation even after the applause. People stopped her in the aisle, on the stairs, and in the reception area to express their pleasure with her playing.

The Lees went through a year and a half of soul-searching and finally came to the decision that Marjorie would *not* pursue a career as a concert pianist. It was a decision made by all of them. "If she had really wanted to do it, we would have supported her," said Mrs. Lee. But Marjorie's determination was not strong enough. She will continue to take piano lessons for her own pleasure.

HOW TO DECIDE

Rosato is concerned that talented children be happy, not give themselves over to their talent for the wrong reasons, such as to make their parents or teachers happy. He wants them to have time to socialize, to make friends, to have fun. He advises parents of a talented child to "sit down and list just what the commitments would involve and tell the child, 'This is what it would mean. The choice is yours.' If the parents try to avoid the discomfort by making the decision for the child, it does not help the child to grow up." And the main objective is still to develop an emotionally healthy child.

"START YOUNG. . . NEVER STOP TRYING!"

Below is an interview with eleven-year-old Julie Dobrow of Franklin Lakes, New Jersey. It originally appeared in the *Gifted Children Newsletter* (now *Monthly*). Julie was a member of the *Monthly* student advisory board who describes her life as a performing artist in the theater. Her remarks illustrate — especially for children who aspire to a career as a singer, dancer, or actor — the kinds of commitment such careers entail, as well as the inevitable hardships and setbacks that one must get used to in these fields.

GCN: How did you get started in the theatre, and what role do your parents play in the development of your artistic talent and goals?

JD: I became interested in the theatre when I was about 7 years old and got the lead part in a summer camp show. Afterwards, I joined a local theatre group and had the lead roles in "Annie," "The Wiz," "Barnum," and "The Me Nobody Knows . . ." My parents were very supportive. They arranged for lessons in ballet, tap, jazz, and piano so I could accompany myself. . . .

When I was about 9, I wanted to audition in New York. My parents said it was okay, but that I couldn't tour — I could only accept a Broadway part. So I auditioned and was chosen for a part, but I didn't realize they were casting for a touring company only. That was a big disappointment. . . .

Although my parents want to give me a chance at a professional career, they still set limits on where I can perform. They'd like me to have an academic career as a back-up. Also, if I were to travel, we would lose our closeness as a family. (I have an older brother and a younger sister.)

GCN: Have you had any mentors along the way who have had a special influence on you?

JD: Yes. I belong to a professional students' workshop in Glen Rock, New Jersey called ACT II. The director, Ron MacFarland, is special — not only because of his talent and how he develops ours, but because he cares about kids' feelings and makes us all feel successful.

GCN: What kinds of things do you do at the workshop, and what kind of time commitment is required?

JD: Well, in addition to acting we write original material, such as monologues. We meet every Saturday from 11:30 to 6:00 and even on weekdays for productions. . . . We play for community groups, schools, senior citizens, and dinner theatres, so it gets time-consuming. I miss parties and trips and days with friends, but it's worth it because I love the theatre!

GCN: Talk a bit about auditioning. What's it like? What do you have to do? Are you upset when you don't get the part?

JD: I started auditioning at age 9, so I'm used to it now. The first rule is to be well prepared. Bring music, pictures, and dance clothes. You have to speak clearly and try to "sell" yourself. In other words, you have to give the best impression that you can and try to convey that you're right for the part. I think they're mostly looking for an outgoing personality.

I've auditioned for a lot of commercials, too, like Duncan Hines, Kenner dolls, and Kelloggs, Hi C, and Kool-Aid. But I haven't been chosen for a commercial yet. Although it's disappointing, you can't see it as a failure. If you're not selected, it's usually because you're the wrong size, coloring, or "look" for the part. . . . At this level, not many adults [involved in making commercials] care about kids' feelings. I've learned to forget all about it and never wait by the phone.

GCN: What happened with "Christmas Caper," that Broadway show you were going to be in?

JD: Well, I got the part of Holly, which would have been the lead part for the kids. The show was supposed to open at the Princess Theatre, but it was cancelled. I was told it was because the producers didn't want to pay us kids at union rates. Meanwhile, I had told all my friends that I got the part. . . . I learned from this that in show business nothing's definite. Still, I'll never stop trying!

CGN: What advice would you give other kids who may be interested in seriously exploring the performing arts as an avocation or career?

JD: Start early, no later than 10 years old if possible. And if you're seriously interested in a professional career, don't take on too many other outside activities. . . .

Make sure you pick well qualified vocal, drama, and dance coaches. Have them explain the curriculum to you and ask for a lesson before you decide. . . .

Don't sign a contract with any manager until they've proven they have good audition contacts. My manager [Shirley Grant] sent me on several auditions before I signed with her. . . .

Don't let rejection stop you from trying. . . . And most important, make sure you're doing it for yourself and not for your parents or friends.

Counseling the Gifted Child

A GIFTED CHILD is, above all else, a child who needs nurturing, understanding, and love. In fact, gifted children depend as much as, if not more than, other children on consistent adult guidance, examples, and perspectives. However, parents of gifted children are sometimes intimidated by their child's mental abilities and verbal prowess, and they fear the risks of guiding and advising. "I'm afraid I'll make a mistake," they may say. "I think I need the advice of a professional" is a frequent comment.

Of course, there are situations that require professional counseling — especially if you wait too long to address a problem. But parental counseling and guidance — based on wisdom, experience, values, an understanding that being gifted is not the bed of roses it is often assumed to be, and careful listening to the child's concerns — are essential to the growth and development of the gifted child.

Most important, parents must realize that giftedness does not go hand in hand with maturity and self-actualization. Gifted children are not perfect. They, like other children, must be expected to have flaws and limitations, to aggravate and disappoint as well as bring joy. Basic aspects of human personality development, such as love, humanity, sharing, and compromise are *unrelated* to giftedness and must be developed. Acquiring values, standards, and principles demands the same discipline and rigor for all children.

PERSONALITY PATTERNS OF
GIFTED CHILDREN

In order to guide our gifted children and help them develop in positive, self-fulfilling ways, it is important to understand their personality traits and the common misunderstandings about them.

Recent psychoanalytical theory underscores the long-recognized tenet that the acceptance of imposed emotional or intellectual expectations limits everyone's potential. Parents are pressured to conform to what *their* parents, employers, neighbors, spouses, and even children expect of them. Gifted children unfortunately bear the heaviest burden of expectations for two reasons. First, the more exceptional the child, the more likely that expectations of him will be inaccurate or unfair. Second, because of the prevalent myths about the nature of the gifted (for example, they will always make it on their own; they are excellent students; they are always agreeable and charming), formal identification in school may serve only to reinforce distorted self-concepts.

Because of their exceptionality, if the gifted blindly accept others' expectations, they have more potential to lose than the less gifted do; if they reject group norms outright, their rebellion may be so extreme as to invoke severe penalties.

According to Susanne Richert, director of gifted education at the Educational Information and Resource Center, gifted children and adults seem to develop one of four survival stratagems in response to externally imposed values: conformity, withdrawal, rebellion, or independence. Each of these responses fosters or hinders the development of certain aspects of the self — including one's ability, productivity, creativity, values, self-concept, social relations, and sensitivity. The ideas that follow are Richert's.

Conformity: The "Closet" Gifted Child

For the sake of survival, most people, including the gifted, take the path of least resistance and accept what others require of them. Many gifted children accept, conform, and perform accordingly. First they learn to please their parents and teachers, then their friends, and later on employers, spouses, and others. The level of achievement of some very successful gifted children is often based on what others want in order for their acceptance to be gained. The excellent grades, intense competitiveness, and need to excel of the gifted may be motivated not by confidence, but insecurity. These children are dependent on continual external reinforcement of their worth through grades, test scores, parental praise, and friends' admiration.

As adults they can become ambitious workaholics who are never satisfied by their achievements, but continually crave another credential, promotion, raise, award, or public recognition of their worth. This is hardly surprising, since our society encourages people — males in particular — to value themselves according to how many of these external status symbols they acquire. Personal relationships, too, can be based solely on expediency. *Whom* one knows may be meaningful solely because of others' status or what some person can do for one's career, for example.

For girls in our society, pleasing others — whether teachers, parents, or friends — can become far more important than other measures of achievement. Gifted girls in particular are pressured to be "well rounded," not just to be good students, but also to be "popular." "Closet" gifted girls may fear social ostracism more than academic failure. Thus they sometimes engage in a frenzied round of social activities and club memberships, which they may not necessarily enjoy, but which they participate in because they do not want to feel excluded.

The pressures to conform are great. Unquestioning acceptance of conventional academic standards is counseled by many parents and advisors because it offers the most immediate rewards and ostensibly the surest route to success in the world. However, such conformity is based on a denial of individual values, a reluctance to accept mistakes, repression of creativity and independence, and fear of being unmasked or rejected. Without the development of creativity, a child can be successful, but not gifted.

But even more serious than the repression of creativity is the emotional dependence that in the long run makes these children inordinately susceptible to external criticism. However exceptional the child, sooner or later he or his work will not meet someone's standards. Neither past laurels nor the arbitrary nature of judgment can protect an insecure person. Some "closet" gifted children — and adults — can be so devastated by what seems to be the exposure of their true worthlessness that they can become self-destructive.

Withdrawal from Competition

Other gifted children may accept external standards, but unlike the "closet" gifted, feel they cannot meet them and withdraw from competition before they can be defeated or rejected. While some gifted children's fear of failure may keep them on a perpetual treadmill of exceptional achievement, some fear success as well because it can heighten the pressure to perform. Therefore, they hedge their bets psychologically by avoiding both failure and success. They become so adept at underachievement that they perform and achieve like "average" children. By consistently delivering less of themselves — both personally and academically — these children lower others' expectations to where they can deal with them, either by meeting them or at least not being burdened by them.

Some boys respond in this way to pressure to succeed especially if they have an older sibling, male or female, who is very successful in school. However, withdrawal is probably most typically a feminine response. For females, the academic, professional, or financial achievement that males can rely on for self-esteem may endanger personal relationships. Given cultural conditioning, boys and men expect to be first or best in certain areas and may feel threatened by girls and women who refuse second-class citizenship. Some males will have little to do with females who are as aggressive or competent as they are — particularly in the science, math, or business fields. So if girls win in one area, they may lose in another.

The worth of females in our society is apparently still judged differently from that of males, according to Matina Horner, the president of Radcliffe College, who laments the fact that many women fear or avoid professional success because their self-esteem is based instead on how well they please males in general. Some females may still not dare risk the emblems of their value — awards, promotions, higher salaries, and the like — so they may settle for "safe" mediocrity. This path is the most debilitating, because it allows for the least development of the individual.

Rebellion

Some gifted children, frequently those whose thinking is most divergent, respond by totally rejecting any external expectation.

They choose to rebel against rules or restrictions they find in any way confining. However, the vociferous assertions of rebels are indications of dependence rather than independence. Unlike revolutionaries, who object to the status quo because they want to establish a superior order, rebels are reacting only against rules or norms. Parents can mistake the aggressive protests against cleaning rooms, completing homework, or arriving at meals on time as arrogance or self-confidence. But in counseling sessions, rebels often reveal that while they are rejecting rules, they still believe in the judgments others impose on them. They accept the "bad" label, but because they feel rejected and betrayed they use their divergent thinking abilities to undermine authority figures and risk the punishment or failure that might result.

In school, if the various indicators of their creativity — wild ideas, daydreaming, tolerance of disorder, sloppiness — are not accepted, or they are punished for them, creative children can feel rejected and may respond by rebelling. For some exceptionally creative children, being a rebel can become a life-style with many more risks than rewards. For other children this stance will emerge only in very rigid, restrictive situations or in adolescence as they strive to become unique.

While "closet" gifted children strive for acceptance by revealing no less than their best and hiding their weaknesses, rebels use the opposite tactic. They present their anger, impatience, sloppiness, and selfishness, calculating that if their worst is accepted, then they are indeed loved.

Independence

The most constructive approach, which leads not only to development of all aspects of the self, but also to self-satisfaction and to resilience when faced with limitations and conflict, is to transcend group expectations and work toward independent values that foster self-actualization. When the child's self-esteem is liberated from external approval, potential and energy are unleashed. His achievement becomes motivated by interests and personal values rather than a need for grades, approval, prestige, or money as proof that he is a worthwhile person.

The behavior of the child who is motivated from within may look like that of any of the other personality types, since he will appear to agree or disagree with rules, but the critical issue is *why* he has made that choice. One of the key indicators of such a person is the ability to make choices based on personal commitment and to accept the consequences of those decisions. For gifted children who have the ability for original contributions, the willingness to take two kinds of risks is essential for the full development of their emotions and creativity.

The first risk is the disapproval of others. Gifted leaders must be willing to take stands that are unpopular, as Seward did in purchasing Alaska, or Jefferson in buying Louisiana. Visionary artists must be able to put up with the ridicule of professional critics in forging new styles, as did Vincent van Gogh in painting, Gustav Mahler in music, and James Joyce in literature.

Acceptance and endurance of another kind of risk are a requisite of giftedness and are exemplified by the careers of Edison and Einstein. Edison wrote that he had to be wrong over 120 times (he used 120 nonconducting filaments) before he found the single appropriate material for the incandescent light bulb that has become a symbol for original invention. Einstein failed mathematics at one point in his early schooling, had a nervous breakdown, and was thought to be retarded. In our schools and institutions where failure is an epithet and mistakes irrevocably recorded in grades or test scores, the cost of developing creativity can be very high, and the gifted must become strong enough to pay.

STRATEGIES FOR SELF-FULFILLMENT

Richert maintains that to help the gifted develop unachieved potential, it is necessary to create situations that will counteract inappropriate expectations, make children resilient to external judgments, and evoke all aspects of a child's potential (including special abilities, productivity, creativity, and maturing emotions). Following are six goals toward which all parents can work. The effectiveness of specific strategies will vary according to a child's distinctive personality pattern: conformity, withdrawal (avoiding competition), rebellion (rejecting rules), or self-actualization (determining values for him- or herself).

Strengthen the Child's Self-Concept

Giftedness can be a trap if it causes adults or peers to expect perfection of a child. A positive, healthy self-concept distinguishes between the best and weakest parts of the self and accepts the fact that human beings are all imperfect. Point out children's strengths to them: "You know, you're really quite a good creative writer." For the "closet," or withdrawn, gifted child, hidden faults and errors ought to be revealed and accepted so that their eventual exposure is not feared. "Don't worry that your spelling needs work. It can be improved with practice and by taking notice of difficult words as you read."

Rebels have the complementary problem of unconsciously exposing their flaws in a counterproductive ploy for acceptance that results in failure or rejection. Their strengths and interests, whether or not they are academic, should be legitimized. A child who has an extraordinary talent for drawing political cartoons, for example, should be encouraged in this area, not told that her interest has nothing to do with her schoolwork. Patience will be required to regain the trust of rebels so that they become willing to expose their true interests. You must show them that you value what they do well.

Successfully self-actualizing children, too, need their parents to be nonjudgmental, accepting their worst as well as their best.

Help Cope With Failure and Success

and

Help Unleash Creativity

Some strategies achieve two goals: coping with failure and success and evoking creativity. The success of "closet" gifted children is earned at the exorbitant cost of repressing creativity and fearing failure. These children need protection against the inevitable judgments that can devastate them and the rewards that inhibit their creativity.

"Closet" and withdrawn gifted children should be encouraged to embark on new tasks and take risks to be creative: set an arbitrary limitation; tell them not to repeat a safe, successful achievement; require them to find an alternative; help them to brainstorm for other options. The new task may be a different responsibility for a family trip (planning the itinerary rather than packing the car), or another way of approaching a school assignment (composing a song or poem rather than writing a report on a reading assignment). The risk may be the first independent clothing purchase, or the first attempt at negotiating an alternate homework assignment with a teacher. All needn't go perfectly, either. Just a slight dose of mistakes or failure can inoculate them against the greatest danger "closet" gifted students can face — someone's inevitable judgment that their work is not good enough.

Rebels and withdrawn gifted children share the need to overcome the stigma of failure. Too often these children are unfairly accused of being unmotivated, irresponsible, or (the ultimate criticism in too many programs) lacking "commitment to the task." In order to help the child to success, his or her strengths need to be reinforced. This can be done by simply giving rebels the freedom to work in an area that interests them. Underachievement can be overcome by a sensitive teacher who incorporates a required skill into a topic that interests a child. The boy who refuses to learn the multiplication tables will learn if he needs them in order to use exchange rates to assess the value of his coin collection in various currencies. The girl who is impatient with spelling will ask for help if the teacher suggests that were her story to meet spelling standards it might be suitable for publication. Parents, too, should search for ways to make schoolwork relevant to their children's interests.

Rebels with divergent views, which are very often rejected, need encouragement to bring any of their ideas to fruition. Ask them to select among several options — require only that they finish by a mutually agreed-upon deadline. The best possibilities for re-establishing trust between parent and child are accepting options you have previously rejected: mowing the lawn in a zigzag rather than rectangular pattern, baking cookies in a frying pan, using old pipes as a sculpture in the perennial garden, or setting his own bedtime for a week. Once the task is finished, the rebel needs recognition both for completing the project and for trusting the parent not to judge him unfairly.

Help your rebellious child negotiate alternative tasks at school or at home. Suggest that instead of saying, "No, I can't do the dishes," he offer an alternative such as "I'd rather set the table and make the salad." This approach helps break the pattern of failure, judgment, rejection, and rebellion.

Withdrawn children need the approaches required by "closet" *and* rebel gifted. Both weaknesses and strengths need to be evoked and confronted without the evaluations they so fear. Ask these questions of children who tend to withdraw from competition and who fear evaluation: list two activities you do best at home and at school; list two activities you do worst at home and at school. Help them to overcome evasion by asking them to commit themselves to carrying out one activity from each category. If your child says she is afraid to speak out in class, for example, have her commit to contributing at least one sentence a day — alternating the subjects from day to day. Upon completion, discuss how they feel after each task they do. Point out that everyone has strengths and weaknesses and discuss some of your own. Knowing that parents have such anxieties, yet manage to cope, will greatly reduce children's fear of being required to do too much. It is important to accept their anxieties as real, yet to encourage them to act in spite of them.

Highly motivated children who are independent need a safety net when they expose themselves to the risks of doing something different. The psychological safety all children who take risks should enjoy is that whatever the quality of their performance or product (and it's unlikely to be terrific at first), they cannot fail, because the major objective is simply to take the risk. The best response to the first wobbly geodesic dome built by the girl who previously got A's is not the dishonest judgment that it's good. Rather, admit that her building skills are not great, but that it is completely acceptable to be imperfect. She should know ahead of time and be reminded at the completion of the task, "You tried something new; you were brave enough to risk making a mistake, and that shows strength!"

Teach Planning

Emotional dependence can be gradually loosened if children are given choices and are required to make decisions and set their own goals. Discipline and motivation need to be shifted from dependence on teachers or parents to a basis in internal feelings and values. This does not mean that children run rampant following every whim. Rather, within the limits of family responsibilities and mutually accepted standards, children choose among alternatives. The parent's or teacher's role should not be to direct but to generate options, to guide discussions of the consequences of each alternative, and to avoid making decisions for children. Such experience is vital for the development of independent decision making and planning skills all children need to survive. However, involvement in goal setting is particularly important for exceptional children, who must eventually function independently if they are to develop their unique abilities.

One good example of teaching planning and goal setting involves family chore responsibilities in relation to earning an allowance and scheduling activities with friends. Point out to your child that he must complete the jobs around the house to earn money for short- and long-term purchasing. Likewise, leisure time and time with friends must be built around responsibilities at home. You might have to remind your children what needs to be done, but also tell them that the responsibility for planning when and how to get the work done is theirs.

Generating options also breaks the pattern of not living up to expectations. The "closet" gifted child is prevented from merely conforming because she is required to choose for herself. The rebel has nothing to rebel against. The pressure to perform is reduced for withdrawn children, yet they too must apply their abilities by choosing. The highly motivated child can develop independence without penalty.

Teach Self-Evaluation

Gifted children are extremely vulnerable to external evaluation, most often in the form of grades, but also to such social signs of worth as parental or peer approval. More than any other, it is the "closet" gifted child who gets entrapped into valuing himself according to his grades. These children crave approval almost as if it were an addiction, and psychologically that is indeed what good grades can become.

The child who continually bends her ideas to please others needs the help of parents and a good school program to overcome her dependence on others for self-esteem. Address the issue of conformity openly, and your child will understand that she is making a decision about whether to act independently or to go by the unwritten, but well-understood, rules of consensus.

When talking to your child about this, make it clear that it's his decision either way, but guide the discussion around the consequences of each choice. For example, if your child is writing a report that contradicts what he knows the teacher's position is on some issue, and is contemplating "toning it down" so as to make it more acceptable, you might ask your child to consider these questions: What's more important — saying what you believe in or what you think others want to hear? What do you think will happen if you disagree with your teacher in this case? Does this concern you? How do you draw the line between "sticking to your guns" and giving in? How will you feel about yourself either way you decide?

All children, but the "closet" gifted child and the withdrawn child most particularly, need to learn self-evaluation skills based on four principles. First, they must learn to distinguish between themselves and their schoolwork. Language is important! Your child may get A's in math, but should not be called an "A student." Productivity may be encouraged in a gifted program, but avoid calling your child a "producer," since it equates her with a machine that is useless when it's shut off.

The second principle is that evaluation should not be based on a comparison of students. The purpose of evaluation is to measure the progress of each student, not how one child compares to another. The essential question self-evaluation should address is "What can I do now that I couldn't do before?" Gifted programs should help students answer that question, but parents can assist in liberating children from unproductive competition. Report cards can be the occasion for discussing not whether grades are good enough, but "What can you do now in math that you couldn't do last year?" "Have you progressed in writing?"

Third, children should be encouraged to evaluate the strengths and weaknesses of their work so they can determine directions for improvement. "Let's look at this paper together. What have you done well and what not so well?" In particular, creativity and originality ought to be important criteria, even if their teachers don't stress them. While children should not be compared, products and performance are compared in the real world. Children need to be aware of the criteria for evaluation in different fields, not just to know why they got a certain grade, but to begin determining whether or not they agree with the grade.

Fourth, personal growth must be stressed. Product perfection, so prized by "closet" gifted children, should receive less emphasis than originality. Withdrawn children and rebels should recognize that their commitment and progress in a task are more important than their less than perfect products. Independent children should be encouraged to launch into new areas of study and exploration and not be content to rest on their laurels.

Provide Role Models

Gifted programs are designed to develop potential, but ironically, if identification or evaluation procedures are inappropriate, they can have the opposite effect. Gifted programs that segregate academically achieving children to have them compete for grades reinforce their insecurity, repress their creativity, and deny them appropriate role models.

If gifted children of all four personality patterns are grouped together, they can serve each other as effective peer role models. Rebels can learn from "closet" gifted children that completing a task does not necessarily require the sale of their souls. Withdrawn and "closet" gifted children can learn from rebels that being creative, risking failure, and making mistakes does not lead to irrevocable rejection. Everyone can learn from inner-directed children that independence can bring strength, but that it also has its price.

The single most important influence parents have is as role models. Parents who accept themselves can do a great deal toward relieving the pressure of expectations on their children. In other words, parents must show their children that they can live with their own foibles, that these are human, and that they do not expect perfection for their children.

SOCIAL ADJUSTMENT

The following two scenarios describe typical ways that gifted children may respond socially to their giftedness. First, consider Craig, a young child in fourth grade, and then Sherrie, a young teenager. The insights and advice following the stories should help you foresee and avoid possible problem areas your child may have with the social aspects of growing up gifted.

People accused Craig's parents of teaching him to read, when all along the parents themselves were wondering how he was learning to read on his own. He began with cereal boxes and road signs. Then came kindergarten. Craig's teacher was intimidated when he walked in and started reading the fire drill procedures. But he did well. In fact, by the end of November, Craig was reading books intended for second graders; by April he had written his first "novel." The next year he completed a sequel! By any definition, Craig is gifted. His accomplishments demonstrate this, as does his IQ. Now he's in fourth grade. He doesn't talk about school, other than to say "It's easy." He doesn't say much about friends, either.

As the parents of a gifted child, you probably know what it's like to be suspected of "teaching" your child too much, too early. And you're probably aware how real the problem of "friendship" is for your child. Who are his real peers? For children like Craig are they the other nine-year-olds with whom he has lunch and recess? The sixth graders in his accelerated reading group? The junior high mentor who challenges him in computer programming?

The answer is, of course, "yes" to each of the above. But how can a gifted child cope with the variety of relationships and social pressures he faces?

First, it's important for you to recognize — and accept — the fact that your child's social situation is different from that of less gifted children who are on the general intellectual level of other children their own age. Your child's peer group changes in relation to specific circumstances.

Second, once you recognize the differences, don't be afraid to discuss them with your child. With a better knowledge of himself, he can learn how to feel comfortable with his relationships and will also understand why he sometimes gets confused and upset about them. He'll know that these feelings are "normal" for a person in his situation.

Take Craig, for example. He may not relate well intellectually to age-mates whose reading preferences lean to Hardy Boys adventures, an interest he had two years earlier. On the other hand, if a resource teacher or well-intentioned aide interrupts him during snack time to "do some science," he may complain or cry. Emotionally he is still only nine, and cookies and milk with classmates may preempt even the most enticing project.

Here is a case where home-based preventive counseling — arising from concerns you and your child share — often requires little more than a listening ear and honest reactions. Counseling focused on locating and addressing areas of potential conflict for the gifted child can help prevent serious problems of under-achievement, negative behavior, and emotional trauma.

Your child's difference from his peers is just one example of a good starting point for communicating with him about his abilities and feelings. Sure, everyone knows Craig is bright — including Craig — but to assume that you don't need to discuss "the obvious" is to practice neglect in meeting your child's social and emotional needs.

The gifted child needs to understand that friendship and gift-edness require accepting the fact that he is different from his peers. Craig, for example, is chosen first for the spelling bee team but last for the kickball squad, and he has to realize that his worth as a person doesn't rise and fall with his popularity. To help your child come to grips with his social situation you can do the following things.

• Discuss *peer group* as a relative term and provide examples from your own life to show that peers are not necessarily age-mates. You might look at your high school or college yearbook. Were these classmates all peers the year you graduated? Are they now? If not, why not. If so, how? You might also mention colleagues at work. Some are peers and some are not, but in either case it's not dependent upon age.

• Talk about the distinction between "friendship" and "popu-larity." Compare the characteristics and behaviors that make some-one popular — good looks, good dancing — with those that qualify him as a friend — caring, dependability. Discuss the overlap and the contrasts.

• Read with your child *On Being Gifted,* a book written by and for gifted children and teens about both the hassles and benefits of being bright. Discuss passages that are especially relevant to your child's own situation.

• Together read other books that provide resources and deal with issues of friendship, rivalry, intelligence, and talent. *Gifted*

Children Speak Out by James Delisle can be a helpful text on these topics. Your librarian can help you find other appropriate books.

Sherrie is fourteen, in her first year of high school. She has a generally charming personality, but tends toward sullenness when under either pressure or criticism, and her posture is often awkward. Her moods change swiftly. She is at the top of her class in grade point average and in peer and teacher awareness of her achievements. She wants to be an electrical engineer specializing in research; she worked during the summer as a research assistant in a local engineering research company.

Sherrie doesn't join any formal social clubs. She is generally a loner. She doesn't assert herself but waits to be called or invited. She is not active in matters other than the academic, where she is fiercely competitive and doesn't take criticism well.

Sherrie's parents have been intimidated by her intellectual prowess. They have not realized that her emotional wellbeing is as important as her academic needs. Sherrie became a very lonely girl. Although she remained disciplined in her academic responsibilities, she seemed to withdraw more.

Recently, Sherrie met Matthew, a thirteen-year-old boy who lived with his divorced father. The two became inseparable. He was one year behind her in school, but was also gifted and quite mature for his age. Sherrie saw herself as a mother figure for him and, at the same time, she saw him as the "man in her life." He filled her needs for male companionship with its accompanying meaning for her peers. Sherrie's and Matthew's lack of social life drew them closer together. Their closeness became their private social world in which they could express their defiance, to explore, to feel safe, and feel isolated but secure.

The attachment was not healthy. It was too quick a step toward intimacy before facing the challenges in the real world of peer groups of each sex. Sherrie's relationship with Matthew did not address her larger problems. She needed to be encouraged to broaden her scope of interests and relationships. Her unhappiness, her sexual fantasies, and the repressions indicated in her poems needed to be discussed with a professional counselor.

Sherrie needed guidance from her parents, but they did not act upon, or even notice, all the indications of her problems. Instead they waited until something happened to jolt them to action. They were shocked to come home one afternoon to find Sherrie and Matthew engaged in explicit sexual behavior. Sherrie yelled at them, "Get out, you damn people, and give me a life of my own!" At fourteen, a life of her own was a life with Matthew. Then the parents sought help.

The right kinds of peer relationships are critical to the development of a gifted child. Through such relationships, value systems are developed, as well as one's identity apart from the group's. But, even given their uniqueness in mental abilities and/or talent, can gifted teenagers measure up to the peer "standards" established by all teenagers? It is not easy for a teen to develop and to uphold moral convictions with a strength born of positive, yet realistic, confidence in him- or herself. Yet the most valid way to facilitate the development and integration of a total person and a complete personality is to be found in teenage peer relationships.

One comes of age with one's giftedness not in a vacuum, not in the center stage of the adult world, but only through the experiencing of oneself through the perspectives of peers. Those peers should include all kinds — not just those who are reflections of oneself or those with whom one competes academically. Above all, peer relationships are essential as part of any authentic understanding of oneself.

No teenager — especially a gifted child — should skip the experience of *group* relationships any more than he or she should miss the challenges in gradually becoming more and more selective, to where the larger group is replaced by a smaller, more intimate one. This kind of selectivity is the living, exploring process out of which friendships are developed.

Friendship is essential for any teenager. It should be an organic process wherein each individual is challenged to use his or her principles, values, and ethics. A gifted child needs friends of the same sex as well as friends of the opposite sex. Without both, the teenager misses out on a vital stage in coming of age.

While the teenage clique is an understandable phenomenon, involving security and territory, a teenager who does *not* identify with such a group — usually identifying with only a few peers — is telling adults a lot about his or her self-image. If it is not compensated for, this lack can lead to premature obsessions, intimacies, and even self-destructive behaviors. It often signals the presence of severe loneliness — as in Sherrie's case.

Because gifted teenagers usually become accustomed to being right academically, they often denigrate those authority figures they have not conquered, those subjects they have not mastered, and those peers they think have rejected them. All too many young and gifted teens are lonely. Because of their intellectual insights they appear to be on top of the world, but they alone know these veils cover their actual concerns about wanting to be liked and accepted.

Lonely gifted teenagers need guidance to help in the difficult process of becoming integrated and unself-conscious individuals. They need to learn how to become part of a group, a team, an activity — without becoming the whole activity or needing to be in the spotlight of that group or team. They need to win, but they also need to learn how to fail. They need to learn that every challenge will not become their personal victory. They need to learn how to receive from others who may not be as gifted, and to give to them as well.

Unless this kind of counsel is provided, lonely gifted teenagers like Sherrie see themselves as apart and seek for a "treatment" or solution that is unhealthy, as she did. Their loneliness may be dangerous to themselves and others.

Though the school has a formal role in counseling the Sherries, the Matthews, and others like them, the major responsibility lies in the home. Gifted children do not grow into and out of their teens as healthy persons without parental assistance and direction. In addition, nothing is more critical to the coming to terms with one's giftedness than appropriate, diverse peer relationships, through which children can reinforce each other's strengths for mutual growth.

Once her parents were shown how to help her, with the support of professional help, Sherrie was able to use the depth of her perceptions and intellectual judgments to understand her problems.

WHAT CAN PARENTS DO?

All parents of gifted children need to understand the nature of a healthy relationship. Then they will be able to nurture those friendships and activities that are positive and constructive forces upon the lives of their gifted children, and their influence will withstand the usual pressures outside of the home. The following checklist can help parents recognize the factors present in a healthy adolescent peer relationship:

• Visibly happy social-emotional behaviors; enjoyment of being with others;
• Open patterns of communication with parents about activities;
• Inclusion of other people, both peers and adults, in their lives;
• Involvement with a variety of experiences, activities, and interests;
• Equal contributions to and reception from the peer relationships; not requests to do favors all the time;
• Activities in groups as well as pairs;
• Involvement with both sexes in activities;
• Respectful behavior toward others;
• Positive personal attitudes and mannerisms;
• Variety of time patterns — not with peers every day or even every week;
• Reinforcement of growth in social behaviors;
• Careful planning and open discussion.

Parents should also be able to recognize the warning signs in destructive adolescent peer relationships that cause the child to demonstrate one or more of the following behaviors:

• Unusual sensitivity or rebelliousness toward criticism;
• Unresponsiveness to spontaneous humor;
• Unusual introversion or hostility;
• Unwillingness to share day-by-day details of relationships freely;
• Vagueness regarding future plans within the relationship — particularly involving members of the opposite sex;
• A limited number of personal telephone calls, visitors, and mail;
• Avoidance of outgoing, gregarious activities such as parties;
• A view of oneself as being unpopular;
• A lack of close friends of the same sex;
• A resistance to or lack of variety of personal, social invitations;
• The revolving of all activities around one relationship to the exclusion of others.

Danger signals of this kind should not be used as panic buttons, but rather as preventive beacons illuminating the need for parents to become more involved in the socialization process their children are undergoing. Gifted young adolescents do not just "get through" or "come out" of the growing-up process without careful guidance. Parents can remain gentle observers and then can move into a more active role. With dialogue and a home-imposed system of values that parents try to teach a child, the parents can help start the child on the pathway toward self-fulfillment. They can be alerted by the danger signals to bring the gifted adolescent child back to his or her moorings.

No parent should allow the young adolescent to wander too far away. Such distancing from family bonds can only imbue the child with a false sense of power and a mistaken perception of his or her readiness to assume the roles and responsibilities of an adult. What often follows is confusion between independence and self-indulgence. Peer relationships should exist within the larger context of the total individual and should not overwhelm or dominate all other aspects of one's life.

Juxtaposed between the needs of the gifted adolescent and the means to satisfy those needs, the issue of limits comes into focus. All children need to know and understand the basis upon which limits are established — as the conditions and expectations upheld by the home. This knowledge precedes conflict and helps resolve those conflicts that still emerge in all aspects of adolescent life. Being faithful to the family's conditions and expectations should be upheld by the parent and child alike as an essential value. There can be no double standards.

Within such a framework of positive expectations, the young gifted adolescent will come to know the nature of and the necessity for limits. These expectations must include mutual respect, open communication, sharing of ideas, schedules, and arrangements, cooperation in maintaining the home, consideration for the needs of all, compromising when necessary, keeping everyone informed about plans and whereabouts, embracing appropriate and civil behaviors outside the family, and seeking guidance and direction from within the family constellation.

Children who respect these expectations understand that limits are an extension of the love given by a parent to a child. Specific limits should be set in terms of the days of the week allowed for out-of-school socialization, the apportionment of times (including curfews) viewed as appropriate, the activities and experiences viewed as healthy, the relationships viewed as productive, and the friends viewed as nurturing, supportive, and respectful. These kinds of limits offer guidelines to adolescents and help them simplify their personal choices. Later, through discussion and sharing, the reasons can be explored; and ideally, as the child grows older, limits can be set and modified together.

HELPING WITH SEXUAL MATURATION

The physical realities of sexual maturation affect the gifted child as they do all children. All children require sex education to help them integrate these realities into their psychological, emotional, and intellectual development. However, because of the heightened sensitivities to the world around them and the grasp of the complexities within human experience that this group often exhibits, there is an urgent need for sex education of the gifted to be directed toward present and future mental health and the awareness of an individual's social responsibilities.

The differences in this experience for gifted youth are in both kind and degree. Gifted young people are often persistently curious, needing to search continually into facts, specifics, and experiences in order to act. And the gifted are often intensely willful, impatient with adult authority, and lacking in self-assessment.

In today's permissive, "me"-focused culture, there are many ambiguities and confusions for young people. Hence, the gifted need to learn how to use their intellectual strengths at the same time they are learning how to contain the negative forces within their emotional natures.

The intellectual nature of the gifted makes it possible for them to become involved in open conversation, discussion, and readings related to human sexuality. If they acquire a solid base of knowledge about sex, they are less apt to be sexually self-indulgent and destructive, as Sherrie and Matthew were, and more likely to value personal responsibilities that should go along with sexual experience.

Because of the intensity of their nature, distressing qualities on the other side of that coin called gift might include extremes of aggressiveness, competitiveness, manipulativeness, sarcasm, and general cynicism. Bringing these negatives to sexual development can result in severe trouble.

Gifted children need to be taught that they should not "run" with their sexual energy as they do with their intellectual capacities. The gifted need help in developing positive attitudes toward their own sexuality; they need an understanding of sex as only one aspect of the complete person. They need to be helped to understand the consequences and implications of sexual needs and desires. Parents must be forthright, honest and, if necessary, confrontative in establishing the foundations upon which "life practices" will be based.

Parents must also establish a framework of values within which the gifted child can probe intellectually, and eventually physically, the many aspects of human sexuality. This framework should include an awareness that sexual experience can go beyond self-gratification. They should also know that the total personality and emotional fabric is expressed through sexual energy. And they must learn that sexual activity is enhanced, not diminished, by responsible interpersonal behavior.

Responsibility should be presented to the gifted as a positive challenge to an individual's total inner resources. Responsible attitudes and behaviors enable the expression of "caring" regardless of diverse views related to the sex act itself. Teenagers must come to their own sexual development with the knowledge that it is caring for others that makes a sexual relationship most meaningful.

Gifted children need to know that being able to express oneself sexually is just one part of "doing what comes naturally." The other part is learning how to find sustained fulfillment through sexual relationships, which requires the realistic use of all individual gifts — the application of one's intellectual capacity for reflection or one's artistic abilities for expression, for example. Through this process gifted children can come to understand the responsibilities incumbent upon any sexually active person, regardless of age.

Although they need to realize that denial of sexuality drains energy and causes self-alienation, they also need to understand the implications of sexual intercourse, abortion, venereal disease, parenthood, and the like. And they need specific facts on which to base their own informed judgments as to the appropriateness of their sexual activity. They must be made to realize that rather than giving in to self-indulgence, they will have to learn to integrate sexual and emotional needs so that the expression of those needs, both in terms of enjoyment and a source of energy, is creative rather than destructive. Providing these facts and values is the responsibility of the parent. There is no substitute for good social information gained at home.

As parents provide information for their children, they can guide them to ask questions that will encourage responsible attitudes: Who am I? What am I? How do I describe myself as an individual? What do I value most in people and in things? What kind of person do I want to become? What part of that development includes fulfilling my needs? How do I describe my own sexuality? Why is it important to me? How best do I express it? What do I value sexually? Why?

The following explanation of why sex is important can serve as a model for parents to adapt to their own circumstances and the age of their children and as a basis on which children can frame further questions.

Sexuality is a natural and inextricable part of every individual. Sexual activity is a basic human need, not just for pleasure, but to overcome the human condition of being alone. The urge for physical union goes far beyond the biological and is an expression of the intense emotional and spiritual need for intimacy. Through different expressions of sexual feelings, from affectionate caresses to intercourse, we can have various degrees of intimacy or connections with people we care for. Sexuality, including explicit sexual behavior, is the most intimate way we have of expressing our intense feelings and touching — not just physically, but also emotionally — another person. It is a vital way of communicating and giving of the self.

This kind of communication is important for all humans, but for the gifted, who are often isolated because of their differentness, developing the capacity for intimacy is even more important. One of the worst emotional agonies is the inability to express or accept affection, since that condemns an individual to live alone. Whatever a gifted person's accomplishments or victories, they can be very sterile and even alienating if there is no one really close to share them with.

Sexuality informed by the intellect leads to a conscious and rational understanding of sex, sexual activity, sexual values, and personal morality. Uninformed sexual behaviors can be self-destructive as well as exploitative. During these confusing times, young people need guidance in becoming comfortable with their own convictions, decisions, and choices regarding their sexual activities. The gifted young person ought to be able to respond to his own and others' sexuality with intelligence, assurance, and concern for self and others. The strength and maturity required will not be achieved through "street corner" information, but requires parents to put aside their own uneasiness about the subject of sex and lead the way.

Role Modeling

Besides teaching their gifted children *about* sex, parents have to realize that they are the most important role models for sexual behavior that their children will ever have. For your children, as well as for yourselves, it is important to develop your potential in the following ways.

1. Accept your own sexuality; don't be judgmental about your own sexual needs. Your child can pick up on your own discomfort with sex, even if you try to conceal this.

2. Express your emotions in a wide range of ways, not just privately with your spouse in your bedroom, but with your spouse and your children through verbal affection, acts of concern and sensitivity, and soothing caresses.

3. Trust is something parents earn from their children by accepting them and not judging their sexuality from their earliest explorations or questions. Try not to let your own inhibitions get in the way of honest and candid responses to their questions.

4. Demonstrate responsibility and respect in expression of sexual feelings through the ways in which you relate to people you love. Attempt to have authentic, nonjudgmental, nonmanipulative relationships with your spouse, your family, and your intimate friends.

5. Offer your child the same privacy you need to express your own sexuality! Respect closed doors, private conversations, and intimate diaries or journals. If, out of a need for privacy, you or your children cannot discuss technical aspects of sex, offer ma-

terials, encourage their taking sex or family life education courses, or provide an adult friend or relative your children trust to help them with *their* concerns (*not* the adult's).

Sexuality Resources

Awkwardness about the subject of sex crops up often between most parents and children for a variety of reasons. Some children, the gifted in particular, ask sophisticated questions much earlier than the parents anticipate. Others don't ask at all. At certain ages, a child's embarrassment will prevent his talking about bodies, babies, and lovemaking. Many parents find that as their kids get older, their own discomfort increases.

Whether or not you have one or more of these problems, there are books to make the telling about sex informative, interesting, and even fun. Illustrations help clarify complex biological information, and children will absorb different aspects at different ages and stages of their growth.

In selecting books for yourself or your child, look for these five qualities:

1. Language, whatever the audience (young children or adults), should be direct in referring to body parts and sexual functions, rather than filled with cute euphemisms.
2. Naturalness of sexuality as a basic human need at all ages should be stressed. The tone should be one of acceptance, not judgment.
3. The broad range of expression of sexuality that is natural and normal — including masturbation, and affectionate touching within the family and among friends of the same or different sex — should be introduced and explained.
4. Enjoyment of sensual feelings, alone or with others, should be frankly, not coyly, discussed as a major reason for sexuality.
5. Expression of sexual feelings within a relationship containing affection, respect, and commitment should be discussed.

The following books for children from preschool through puberty are among the excellent resources available.

Most preschoolers are more interested in the birthing of a baby, not the conception. For the precocious ones who do ask about lovemaking, these two books present the subject sensitively: *Where*

Do Babies Come From? by Margaret Sheffield and *How Babies Are Made* by Andrew D. Andry and Steven Scheep.

The younger kids in the primary grades are ripe for any and all new information. They may need you to read books such as the following aloud. When the child is around the age of nine, however, sex becomes embarrassing . . . something to giggle about. In that case, leave the books on the coffee table. Sooner or later, they will be read. For primary graders: *Inside Mom* by Sylvia Caveney, *How Was I Born?* by Lennart Nilsson, and *Where Did I Come From?* by Peter Mayle.

Once the children are past the fits of the giggles, parents of the ten- to twelve-year-olds must confront the fact that the subject is no longer an abstraction about the birds and the bees. Your preteen is on the brink of acquiring his or her own sexuality, and anticipating that period can make you squirm. Your child's exaggerated sense of privacy peculiar to adolescence combined with your own hesitancy can leave you tongue-tied. The following books are warm, reassuring, and helpful: *Period* by JoAnn Gardner-Loulan, Bonnie Lopez and Marcia Quackenbush, *What's Happening to Me?* by Peter Mayle, *Love and Sex and Growing Up* by Eric W. Johnson, and *The Playbook for Kids about Sex* by Joani Blank.

Discussing sex during the teen years can be really difficult. Parents may want their almost-adult children to have a happy and satisfying sex life, while still wanting their not-quite-adult children to wait a while before launching into it. Many teens are sexually active, and gifted children may tend to be more so because of heightened curiosity and a willingness to take risks. There are two books that emphasize responsible choices: *Love and Sex in Plain Language* by Eric W. Johnson and *The Teen-Age Body Book* by Kathy McCoy and Charles Wibbelsman. The most cogent and readable book on female sexuality, excellent for both boys and girls, is *Women: Our Bodies, Ourselves*.

And finally, transcending all age groups and attitudes, is *The Story of a Baby* by Marie Hall Ets, in picture-book format and found in the juvenile section of the library. It is a classic.

Family Life and Sex Education Courses

As well as guiding their children's sex education at home, parents must be able to evaluate courses and teachers at school. In addition to fulfilling the criteria suggested for materials, such courses should focus on what students want to know and when they want to know it. Integrating themes should be helping students of various ages and of differing levels of sophistication to distinguish for themselves what is normal and abnormal, natural and unnatural, healthy and unhealthy, creative and destructive, and ethical and unethical.

As important as assessing the content of the lessons is evaluating the attitudes of the teachers involved.

1. Will they let student questions (written and anonymous if not spoken), rather than a preordained curriculum, be the focus of the course? Are they ready to suggest topics of discussion among which students can select?

2. Can they be nonjudgmental and accepting in discussing these critical issues?

3. Can they deal with a diversity of views and opinions?

4. Can they distinguish between their own values and attitudes and the range of views on the issues under consideration?

5. Finally (only the students will be able to appraise this), does the teacher create the nonjudgmental atmosphere that will evoke the trust necessary for children to ask what they need to know?

Parents should ask the first four questions of the sex education teacher and monitor their children's instruction through discussion with their kids. "How are you doing in the course?" "Do you understand everything?" It's a good idea to read the material yourself. Also, be aware that children may not always wish to discuss sexual matters in an open discussion. Recommending a private chat will often do the trick.

Gifted Girls:
A Neglected Minority

ALTHOUGH Lewis Terman could find only five girls for every seven boys in his famous study of gifted elementary school children in 1922, girls are now being identified for new elementary school gifted programs in numbers that often outstrip those of boys. But the eventual success in life of these girls is going to depend on how well they are able to overcome the pressure of prejudice about sex-role behavior — the feeling that females should be or are passive, dependent, and tend to be self-sacrificing — that pervades our culture and inhibits girls' emotional and intellectual growth in even the best of circumstances.

The point will be self-evident when you give yourself the following test: name five male classical composers. Now name five female ones. Having trouble? Try artists or outstanding Pulitzer Prize winners or corporate executives. According to Carolyn Callahan, associate professor at the University of Virginia, while underachievement in school is usually considered a problem of boys, the reverse seems to be the case in terms of lifetime achievement.

Since the onset of the feminist movement, more and more subtleties of the inequities women face have become evident. And gifted girls and women are in double jeopardy. They have to overcome all the difficulties of being female as well as the stereotypes associated with the gifted. This chapter will give parents some insights into the problems and some ideas for helping their gifted daughters achieve to the best of their capabilities. It will deal with the influence of parents and society on gifted girls, the bias against these girls in the schools, and specific ways parents can help their gifted daughters — particularly in the math and science areas — and, finally, it will present a report by a preeminent scholar and researcher on creativity, E. Paul Torrance of the University of Georgia, on the future for creatively gifted girls.

THE ROLE OF PARENTAL AND
SOCIETAL INFLUENCE

Parents influence their daughters' options with their choice of toys. Patricia Lund Casserly of the Educational Testing Service found that for the 161 gifted high school girls she studied, construction toys, especially Legos, had been as popular as dolls. Microscopes and chemistry sets were also part of their childhoods. As they grew up, the girls tended to become "tomboys" — assertive tree climbers and fort builders.

Carolyn Callahan, cited above, observes that boys are given toys that come apart; girls typically get toys to be played with as a whole, not to be taken apart to see how things work. This is the reason, she surmises, that as problem solvers girls tend to be more global — seeing the whole intuitively — and boys more analytical.

Add to these subtle environmental biases that begin in early childhood the cultural and social pressures of adolescence, and a gifted girl's problems are compounded. Girls actually fear success, Callahan claims, because it may make them appear to be unfeminine and cause boys to be uninterested in them.

In addition, Callahan notes that the lack of female role models (literature assigned in school, for example, is usually written by men and about men, and textbooks still tend to portray females as the weaker, dependent sex), reinforces the conforming, dependent behavior that can be a subtle barrier to achievement for gifted girls.

Recent surveys reveal that the activity gifted girls seem to pursue most avidly is reading. When the girls surveyed were young, their parents say they limited TV watching and guided their daughters' reading to children's "classics," often choosing stories about women who accomplished feats of courage or intellect that girls could identify with. (Nonsexist bibliographies are available from the Feminist Press, P.O. Box 334, Old Westbury, NY 11568.)

These girls also reported an exceptionally close relationship with their parents, a fact that points to a potentially significant factor: they were treated as intellectual equals at a very young age. "They respected what I said on the same level that they talked to their friends," said one gifted girl. "My parents always talked to me as if I were an adult," said another. "They didn't just make rules; they explained why, so it made sense." Said the mother of one high school senior: "From early on we talked without inhibition about things kids usually don't talk about. We were just like friends."

On the other hand, too much parental pressure and involvement can create problems. Carol Copple observed preschool girls in a program for gifted children at the Educational Testing Service in Princeton. She found that young girls who were "intellectually independent and free-ranging in their thinking [were] not being pushed by their parents. But girls who were pressured to get right answers so they could move to the next intellectual level were more likely to be quite conforming — trying to figure out what the teacher wanted them to say."

Said one seventh grader about her parents: "They have high expectations for me, but they encourage me to do things on my own, to experiment." And the mother of a college freshman responded, "We always asked her to solve her own problems. After she had exhausted all possibilities, we were glad to help."

"The main thing parents have to do," says Alexinia Baldwin, of the State University of New York at Albany, "is to give girls a feeling of self-confidence by building up early successes at home. Let them plan a garden, design a room or a quilt (which develops abstract thinking), invent new games, create a new recipe, or plan a route for a vacation." Baldwin also stresses the importance of carpentry and electrical and plumbing skills for girls, and the need to share experiences with fathers. "They should go camping or build a playhouse together," she says.

Of course, gifted girls need the same cultural and intellectual stimulation as gifted boys — visits to museums, concerts, the theater; access to creative materials at home; information on subjects that interest them. They also need special encouragement to be scientists and engineers, says Max Fogel, former director of science and education for Mensa (a society for people with high IQs), because many girls still perceive these as masculine occupations and avoid development in these areas. Experts agree that problem-solving skills should be taught at an early age. For girls, involvement in some aspect of financial planning is particularly useful.

Bias in the School

Schools continue to reflect the sex bias of the culture in administrative staffing patterns, curriculum materials, and teacher attitudes — despite antidiscrimination laws. "Teachers can be hostile toward the gifted of both sexes," says Fogel, "but they seem to be more prejudiced against girls than boys." In one program for gifted adolescents, teachers gave their lowest ratings to female students who were analytic and preferred nonconventional approaches, while boys exhibiting the same characteristics received the highest.

Parents who feel their daughters are not being properly challenged should have them tested privately so they can present the school with data to reinforce their concerns. Or parents may show their daughter's teacher examples of exceptional work the child has done outside the classroom. Some parents develop home seminars to provide stimulation and companionship for their children as well as a vital idea-sharing support group for themselves. One New Jersey couple arranged with their gifted daughter's school to teach the child at home two days a week to discuss topics like auto mechanics and career choices.

Adolescence can present particularly serious conflicts for gifted girls as they begin to hide their intelligence in order to attract boys. Studies show that girls perform well in all-girl or neutral situations, but shy away from competition with boys (who often become even more competitive around girls at this age). Suzanne Schneider, a Philadelphia psychologist, feels that fathers play an extremely important role for gifted girls at this time. It is up to the father, she believes, to validate both his daughter's sexuality (making her feel that she is a desirable member of the opposite sex) and her competence. Mothers of gifted girls say that they point out women who are successfully combining careers and motherhood and encourage their daughters to begin career plans early. Mothers, teachers, and other women who manage to integrate their working lives with their private lives are especially important as role models for adolescent girls.

But most girls are not lucky enough to find such encouragement and role models, particularly in the sciences. Although girls perform as well as or slightly better than boys in math until the age of eleven, their interest in math and science drops off in junior high; girls' test scores at this stage begin a steady decline. A large sample of seventh-grade girls scored an average of 31 points below boys on a recent Scholastic Aptitude Test (SAT) for math, conducted by Johns Hopkins University's Office of Talent Search and Development, as part of its nationwide search for youngsters precocious in math.

High-scoring girls not only feel their femininity is threatened, says Lynn Fox of Johns Hopkins, they also "fail to see science and math as having socially useful applications." She continues, "We've found these girls have fewer theoretical interests than the high-scoring boys, so we've created a special summer program to show them how these subjects can be used to solve human problems (in architecture, engineering, psychology). Women scientists who [speak about] their fields become role models for the girls." Fox feels that career education of this type is particularly important at the junior high school level to keep mathematically and scientifically gifted girls from withdrawing from these fields and to allow them to plan a comprehensive high school program.

Patricia Lund Casserly, mentioned earlier, reports that high school girls in advanced placement courses often attributed their academic success to teachers who recognized their giftedness when the children were eight or nine, helped them develop their skills, and inspired them to do something significant with them. The mother of a gifted writer says, "My daughter was turned on to writing in sixth grade by one of those magical teachers. All through high school she has sent stories to her for comments."

For gifted girls who haven't found that "magical teacher," parents may want to look outside the classroom at a variety of special programs. In her study, Casserly discovered several ten- and eleven-year-old girls who had been tutored in math "for fun" or who had taken science courses at university museums and laboratories. In some instances the girls had helped graduate students collect data for doctorates. Speaking for a group involved in a special science project, one girl said, "We didn't start off as scientific 'geniuses.' Our parents sent us because they thought we weren't challenged in school, but before long we were hooked."

SPECIFIC IDEAS FOR HELPING
GIFTED DAUGHTERS

Carolyn Callahan believes that most of the blame for the fact that the overwhelming percentage of adults who are considered to be gifted and creative are men rests on the social and intellectual environment created for girls at home, in school, and in the environment in general. She suggests that parents can do the following to cut down the negative influence of environmental experiences and give gifted girls an equal chance to develop their talents and achieve in life:

• Encourage and allow girls to manipulate mechanical toys, explore electronic devices, and try other such things at the same age at which boys do;

• In answering the question "How can I be both feminine and professional?" expose girls to successful professional women — in the home and community, on TV, and in books — as role models;

• Be sensitive to what your child of either sex is watching on TV and how women are portrayed. Are they constantly seeing women portrayed as "dumb blonds," rather than intelligent problem solvers? Discuss the dual roles today's women are shown to embrace — as *dependent* and subservient, whose main daily activities are still cleaning the house and preparing dinner; as *independent* professionals and heads of households.

• Monitor the kinds of advice your school's guidance counselors are giving. Make sure they are not dissuading your daughter from certain fields or areas of study that have been characteristically male-dominated.

Make sure your child's school and teachers are not assigning classroom tasks on the basis of sex-role stereotyping (girls correct papers; boys wash blackboards); providing activities that allow her to practice visual-spatial problem solving from a young age, such as working on puzzles; providing activities that emphasize the impact that gifted girls can have on their own success, and that build their confidence in their ability to control what happens to them, like teaching them to choose what clothes they wear, what subjects they study, etc.; providing activities that encourage girls to establish personal goals; providing equivalent standards and opportunities for boys and girls; providing co-ed athletic activities in which boys and girls can play together and enjoy the same facilities; providing counseling that exposes bright girls to learning programs that challenge them intellectually and present a wide variety of career options.

Parents should inquire about these things from time to time throughout the school year, not just in formal parent-teacher conferences.

How to Encourage Girls in Science and Math

Robert M. Byers, Director of Admissions at Massachusetts Institute of Technology, explained the importance of mathematics in a letter to a girl enrolled in a gifted program: "Mathematics underlies everything. Please try hard in arithmetic and in the mathematics courses you will encounter later on. It's so important for almost anything you want to do in life.

"There is something else I want to tell you. Sometimes you will hear people say that boys can do math and girls cannot. Don't you believe them, Erin. Math is no harder for girls than it is for boys. We have many young women at MIT. They do just as well as the young men. So if you hear someone say girls cannot do math, you tell them they are wrong. And if you know girls who think they cannot do math just because they are girls, you tell them they are wrong, too."

At a state conference for parents and their gifted children in Connecticut, approximately seventy-five students from grades four through six had the chance to select a two-hour afternoon workshop in one of three areas: drama, television production, and chemistry. Predictably, twenty-five girls and no boys selected drama, and twenty-five boys and only two girls chose to participate in the chemistry class. The issue continues a frustration to concerned teachers and parents. Bright young girls rarely display as much interest in math and science as bright young boys, and, on the whole, they do not do nearly as well in math on their SATs.

While argi *n* ents continue to be waged over whether these differences are ?. result of innate abilities or environmental conditioning, a critical issue is often ignored. Unless we can stimulate the interests of young girls in math and science, they will not become motivated to pursue high-level courses or careers in either area.

Lynn Fox of Johns Hopkins, in her study, reported in the attitudes of gifted girls differences that accompanied the distinct differences she found in math scores on the SAT. Fox found that girls who did display an aptitude for mathematics were far less likely than mathematically gifted boys to have the following: self-confidence as learners of mathematics; strong support from parents, teachers, and peers; perceptions of the importance of mathematics; well-defined goals for their futures; willingness to take intellectual and educational risks; values, interests, and aspirations consistent with their abilities.

What can be done to encourage young girls to work up to the level of their academic ability in the scientific fields? There are some programs that may be established for gifted girls and some strategies that parents can pursue to encourage their daughters' interests and abilities in science and mathematics.

One successful program for young girls in science was developed at Talcott Mountain Science Center in Avon, Connecticut. TMSC is a regional center that provides special science and math classes at school locations throughout Connecticut and at the Talcott facility on Avon Mountain. Because the number of girls attending the science center was comparatively low, staff scientists decided it was time to develop a special program specifically designed to recruit and involve young girls.

The program, called "Action Science," has three unique features. First, only girls attend this program, in groups of twenty-five first- through third- or fourth- through sixth-graders. Second, the program is taught only by women who are working scientists and extremely committed to their field of study. This intensive exposure to female role models has helped to expand the horizons of young girls and has encouraged them to consider science and math as future career options. Third, at least one parent or adult is asked to accompany the girls to this special science program.

Action Science emphasizes two major goals. First, bright girls are exposed to sophisticated science equipment and learn how to handle it successfully. Every girl enrolled in Action Science learns how to use a variety of equipment and to feel pride in her accomplishments as she develops new skills — such as aiming and focusing a telescope on the craters of the moon, using high-power microscopes, dissecting and examining a squid, and operating a laser.

The second major goal of Action Science is to encourage young girls to rely on their own judgment of correctness or quality as they try such activities as dissecting frogs or building electrical circuits. Very often, girls in science or math classes seem to rely more on the judgment of an adult or peer to affirm that something has been done correctly. Their dependence on the judgments and opinions of adults and peers is not a trait exhibited by most young boys in similar situations.

Because parents attend the Action Science program with their daughters, they can learn two ways to encourage their child in science and math. First, they learn not to provide too much assistance as girls confront new activities or unfamiliar equipment. If girls are constantly helped by their parents, their teachers, or their peers, they will never learn to feel confident or successful when they meet a challenge or when they are approaching a relatively new situation.

Second, they learn to encourage independence, self-reliance, and decision-making abilities. Too often bright girls become too dependent upon their parents and peers. While parents often nurture and encourage independence in boys, they often discourage it in girls, fearing that their daughters may be regarded as unfeminine or unladylike if they become too independent or assertive. After receiving instructions and suggestions, the girls in the program are encouraged to make their own judgments about the quality and completeness of their work.

Another possible option parents can provide is a conference for young girls to motivate them to pursue advanced math and science courses. (A handbook for planners of conferences like this, entitled *Expanding Your Horizons in Science and Mathematics*, is available from the Education Development Center, 55 Chapel Street, Newton, MA 02160.) One such conference held in Connecticut brought together 39 women who have achieved success in math, engineering, and technology. These women interacted with 250 high school girls, parents, teachers, and guidance counselors, and urged the girls to enroll in advanced math and science courses.

Girls who are considering any type of future career in science should be encouraged to study calculus and physics in high school. Otherwise, they will not be prepared for appropriate college courses.

Parental encouragement can make a tremendous difference when teenagers of either sex are considering course selection in high school and college.

Another way in which parents can provide role models in math and science for their daughters is to locate books that provide exposure to successful female mathematicians and scientists. One book that has proven to be popular with young gifted girls is entitled, *Math Equals: Biographies of Women Mathematicians and Related Activities*. It provides summaries of the life and work of nine women mathematicians from Emilie Marquise du Châtelet to Emmy Noether. Simply having such books available for girls may provide a subtle reminder that women can do and can be what they desire.

A LOOK TO THE FUTURE FOR GIFTED GIRLS

Now that you are more aware of some of the problems gifted girls face in our society, as well as some strategies for overcoming the various forms of cultural conditioning and sex-role stereotyping, as parents you need to know the current career trends for bright young women and some of the major frustrations for them that still crop up. In this way you can better help your gifted daughter anticipate and understand some of the important career and life choices she will have to make.

E. Paul Torrance, Alumni Foundation Distinguished Professor at the University of Georgia and a pioneer in creativity testing and development, has conducted a twenty-five-year longitudinal study of two groups totaling nearly 500 gifted girls and women first identified as gifted in 1958 and 1959. In addition, another 2,000 students in grades 4 through 12 from across the country recently wrote scenarios describing where they thought they'd be in their careers in the year 2010.

Marriage and Children

Torrance found that "today girls' career expectations are dramatically different from anything we have ever known." Since 1970 gifted women have been pursuing career and family concurrently, a trend that accelerated significantly in 1980 and was projected to have been increased even more by the "women of 2010."

The most frequently mentioned source of frustration for the gifted women in Torrance's studies was that of combining career and marriage. Despite the inroads women have made in professions that have previously been closed to them (see below), family and motherhood, as a rule, seem to intrude and disrupt a woman's career plans and life more than family and fatherhood disrupt a man's.

The specific patterns with respect to marriage and children, however, show an interesting shift. Between 1970 and 1980 the percentage of gifted women who married decreased significantly, and an even sharper decrease was noted in the number of these women who had children. The "women of 2010" project somewhat of an increase in marital status for themselves and a concomitant increase in their intentions to have children. Although it is impossible to predict whether these trends will hold, it seems safe to say that some of today's gifted girls believe they can juggle all three elements — career, marriage, and children.

Education

Among all groups of gifted girls and women in the Torrance studies, past and present, there is an increased trend in attaining (or planning to attain) doctorates or other advanced professional degrees. Likewise, since 1970 there has been a big shift away from entering the profession of education and toward such fields as law, medicine, business management, civil engineering, and psychiatry.

The information gleaned from students today, the scenario authors, points to what might be taking shape as another important trend. The majority of these youngsters described self-directed and experiential educational programs, rather than traditional university or professional school experiences, as a desirable way of obtaining career expertise.

This trend had begun by 1980 with a considerable number of gifted women dropping out of college to acquire their eventual career expertise in more unorthodox ways. But many of them encountered difficulties, Torrance reports, and had to return to school for "acceptable credentials." Many of the scenario writers foresee the need for society to establish alternative means by which self-directed and experiential learning might be validated. In the meantime, it appears that among women the more conventional educational routes are still enjoying the greatest acceptability and success.

Troubleshooting

B Y NOW you realize that parenting gifted children is no sinecure. Special abilities bring along special needs and special *problems*, too. What follow are answers to questions that are most often asked by parents of the gifted. In each case they are *actual* questions; the responses were made by members of the advisory board of the *Gifted Children Monthly* (at that time *Newsletter*) and by other authorities, in a department of the publication called "Ask the Experts."

EXPLAINING GIFTEDNESS TO YOUNG CHILDREN

What are the best ways to explain giftedness to young children in order to make them feel more comfortable about being gifted?

The question posed on how to explain giftedness to young children, in order to make them feel more comfortable about being different, reminded me of a situation concerning a parent of a very bright five-year-old who was not doing well at school. The teacher reported that he was asking silly questions, talking incessantly, and demonstrating bossy behavior with the rest of the kindergarten group. These behaviors were not new to the parents, for Kenny was demonstrating similar aggressive, active behavior at home and in the neighborhood. And as a result, many children his age and older were reluctant to play with him; consequently Kenny was becoming a lonely and unhappy child.

Kenny's mother said that when the five-year-old next door wanted to talk about his pet puppy, Kenny wanted to discourse on galaxies and how many stars there were in them. In fact, just that morning he had blurted out that there were 150,000 stars in . . . and his eight-year-old brother had stomped from the breakfast room muttering, "Not again."

Kenny's mother, a remarkably sympathetic and wise woman, took her young son on her lap and said, "Kenny, have you noticed that the other children often don't want to talk about what you want to talk about and they really don't like you telling them what to do?" The child nodded and sadly said, "Yes." Then with a deep sigh, she continued, "Kenny, you know about the early explorers who sailed far beyond their own lands and discovered new lands?" "Yes," Kenny eagerly nodded, as he loved it when his mother told him interesting stories. "Well," she continued, "when they returned with tales about people with brown skin, who wore fine silk of many colors and ate rare and strange food, the people did not like hearing this and disbelieved it. In fact, they stayed away from the explorers."

Kenny's eyes opened wide, displaying a curiosity and empathy that often helps parents and teachers identify giftedness, and said, "That wasn't nice." "Well," his mother went on, "You are like those early explorers, but where they explored new lands, you explore new ideas in your mind and you go places other children cannot go." Breathing deeply, she continued, "The children are like the people who didn't believe or understand and that is why they pull away."

Kenny sat quietly looking at his mother, and she thought, "I've gone too far over his head and he doesn't understand." Then Kenny nodded and slid off his mother's lap, giving her one of his wide grins and said, "I wish you had told me that last year; I thought there was something wrong with me."

Kenny's mother said that she quietly wept for her own son's deep understanding and also for the heavy burden that all young gifted children bear — that of being different. All gifted children are different, and they will perceive this differentness to the degree that they do not have age mates at school and at home who are also gifted.

Helping Children Understand Their Giftedness

First, unless the child is suffering from his giftedness and consequent interaction with others, I would not have a heart-to-heart discussion on the problems of being gifted. However, if such problems do emerge, an analogy similar to what Kenny's mother used should prove helpful. Still another way to explain giftedness to young children is through the use of "bibliotherapy."

There are three steps to bibliotherapy. They are *identification, catharsis,* and *insight*. I would add another, that of *action* or changed behavior on the part of the child.

For a young child to understand differentness, a delightful book entitled *Flutterby*, published by Serendipity, might be helpful. In this book, Flutterby, who is a wonderful flying white horse with a unicorn horn doesn't know who he is. In exploring an ageless theme, the author has Flutterby thinking he might be an ant, because he likes to work, but disaster befalls him when he tries to help roll a cookie down an ant hole. His travels take him to many places with as many misadventures, until finally Flutterby realizes that he is satisfied and happy to be who he is.

That simple message can be the insight that young gifted children gather. They need to hear, accept, and adopt the notion that "I am different and I prize that differentness. I am who I am."

Identification comes about when the child can say, "Gee, I'm like that unicorn and I feel that way too." *Catharsis* takes place when the child feels sad when Flutterby is misunderstood and even stung by a bee! *Insight* comes when he grasps the notion that it is truly all right to be different and that he, too, is different. *Action* is when the gifted child evidences less concern about being gifted and pursues his unique interests, needs, and abilities.

Parents can do much to encourage this understanding through gentle unobstrusive questions such as "Do you think Flutterby likes himself now?" or "How else could Flutterby have found out who he was?" or "Have you ever felt like Flutterby?" The atmosphere should be relaxed and casual. Gifted children can feel when they are being probed. Remember they are very sensitive to "con acts" and will sense your anxiety if the timing is not just right. Easy does it!

Don't Deny It!

The importance of gifted children accepting their giftedness and developing it cannot be denied. Being gifted is being different, not better than other children or more precious to either parents or society. Yet, many times when gifted children are misunderstood or confused about other people's actions, they misread their own personal dignity and worth.

Too often, we try to pretend that a child is not gifted and we attempt to shield that gifted child from recognizing his giftedness or differentness. Leo Buscaglia, in a favorite book of mine entitled *Personhood: The Art of Being Fully Human*, says the following: ". . . the most damaging course of action is attempting to keep children from experience or protect them from pain, for it is at this time that children learn that life is a magic thing . . . if not a rose garden. The parents' role is primarily to stand by with a goodly supply of bandaids."

— *Dr. Dorothy Sisk, professor of Exceptional Child Education, University of South Florida, Tampa*

HELPING CHILDREN TO ACCEPT FAILURE

My daughter expects perfection from herself in all situations. How can I help her to accept failure?

All the children in the neighborhood get around on bicycles, including 4½-year-old Nadine. All except Mark, that is, who is reluctant to try even at eight. "It hurts when I fall," he says. His fear, of course, is greatly exaggerated.

Mark, with a fairly high IQ, is an example of a child who often clings to what he knows well in fear of making mistakes. Among gifted children, these individuals tend to be perfectionists.

In examining Mark's state of mind, it becomes apparent that Mark's fear of falling, or more precisely, his uncertainty about something he is not familiar with, makes him skeptical about the new adventure. Why does Mark behave this way? The uncomfortable feeling of confronting something unknown creates a tension for him. Instead of facing the challenge, he protects himself by building a shelter. He looks for excuses for not trying. Yet it is this psychological shelter which gives him the sense of false security that prevents him from progress.

On closer inspection, Mark's uneasiness about something he has never experienced before really comes from his eagerness to have positive results to assure himself right away. In contrast to taking things as they come, he is far too conscientious about what he is doing.

Sometimes all of us, like Mark, are trapped in our own psychological closures. We want to succeed right away. We want to know as soon as possible if we are doing all right. Without being aware, we constantly judge ourselves on the immediate outcome, whether in mastering a skill or in producing something.

If we fuss too much about the immediate result, we may deny the opportunity for ourselves to grow. In other words, we not only create stress for ourselves but also greatly limit our vision, missing the entire process of experiencing and the spontaneous way of discovering and learning.

Focusing on the immediate result determines why some people take only superficial excursions; others cannot stop exploring. Results can be signals which expand or terminate our mental journeys. When the result is a failure, we may be discouraged from trying again. Mark's reluctance to ride a bicycle is an example.

Psychological Openness Required

Just what is the quality, the prerequisite, that makes a person a "persistent explorer"? Willard Van Dyke wrote about Dorothea Lange, a genius for seeing through the camera, "Her method is to eradicate from her mind before she starts, all ideas which she might hold regarding the situation — her mind like an unexposed film." This "psychological openness" is what makes Dorothea a persistent explorer. Referring to her style of operating without preconception, she said, "I have no habit . . . growing up in the quiet of my own soul."

The meaning of psychological openness, then, lies in being receptive; it is the way to increase our capacity to absorb new information. Our eagerness to go on experiencing without being overly cautious on the way is the very secret of learning and forever growing.

How can we apply this in raising our gifted children? Several pointers may be considered for nurturing psychological openness:

• Suspend judgments. Don't frighten the child by being overly critical. Let the child enjoy "doing his own thing" for a while. As Jane Cooper Bland, author of *Art of the Young Child*, pointed out, we should view growth in terms of fairly long spans of time and not judge a child solely on his products. The things a child makes may not be attractive to an adult, but have real meaning for him. The stage which appears sloppy and unfinished may represent a new effort or a more challenging exploration.

• Gradually let go of parent and teacher supervision. Try not to be overly protective or to monitor too closely. Provide a firm boundary and a set of general rules instead. As a child grows up, cultivate his responsibility to be independent. Constant overevaluation or oversupervision can restrict a child's growth.

• Help the child to break her goals into "goal gradients" when she sets too high a standard for herself. Show her how to take a step at a time toward the end and then encourage her to keep up.

• Encourage the child to be a "persistent explorer." Help her understand that making mistakes or being imperfect is a normal part of learning. Help your child to get over quickly the frustration of not succeeding right away and to have the courage to try again. Many biographies are good examples of the inevitability of setbacks and failures en route to great accomplishments.

• Create opportunity for new experiences. Make it a gradual but continuous commitment, whether to try a new food, to meet a new friend, to visit a new place, or to learn a new skill. Each small step of success is a reinforcement for psychological openness. For instance, Mark, the lad whom we met at the beginning, certainly learned a lesson when he finally mastered the art of bike riding. In the process of learning he discovered that it wasn't so bad to fall after all.

— *Dr. Alice Chen, teacher of the gifted, Greece Central School District, Rochester, New York*

SHOULD FANTASY BE LIMITED?

My seven-year-old daughter is the oldest of three children. For the past two years she has delighted in telling "stories" to her friends and our neighbors about a pet caterpillar. She has quite a creative imagination, but seems to carry it too far. . . . I don't want to squelch her creativity, but when should this fantasy world in which she thrives become a concern?

Among children, fantasy is a natural and useful device for coping with developmental problems. Among adults, fantasy is useful not only in coping with life's problems, but for inventing, making scientific discoveries, creative writing, artistic and musical achievement, and the like. For these and many other reasons, fantasy should be enriched and kept alive.

Fantasy is an individual's attempt to bring about a comfortable compromise with some reality. If a child has not learned how to play or to use fantasy, she lacks an important tool for coping constructively with the environment. Fortunately, the constructive use of fantasy can be taught to children and there are a variety of well-tested ways for doing this. Many of them can be applied by parents.

A Case Study

I would suggest that you help your seven-year-old daughter and her two younger siblings to enjoy and make constructive use of fantasy. I realize that when situations such as the ones you described occur there is a tendency to conclude that things "have gone too far." The logical solution then seems to be to make the child stop telling fantasy "stories." However, the consequences of this may be tragic.

Let me relate the story of Tammy, one of the children in my twenty-two-year study of some elementary school children I began studying in 1958. Tammy was six years old, had an estimated IQ of 177, and had the highest score of any first grader on the *Torrance Tests of Creative Thinking*. The teacher told me in horror that this child still had imaginary playmates. The parents, the teacher, and the school social worker were all trying to rid her of these imaginary companions. Apparently they succeeded, but by the third grade her IQ had dropped to 105 and her creativity was below average for third graders. She dropped out of school in the tenth grade, was married at age nineteen, and now has three boys and daydreams about going back to complete high school so she can take nursing training. She despairs, however, saying, "I am not very bright, so I probably won't do it."

To teach a child to use fantasy constructively, parents need to enrich rather than squelch creativity. In the example about the pet caterpillar, this could have been done by having the child describe imaginatively the caterpillar's behavior, imitate it in movement, draw and color it, tell or write a story about it, make up a song about it, or in some other way elaborate and concretize the pet caterpillar.

Only when a parent perceives that the child is completely obsessed with fantasy — to the point where he or she appears unable to communicate or function normally — should there be concern and should professional help be sought.

Reading on the Subject

There are many excellent books that help parents teach children how to use fantasy constructively to solve developmental problems and to cope with the environment. Let me tell you briefly about some of these.

One of the most comprehensive is Mary M. Wood's *Developmental Therapy Sourcebook, Volume II (Fantasy and Make-Believe)*. This book explains clearly how fantasy and make-believe are used by children to solve their developmental problems. It shows how this can be taught through puppetry, making up stories, role playing and drama, socio-drama, and creative writing.

Some very useful procedures have been developed, tested, and taught by Robert Strom for use by parents and grandparents in participating in the fantasy and make-believe activities of children. One of Strom's books is *Growing Together: Parent and Child Development*. Parents with problems such as yours will find particularly helpful a chapter on "Partners in Fantasy" which gives many practical suggestions for parent-child fantasy.

Richard A. Gardner has also developed excellent procedures for teaching children to use fantasy constructively in solving their problems. A technique that might be especially suitable with your seven-year-old daughter is his Mutual Storytelling Technique. In this technique the parent or other adult joins the child in making up a story, as though they were doing it on radio or TV. The technique is described quite well in Gardner's *Therapeutic Communication with Children*.

Some of the best research on the fantasy and make-believe behavior of children has been done by Jerome L. Singer and Dorothy Singer. Perhaps the most illuminating of Singer's books insofar as parents are concerned is *The Inner World of Daydreaming*. In it Singer discusses imaginary playmates and other matters related to children's fantasy.

A Different Perspective

While visiting Japan, I talked with several groups of parents of pre-school children and many groups of preschool teachers. I always mentioned the importance of keeping fantasy alive and not once were any objections raised. In fact, the response was always one of "but, of course!" In similar audiences in the United States, I have almost always encountered arguments. And yet, the acceptance and encouragement of fantasy is evident in books for children, the education materials published for preschool children, testing materials for young children, their many festivals and celebrations, and the curriculum of preschools and primary schools. Much drama is used to bring alive fairy tales, legends, myths, and other historical fantasies. Indeed, many of these fantasies are made concrete through the visual arts.

In summary, I suggest that you teach your daughter and your younger children how to use fantasy constructively in solving their developmental problems. At times, become partners with them individually or as a group in their fantasy and play. Enrich and keep alive their fantasy. Don't try to stop it.

— *Dr. E. Paul Torrance, Alumni Foundation Distinguished Professor, Department of Educational Psychology, University of Georgia at Athens*

DISCIPLINARY TECHNIQUES

I have trouble balancing my desire to give my gifted son plenty of room for experimentation and independence with my insistence that he follow the rules of the household. He constantly questions my decisions, and tries to negotiate changes. How can parents nurture independence and impose discipline at the same time?

Discipline is an emotionally loaded word which is often associated with authoritarianism, coercion, and punishment. Those of us who consider ourselves to be enlightened and fair-minded may well react negatively to the notion of imposing discipline on a child. It may be argued that the more important considerations when raising a gifted child include fostering divergent thinking, inquisitiveness, a need-to-know, and an independence of spirit. How can parents nurture such independence and impose discipline at the same time?

The primary factors in raising an emotionally healthy child are quite basic: the child must know that he or she is loved, and the child must know the "rules of the game." Discipline plays an important role in both of these areas.

Love is something too often taken for granted. A parent might say, "Of course I love my child," and expect that attitude to be communicated to the child in some way, or expect that the child "just knows" he or she is loved. This is not enough. Children must have parental love demonstrated — the more the better. Just as important, the demonstration must be appropriate to the child's developmental age.

Spending time with the child is a very important factor. Parents of infants should spend time holding, rocking, and talking to their children. As the child becomes a toddler, encouragement and descriptive praise gain importance. Descriptive praise is praise that goes with something in particular. "I like the way you're sitting," or "I'm happy to see you playing so nicely with your brother" are much more useful to the child than simply saying "You're a good boy today," because it tells him *what* he's doing that earned the praise.

As the child grows older, other demonstrations of parental love should be added. For example, giving children responsibility shows them that they are competent in their parents' eyes. It is important that the responsibility be age-appropriate. A five-year-old is perfectly capable of setting the table or deciding whether to wear his red shirt or blue shirt to school. That same child is *not* capable of deciding what constitutes a balanced diet or whether the family should visit Aunt Mildred on Saturday. Giving a child child-size responsibilities helps develop a sense of competence and self-worth. Giving a child adult-size responsibilities leads to insecurity and inappropriate behavior. Children need to know that the world is an orderly place with a degree of predictability to it. They depend upon their parents for that orderliness. When parents do not fulfill their parental roles, the child's world-view becomes chaotic and the child can become maladjusted.

Demonstrating respect for your child's ideas is another way of showing love. There should be times for family conversation, when the children may express their thoughts, feelings, and opinions. The dinner table was the traditional setting for such conversations, and where circumstances permit, this is a tradition well worth preserving. The open forum or brainstorming atmosphere should prevail, and gifted children should feel free to express their own ideas on politics, religion, sex, or Baskin-Robbins' flavor of the month without fear of ridicule or censure. Equally important, the child should be taught that most conversations (those that take place away from the dinner table) are *not* open forums and that it is a matter of courtesy not to intrude on others' conversations (not even one's parents').

Perhaps the most common discipline problems with gifted children are related to their reasoning skills and verbal facility. In my practice, dealing with gifted children, I have seen many four- and five-year-olds lead their parents into lengthy debates over matters that were quite properly within the parents' sole province. Gifted children learn quickly that their parents are loath to use the intellectually stifling "because I said so," and therefore almost any edict can be questioned, argued, and debated, with the resulting reinforcement of parental attention.

An important parenting skill involves learning to limit and structure a child's choices. In the previous example of red shirt versus blue shirt, the parent should define the *range* of choices: the child may choose among styles, colors and patterns, but the parent has already selected a group of shirts appropriate to the season and occasion. Similarly with bedtime — the child may be given the choice of bathing before or after a favorite program, what bedtime story is to be read, what kind of snack (within limits set by the parent), and so on. The child may even decide whether to sleep or stay awake. But no matter what, it's "in bed and lights out" at a specific time.

Sure, children will test the limits. They'll complain. They'll try your patience. That's their nature. *But despite their protests, children are more comfortable, and therefore happier, when their parents are the final authority.* An anecdote will serve to illustrate this point: A few years ago, I was doing counseling and crisis-intervention in a junior high school. One day, one of my thirteen-year-old clients was complaining bitterly that his parents would not let him stay out until eleven o'clock on a school night with his friend. I asked whether the friend's parents allowed this, and he replied "Oh sure. They don't care about him." This boy realized, even though he would not openly admit it, that it was not appropriate to stay out that late and that his parents were enforcing the rule because they cared about him. It's also a lot easier to resist peer pressure when one can "blame" one's parents for not allowing something.

Enforcing rules is what we usually mean when we talk about discipline. The best way to enforce a rule is through its consequences. This simple principle has gained a lot of fancy terminology. There are books about behavior modification, contingency contracting, positive reinforcement, and so forth, but much of it is plain old common sense. Psychologist David Premack's name is associated with the Premack Principle, which states that more frequently occurring behaviors may be used to reinforce less frequently occurring behaviors. If this sounds a little technical, a more down-to-earth explanation is given by Wesley C. Becker in his excellent book *Parents Are Teachers*. Becker simply calls it "Grandma's Rule," which is: "You do what I want you to do, before you get to do what you want to do." This means homework before TV, bed made before leaving the house, and peas before ice cream. Maybe I shouldn't let the secret out — grandmas could put psychologists out of business.

Besides Grandma's Rule, there are some other common-sense principles worth following:

1. *A rule is a rule.* Just ask any four-year-old whether it's OK to change the rules of a game. They'll tell you — absolutely not. Therefore, it's best to be consistent. If you give in to your child's challenge, you've taught him or her several things: Rules can be broken. If you push long

and hard enough you'll get your way. Parents are not really in charge.

2. *Choose your battles.* When you decide to draw the line, be sure it's fair and appropriate. It's appropriate to demand that a four-year-old stay out of the street, or that a thirteen-year-old be home at a reasonable hour. On the other hand, it's not appropriate to demand that a four-year-old stay out of puddles, or that a thirteen-year-old conform to your tastes in clothes or hair style.

3. *There's a time and place for discussion.* Children *should* have *some* say where rules are concerned, and often they're tougher on themselves than their parents are. But negotiations and discussions should take place at a time when calm and reason can prevail. This means you do not renegotiate a curfew while your child is walking out the door.

4. *Let them act their age.* A gifted child with an adult vocabulary is still just a kid. Don't push your child to be a miniature adult. For some bizarre reason, our society is not content to let children be children. In his book *The Hurried Child,* David Elkind describes the emotional damage inflicted on children by pushing them to grow up too fast. Obviously an extensive recapitulation of Elkind's book is beyond the scope of this column, but I think it is particularly relevant to raising gifted children, because the temptation to push a child too fast and too soon is perhaps greater when the child is already advanced for his or her years.

These few hints and guidelines were not intended to be an exhaustive "how-to" manual. There are plenty of those on the market, and some are quite good. The main points made here are simple: Parents should fulfill their parental roles. Children need love, respect, and consistent guidance. Discipline is not a dirty word — it is part of the foundation upon which self-esteem, moral judgment, and good work habits are built.

— *Dr. J. Kent Hollingsworth, a school psychologist in Bogota, New Jersey*

SIBLING RIVALRY

What do you do about sibling rivalry?

For two years, Craig has played piano. At first, practice was tedious and success came hard, but now, the music flows when Craig's energies congeal onto the black and white "ivories." At eight years old, Craig plays piano as no one else plays piano.

Julie has just started lessons. She's Craig's younger sister, and already notes flow from her fingers with equal precision as they do from her brother's. And something else — a flair, an elegance, a quality that adds texture to the techniques that both have learned. Everyone notices, especially Craig.

Now, someone else plays piano as Craig plays piano — and she's only six. The competition has begun.

From "Special One" to "Special, Too"

Sibling rivalry — the competition among offspring — has existed as long as families have. As far back as Genesis, Joseph was despised by his brothers for finding special favor with his father, and without sibling rivalry, there would have been little premise upon which to write the story of Cinderella. Indeed, some degree of sibling rivalry in childhood appears inevitable.

In its many and varied forms, sibling rivalry is a function of sex, age, and birth order. It occurs in most families where education and achievement are priorities. It is generally acknowledged, for example, that firstborns tend to be high achievers who take initiative and assume responsibility. And yet, some studies have found that unequal levels of accomplishment are not sufficient to cause sibling rivalry. It takes something else. It takes parents emphasizing that "more is better."

Parental values and favoritism, whether overt or covert, figure as key factors in precipitating often intense and destructive competition among children. Perhaps, as parents with well-intentioned, high expectations for our children, we tend to reward most lavishly the accomplishments of whoever does "the best," and maybe our children themselves begin to compare, placing themselves in a race for our attention, love, and recognition.

For the gifted child — and especially for the youngster who is one of several siblings with above average abilities — the competition can be especially keen.

Catching Up to "Number One Son"

Craig is in third grade doing fifth grade work. Julie's in first, but already challenges some of her brother's reading and musical talents.

"Better be careful," Mom warns Craig, "Julie'll be ahead of you soon."

All of a sudden, Craig is vulnerable and distressed. Faced for the first time with the possibility of second-place status, he has several options, some of which you may have observed with your own children.

• Deny his sister's abilities, or brush them aside as inconsequential, "the work of a little kid."

• Attempt more, trying to gain parental attention by seeking perfection in new or unusual areas of achievement.

• Rebel by becoming "first-worst" instead of "first-best." Be the most feared, perhaps, or toughest, or least likely to succeed.

• Neglect those areas of common talents — eschew the piano and reading — in favor of new areas, where competition is not home-based or so fierce.

• Realize that different people have similar abilities, and that being "number one" is not a prerequisite to gaining parental affection.

Although many gifted children "talk a good game" about understanding individual capabilities, their outward behaviors may display little of this comprehension. So, they may pout, or be insulting or resentful, or repress their feelings and anxieties. Their goal, though, remains the same: a reaching out for parental acceptance "the way it used to be," before the reality of equally-able siblings intruded upon their world.

As parents, our roles become those of mediator and interpreter for our children's overt rivalries and resultant internal conflicts. What follow are some major "do's," "don't's," and clarifications of ways to reinforce siblings' efforts and performances, while minimizing the negative competition that often accompanies such strivings.

Some Don't's

• DON'T expect perfection. Speaking of his parents, a young gifted teenager wrote recently, "[They] made me feel inadequate and frustrated if I was not constantly performing at my best." Subtle cues — like the refrigerator displaying only papers marked 100 percent — and blatant comparisons — keeping a chart to record each sibling's number of report card A's — are equally destructive to a child's present and future self-worth. Perfectionism, by its very definition, is never fully attainable, yet some of our best efforts to praise and encourage imply that, indeed, only perfection is our goal. Learn to accept outstanding effort as well as accomplishment — from yourself and your children — to avoid the psychological trap of never being quite good enough.

• DON'T compare. For parents of gifted children, the comparison of one child with another is the most flagrant misuse of parental persuasion — and the least effective. When younger Julie is reminded of Craig's accomplishments, or elder Craig gets chided for "losing ground" to little Julie, any resultant change in their behaviors will involve either resentment (of parents, self, or siblings) or loss of family status, both to the detriment of self-esteem.

Instead, separate goals should be encouraged and comparisons made only in relation to one's own previous efforts. The goals, as well as the "acceptable" levels of effort and accomplishment, should be set by children with parental guidance, but without parental pressure.

• DON'T dismiss or suppress resentment. The real world is seldom equal or fair; and competition in our society is "the name of the game." But it doesn't have to be debilitating, even among siblings. As some studies indicate, sibling rivalry can even be fun and motivating. But when quarrels, disappointments, and resentments invariably arise, they should be discussed and worked through. More often than not, however, siblings rarely talk about their rivalry per se. So, it's up to parents to initiate the dialogue. To shelter your children from such encounters can cause more problems in the long run. Research has shown, for example, that brothers and sisters of parents who are "conflictophobes" — people who forbade quarrels — often carry their sibling problems into adulthood.

If an emotion exists — positive or negative, strong or subtle — then it will surely have an effect on outward behaviors. As a parent, you can share with your children avenues of expression for voicing their feelings and should encourage them to do so. ("When you tell me Julie's gonna catch me in piano, you make me feel like I'm lazy . . . is that what you mean?") Telling them to disguise their hostilities and resentments, or to dismiss them as passing moods, encourages dishonesty and is not the path of true family harmony.

Some Do's

• DO be honest and accepting. As much as most parents would like to believe that each of their children is "omni-talented," the fact is that different people — including gifted children — have abilities and talents in different areas. Talk openly about this reality with your children so they can begin to develop appropriate self-expectations. You can do this by comparing your strengths with those of your spouse, your own siblings, or other family members, or friends. The emphasis should be twofold: one doesn't have to be, and shouldn't expect to be, great in everything; and recognize, feel good about, and develop those areas of strength you do have.

Help your children make the same comparisons between and among themselves, with the goal being greater understanding, caring, and respect for each other.

You may also discuss with your children those strengths you wish you had, but don't have. Be a role model of self-acceptance of your own areas of weakness — in scholastics, sports, business, homemaking, whatever they may be. Help your children do the same. Certainly it is an admirable goal to strive to strengthen areas of weakness as well, but not to the point that major concentration and emphasis are on one's shortcomings.

Above all else, honesty and acceptance are the greatest consideration you can afford your children in discussing the ways they are alike and unlike.

• DO encourage different areas of interest. Ofttimes, children develop interests and goals that parallel our own. This is fine, and to be expected and encouraged. However, for the child who pursues computer programming (when you can't even type!), or auto mechanics (though you can't distinguish a carburetor from a cylinder), an occasional boost must be supplied here as well. Remember, too, that later-borns may deliberately avoid direct competition with an older sibling who excels in a certain area and compensate by channeling their abilities in other areas. You want this to be something healthy and productive and not the "first-worst" distinction. So, don't throw up your hands with the defeatist rejoinder: "OK, but you're on your own!" This leaves your child further isolated from the attention he seeks and needs. Some gifted children tend to experience more than their share of isolation as it is.

Instead, bolster his enthusiasm with the encouragement to pursue that different interest. React in the same positive way to this child's activity as you do to the hobby or craft that is "right up your alley." In this way, you will soften the often damaging intensity of competition among highly able siblings, help divert their strengths and energies into alternative areas, and lessen the likelihood of one child developing a sense of failure or inferiority for not measuring up to the other's standards of performance in a specific area.

• DO use praise appropriately. A common mistake when applying praise is an error of focus — we praise the child instead of the act. Witness the distinction in these two examples: "What a smart girl! Look at that report card!" versus "A report card with five A's and two B's shows real effort!" In the first instance, evaluation of the child's work as reflected in her grades is secondary in emphasis to bestowing flattery upon the child. While this seems like appropriate reinforcement, a child can come to associate her "smartness" and her "goodness" with her school performance. Consequently, if the next report card (or test, or footrace, etc.) falls short of this present effort, "I am bad" can be the self-judgment. The second statement lauds the act, primarily, not its performer, which is the appropriate focus for a well-deserved tribute.

Likewise, an inappropriate manner of praise can have a demoralizing effect on the sibling who may not be achieving in school, no matter how high his potential. In fact, using the same barometer (in this case, grades) to evaluate all your children's efforts and accomplishments may not always be suitable. There is an implicit comparison operative here, possibly between apples and oranges. Although it may be necessary and even advisable in some cases to encourage better schoolwork, recognition for achievements in outside interest areas is important for the child who isn't the "bookworm" his brother or sister is.

— *Dr. James R. Delisle, assistant professor of Special Education, Kent State University, Ohio*

"GAME PLAYING"

How can I help my funny, creative, curious child play whatever game is necessary to succeed in school, yet not totally alienate her to learning?

Nikos Kazantzakis suggests that ideal teachers are individuals who see themselves as *bridges* over which students can cross, then, having facilitated their crossing, joyfully collapse, encouraging them to create their own bridges. I would like to suggest that parents become bridges for their gifted children.

Leo Buscaglia, a professor from the University of Southern California, tells of talking with a group of gifted students in a California school district and suggesting that the only way of really knowing something is to experience it. This suggestion was followed by a lengthy description of knowing a tree by climbing it, feeling the tree, sitting in the branches and listening to the wind blow through the leaves. Following Buscaglia's presentation a group of students met him and said that a terrible thing had happened: one boy had seen a tree and climbed up in it, and as luck would have it, the vice-principal passed by and dragged him down, suspending him from school for two weeks.

Buscaglia immediately met with the vice-principal and found that he was irate and unwilling to change his mind. In talking with the expelled gifted student however, Buscaglia heard the following telling statement: "I think the thing I've learned from this is when to climb trees and when not to climb trees."

The boy's statement is certainly insightful, for in society and in school there are many rules and assignments to which one must adjust. The secret is to meet the needs of society and school, but not lose yourself in the process.

No One Teaches Anyone Anything

One very important concept to remember in dealing with under-achieving gifted students is that people learn things when they want to learn. If teachers act as facilitators and help students see how exciting and wonderful learning can be, students will learn. The sad fact is that not all teachers see themselves as facilitators and concentrate on infor-mation gathering rather than the exciting business of application.

In becoming a bridge parents must instill a *sense of purpose* in their gifted children. Through a discussion on the child's level, the parent can help the gifted child realize that the purpose of life is to have made a difference by living. This is pretty heavy stuff, but gifted students can grasp the significance of a life that counts or matters. One excellent way to get this point across is to identify individuals who have dedicated their lives to the service of others. These people can be found in history, in the biographies of Albert Schweitzer or Madame Curie, for example, and in today's news stories on Sister Teresa, Margaret Thatcher, and Norman Cousins.

Develop a Sense of Compassion and Harmony

Another important quality to develop in the gifted child is a *sense of compassion*. Through exercising compassion, gifted students can come to understand that sometimes people do things differently than they would want them to, and that there are several alternatives to handling a situation. One way is to acquiesce and be accommodating. A second way is to insist on one's own way.

In the classroom, a gifted student might suggest an alternative assignment to a receptive teacher in exchange for the more routine assigned activity. The gifted student might also go through an individual lobbying for curriculum change or at least a more lenient grading practice or atmosphere by talking, say, with the principal. This last suggestion can be deadly if the principal is not receptive to student input and ideas. As a parent, you can help your gifted child explore the alternatives and choose the one that is most likely to prove successful.

The notion of accepting the natural flow of life is not new and yet so many gifted children and adults are like moths flying directly into the fire. They literally rise to every occasion, railing against seen and unseen injustices. Righteous indignation and anger have their place in everyone's repertoire, but to be able to "go with the flow" or to resist "pushing the river" is wise. Talk it over with your gifted child. Ask her what she thinks harmony means and give examples of how nature exhibits harmony such as a bee gathering pollen from a flower. In examining nature, she will soon realize that there is a great deal of give and take in nature and that she, too, is capable of giving and taking.

Provide Joy and Inspire Excellence

If school has become a joyless place for your gifted child, find some outside activities that are fun. All of us need to sing, laugh, and dance now and then. Seek out community activities such as Girl or Boy Scouts, children's theater groups, dance troupes, and sports activities where children are encouraged to experience joy. These experiences can then be "joy catchers" for the daily ritual of school. If children feel good about themselves part of the day, they can withstand much more apathy and boredom.

Seeking to do one's best is essential in realizing goals whether they are life goals or just day-to-day objectives and assignments. A child's life is primarily taken up with school, whereas an adult's life is taken up by work and family responsibility. Yet to children and adults alike, it is desirable to give one's best in life.

As a parent, one must be receptive to questions, pointing the direction toward information and answers, and praising the "questing mind" and the work that grows out of this quest.

The goal for parents of gifted students should ideally be to create lifetime learners of them, and this must be done in a loving, caring way. The problem that many gifted students have is that excellence is offered in such a traditional, inflexible way that they seek mediocrity the only way they know how — by underachieving. Each parent must do everything possible to keep the love of learning and high quality alive.

Above all else, help them to maintain their dignity and integrity in their schooling. If the school situation is indeed unfavorable and unfair, it might be worth the time to seek alternative school experiences that are individualized and where children are prized. Schools like this do exist and oftentimes can be approximated in "home schools" when parents band together to discuss issues with school administrators and school boards. The alternative of having gifted children underachieve and become lazy learners is too great an individual loss as well as a loss to society. Consequently, parents must become their children's bridges and advocates in seeking appropriate education. Yes, gifted children must learn how to "play the game"; but the price of success should never be the loss of self.

— *Dr. Dorothy Sisk*

GRADING GIFTED CHILDREN

Should gifted students receive grades for all of their work? What's a good grading policy and how should it be carried out?

Aha, grading! The ancient quagmire of education in general and the veritable quicksand of programs for the gifted and talented. Any discussion of grading must first begin with a couple of general concerns about the definition of a grade or mark and the major purposes for using this practice. There are several issues that must be considered when we try to analyze grading policies and their effect on the overall development of gifted students.

What Are Grades?

Let's begin with a few thoughts regarding the definition of a grade or mark. Most people consider a grade to be a single summary symbol (either a letter or number) given by an instructor or teacher for a particular piece of work. A grade may also represent the sum total of all the work completed in a given marking period or throughout the course of a year. For example, an A− in honors English or fifth grade arithmetic represents a teacher's assessment of a student's work over a given period of time.

Grades do not provide diagnostic information about specific aspects of the quality of a piece of work, or the success of a student in a course, nor do they generally provide the feedback that would allow students to understand *why* a specified value has been assigned to their products or courses. If grades or scores must be assigned, it is, of course, highly recommended that written and/or oral feedback also be provided. This feedback should focus on specific strengths and weaknesses of each aspect of the work — such as factual accuracy, organization and structure, originality, mechanical correctness — and a variety of other characteristics that I'll discuss in more detail below. It is equally important that students should know *in advance* the criteria for which their work will be evaluated.

What are the purposes of a grade? Does a grade represent varying degrees of mastery of skill material? Or does it constitute "time spent" in a given class and a number of attendant factors such as neatness, interest and effort, punctuality, personal agreeableness and "getting along" with the instructor? If we answer "yes" to both questions, we are immediately faced with somewhat of a dilemma. Suppose that a very able student can demonstrate high degrees of mastery or competence on all of the material in a given course on the first day of school! Does this student deserve an A or A+ and should the student be required to sit throughout the semester or year even though the material has been mastered? And further suppose that in spite of outstanding mastery of the material the student is bored and therefore becomes a "psychological dropout" or even a behavior problem in class. Should the student then be "graded down" even though mastery has been clearly verified and documented? *I believe that formal grades should be awarded for mastery of the regular or required curriculum.* If highly able students can demonstrate mastery through acceleration or curriculum "compacting," then grades should be given on the basis of mastery rather than the amount of time spent in a given course or the number of assignments completed. When it comes to assessing work that clearly represents departures above and beyond the required curriculum, *I believe that we should abandon the use of formal grades and replace them with procedures that guarantee students comprehensive evaluative feedback.*

Another important issue related to grades is the evaluation of student performance in relation to his own potential, on the one hand, and in relation to the performance of a given group, on the other. In the first case, if a student is brighter than other youngsters, does that mean he or she must produce "more" or demonstrate higher levels of competency in order to earn the same grade as his or her not-so-able peers? If the answer is yes, then are we not in a sense penalizing a person for being bright?

Appropriate "Grading" Procedures

My own efforts over the years have avoided the issue of assigning single summary grades to given pieces of work. Instead, I believe in providing students with the evaluations that serve a diagnostic purpose and that will enable them to recognize their areas of strength and devote future attention to skills that may need further development in future assignments. In other words, *students should be encouraged to strive for excellence and personal growth rather than earning an ink spot called an A!*

When we evaluate the overall participation of students in gifted programs based on the Enrichment Triad Model, we attempt to provide this feedback in two ways. First, in a conference with the student we analyze the types and numbers of general enrichment experiences in which students have participated.

We try to plan future experiences which will heighten student interest in advanced topics. This information is sent home to parents in a progress report on a regular basis. The second way we provide students with feedback occurs when the student has been involved in the development of a product as a part of the gifted program.

Product Evaluation

The evaluation of products is achieved by the use of an instrument called the *Student Product Assessment Form* (SPAF). This form consists of eight specific indicators of product quality and seven overall estimates of the general characteristics of a given student product. The items in SPAF are:

1. Early Statement of Purpose
2. Problems Focusing
3. Level of Resources
4. Diversity of Resources
5. Appropriateness of Resources
6. Logic, Sequence and Transition
7. Action Orientation
8. Audience

Overall Assessment
1. Originality of the Idea
2. Achieved Objectives Stated in Plan
3. Advanced Familiarity with Subject
4. Quality Beyond Age/Grade Level
5. Care, Attention to Detail, etc.
6. Time, Effort, Energy
7. Original Contribution

Each item consists of a key concept, descriptive statements about how the concept might be reflected in a student's product, and an actual example of a product that is illustrative of the key concept. When we are evaluating the unique products of students, we do not have sets of norms or standard scores by which to judge if a product is truly creative.

Parents should discuss the issues raised in this article with their child's teacher so that everyone is clear about student evaluation procedures for a given subject.

Find out precisely how your child's teachers evaluate student performance, what constitutes "excellent" work, and whether a student's "entry level" of knowledge is assessed so that material already mastered does not have to be "learned" again. If necessary, you may have to point out to school personnel where your child's grasp of subject matter transcends the normal grade-level understanding, so other provisions can be made — and other criteria set — for measuring your child's progress.

— *Dr. Joseph Renzulli, professor of Educational Psychology, University of Connecticut at Storrs*

SOCIAL AND EMOTIONAL PROBLEMS OF GRADE SKIPPING

When children skip grades, are there any social or emotional problems I should be aware of? If so, how do I handle them?

As one of various forms of acceleration, grade-skipping used to be rather popular, particularly in the post-Sputnik era of gifted programs. Prior to that it was even more popular, but began to be questioned as the social needs of students were being investigated more closely. It has gone out of favor in some districts, in most instances because of either unsuccessful experience with it or a misunderstanding about the various educational needs of gifted children.

It is hardly surprising that there have sometimes been poor results from removing well-adjusted achieving students from successful learning situations where they have friends and, without any preparation, dropping them into a new situation. Those of us who have friends or relatives who were skipped with unhappy consequences have heard of the difficulty of making new friends, the pressure of meeting higher teacher expectations, and finally of never being able to go back if it didn't work out. Using these procedures generated problems for some students who previously had none.

Any academic change or intervention for gifted students should resolve rather than create problems. Before even considering criteria for having a child skip a grade, it is essential to clarify the rationale for the procedure. Grade-skipping, just like other program options for the gifted, should reduce obstacles to growth and foster the realization of children's psychological and academic potential — not to remove children from successful learning situations.

Indications of Need

The following are indications that a student may need to skip or may benefit from skipping a grade. (At least two out of three of the following):

ACADEMIC INTELLECTUAL ADVANCEMENT

1. Scores in the 99th percentile or two or more years above grade level in *both* reading and mathematics standardized achievement tests.

2. IQ of 135 or more.

3. Either good grades, but frustration or boredom with class work, or average or poor grades, indicative of boredom or frustration.

EMOTIONAL MATURITY (teacher observations are useful for this)

4. Compared to other children in class, she can work independently on projects that interest her.

5. Compared to other children her age, she is better at

- making decisions about her work
- evaluating her own work
- expressing agreement or disagreement
- expressing feelings

NEED FOR AN OLDER PEER-GROUP

6. Either the child gets along well with age-mates but prefers the company of older children or adults outside of school (particularly telling between kindergarten and third-grade level; or the child has problems with age-mates, but has productive or satisfying relationships with adults or older children outside of school.

7. Either the child can comfortably follow teacher instructions and rules in class, but outside of school is more independent in decision-making or carrying out responsibility she takes on herself, like hobbies or other projects; or the child is having difficulty accepting teacher instructions for rote homework or details in classwork, but at home can work independently with friends and family on projects or hobbies.

If the answer is yes to all seven criteria, then a child is a good candidate for grade-skipping and it should be considered as an option for meeting some of her needs, provided that it's on a trial basis. This procedure need not be an irrevocable one-way street. If it doesn't work out, if students do not feel comfortable or cannot adjust, it is the intervention, *not* the child, that has failed. Enough time, about a semester, is necessary for a fair trial, but even before starting students should know they can go back if they prefer. Reducing the pressure on the child will increase the likelihood of success.

Also, students should participate in the decision-making process, both in the initial decision and the final assessment to stay or go back. No programmatic decision is likely to be successful if a recalcitrant child is forced to go into another grade. Students are far more likely to achieve if they feel they are involved in the process.

It is likewise important that students should not be put under unreasonable pressure to perform brilliantly, to please the new teacher(s), or to make friends instantly. They and their teachers should be told to expect that some time will be required to adjust to the new situation. This should not be taken as an excuse not to fulfill class requirements, but to have reasonable expectations for quality.

Who Should Assess Success?

Teachers are the appropriate judges of the quality of the *work* produced. The work need not immediately be extraordinary, but simply good for that grade level.

The children themselves are best judges of whether the new situation is developing their potential, both intellectual and emotional. There are essentially three questions to ask:

- Are you learning more or better?
- Are you happier with this group of students?
- Do you prefer to stay?

A "yes" to two out of three indicates that children are in a situation that is conducive to their growth and should probably stay unless the teacher has major objections.

In addition, certain times are better than others to skip a grade, particularly for the purpose of psychological adjustment. Generally, joining a new class of students is far easier than unnecessarily leaving or joining an established class. Beginning a new cycle early — for example, kindergarten — or skipping the last year of a cycle — such as the last year of elementary, middle, junior high, or senior high school — and starting the next level of schooling a year early, are among the easiest times to adjust.

— *Dr. Susanne Richert, director of gifted education, Educational Information and Resource Center, Sewell, New Jersey*

DEPRESSION AND SUICIDE

Readers have written us to express worry about the vulnerability of gifted children to depression and suicide. One reader asked, "What are the danger signals to watch for in an intense, extremely bright youngster?"

In our world of increasingly high tech (and high pressure), adults must become more aware of the subtle and obvious clues that precede childhood and adolescent suicide. We must be able to look at gifted children as *vulnerable* as well as *capable*.

The statistics are well documented: among ten- to twenty-two-year-olds, suicide is the second leading cause of death — 5,000 per year. Although suicide occurs most often in the fifteen-to-twenty-two-year-old age group, it is far from rare among elementary and junior high school students. The percentage of these young victims who are gifted is open to question, yet our knowledge of gifted children tells us several things about their vulnerability:

- Gifted persons have a hypersensitivity to personal and world problems.

• Personal losses — friendships gone sour, scholarships not attained, relocation to new "rootless" communities — are all strong threats to gifted children's self-esteem and social status.

• The societal expectations for gifted children to be future leaders may seem unattainable, so that life can become aimless and barren.

These characteristics of gifted persons, coupled with the turbulence of everyday adolescence, may combine to create an illusion of life as a series of disappointments. Hope seems to expire and suicide becomes a viable option.

Common Complaints or a Crisis?

When does one intervene? How far is *too* far in the topsy-turvy emotional lives of gifted adolescents? When is the threat of suicide real and not just a passing thought of an active, ambitious mind?

Too often, these questions are asked in retrospect, after the suicide (or its attempt) occurs. Although no psychologist, counselor, or other professional can provide a fail-safe checklist of warning signs, there are several clues to guide parents in sifting normal adolescent concerns from more severe elements of stress:

1. The gifted child or teen — like all of his age-mates — is a social being who craves acceptance. Becoming "one of the gang" — any gang — is important. For the gifted child, who may already feel apart from age-mates because of exceptional intellectual abilities, it is easy to become a "minority of one" — a distinct unit with no true peers, an expendable cog in the family or social sphere. Watch for signs of self-imposed isolation — a child who dismisses social occasions as "trivial," or who continually ignores invitations from friends to enter into games or parties.

2. The self-imposed pressure to be perfect is an influential, yet often overlooked, aspect of being gifted. From the seven-year-old who only enjoys tasks at which she excels, to the teenager who is crushed by his first report card B, to the pre-med undergraduate who relinquishes free time for the sake of straight A's, the striving to succeed often becomes a struggle merely to maintain current levels of performance. Become aware, as a parent, of the emphasis your children place on their own successes and failures. How debilitating are mistakes? How rewarding are accomplishments? For the gifted child who lets perfection be the

ultimate standard, the pressure to succeed may override the motivation to do so.

3. Among the mixed blessings of being a gifted child is the frustration caused by understanding adult situations and world events while being powerless to affect their outcomes. Thus, when a gifted ten-year-old asks, "Why don't we buy food for poor people instead of making bombs to kill them?" all we can sometimes answer is "I don't know" or "Don't worry about such things, you're too young." As parents, we cannot dismiss these questions or fears; if we do, we deny the existence of those very qualities which help define our children as "gifted." It is our job, then, to notice the genuine confusion and sense of powerlessness that can occupy the minds of gifted children. It is important to recognize with our children that changes come gradually, and that inequities in our world have plagued "good thinkers" for thousands of years.

Preventing Youth Suicide

A small scrape or cut, left untreated, invites infection and further pain. The same is true with emotional hurt: left untended, feelings of anguish, despair, or grief become compounded, spreading ill effects throughout the human spirit. There are some preventive strategies that parents of gifted youngsters can use to help children whose anger or depression makes suicide an inviting alternative:

1. *Listen*. Whether the words come readily or only after great struggle, and whether the words be few or many, *be there* to hear your children speak their minds. Don't lecture ("You have your whole life ahead of you"); don't criticize ("I wouldn't complain if I were you; when I was your age . . ."); and, most of all, don't negate true feelings of hurt ("Don't be silly, only an idiot would want to kill himself").

2. *React Appropriately*. If you fear for your child's personal safety, don't sit back and hope that what you observe is a passing fad. Instead, tell him that you have noticed a change in behavior, and that you want to be sure that "things are OK." If you find it difficult to talk openly, suggest that *together* you speak with someone who can help sort things out — a counselor, perhaps, or a friend, clergyman, or doctor. If you believe that your child has considered suicide, don't be afraid to ask about it directly; to sidestep the issue is to avoid a reality that deserves discussion.

3. *Be Supportive and Specific*. Let your child know that you, too, are bothered by world events; that you, too wish people could be more

accepting of each other. Don't take on your child's problem as your own, but let the child know that he is not alone. Tell your child that "the lucky ones" talk out their anger or depression; those who remain quiet stay locked in a very lonely shell. Finally, if suicide is mentioned as an option, help your child to distinguish between "wanting to die" and "not wanting to live." The former is extreme, more related to inner turmoil; the latter is precipitated by external events that at present seem overwhelming.

4. *Follow up*. If you say you will follow through on a plan or suggestion, do so; don't become one more person to disappoint your child. *Arrange* that meeting, *call* that counselor, *schedule* another time to talk.

Suicide is not a pretty topic. The mere mention of the word surfaces everything negative within our psyches. The reality of suicide won't go away. Perhaps it can't in a world as complex and often uncompromising as the one in which we live. Today's gifted children and adolescents can become victims of their own intelligence, hostages to their own special insights. With our help, one child at a time may come to appreciate those facets of our world worth saving and learn how to cope with those realities that exist despite our best efforts to rid ourselves of them. And perhaps, if we are both lucky and skillful, some children that we help will return the favor tenfold in what they offer back to us and their world.

— *Dr. James R. Delisle*

Effective Parent Advocacy for Gifted Children

SOON you'll make your birthday wishes as you blow out eight candles on your cake. I have wishes for you, too, one for each glowing candle, each shining year.

First: I hope you maintain always the joy of discovery that kindles a glow in you.

Second: I hope we see during your school years a growing awareness of the needs of the gifted, appreciation of their contributions, and empathy for their problems.

Third: A satisfying career suited to your talents and interests is something I hope you'll find.

Fourth: Your career must be your own decision, as your life is your own and not an extension of mine. Still I hope you'll offer your talents in some field that helps others.

Fifth: When I think of the difficulties you'll encounter, I wish for you a greater flexibility than you now have.

Sixth: What of your relationships with others? You enjoy your friends so much that I don't worry about your becoming a recluse wrapped up in work and neglecting personal ties. I hope you'll be one of the lucky ones who shares a rewarding marriage. A loving companion will magnify your delights and ease your burdens.

Seventh: I wish for you as a talisman for happiness an inner harmony which allows you to see and accept yourself as you are.

Eighth: I hope that in the future you look back warmly on your childhood as a good time.

As I look back over these wishes for you, I see that some are interior, like spiritual harmony, and some are external, like a satisfying career.

They're dreams that any parent might dream for any child. Yet because of your capacity for complex thought and your heightened sensitivity it seems to me that lack of these things will hurt you more deeply. And fulfillment of these wishes could nourish you more richly, so that in turn you can nourish others. Your gifts won't set you apart from the human race; they'll make you more intensely a part of it.

— *Maureen Melvin, Okeechobee, Florida*

The above winning essay in a "What I Want for My Gifted Child" contest contains universal wishes of parents for their gifted children; but how can parents help assure that such wishes come true? This question raises the issue of effective parent advocacy for the gifted and talented — one of the most difficult roles for parents.

COMMON GOALS

The first thing a parent advocate must do, says Gina Ginsberg-Riggs of the Gifted Child Society, is set aside personal priorities and join with other parents to assume responsibility for making a difference — somewhere between reducing our children to the lowest common denominator and letting them reach for the stars.

Making a difference for gifted children is a multifaceted concept. And although each child's learning needs may be unique, as parents it is important that we recognize the goals we share for changing the attitudes of school personnel, decision makers, and the general public.

First, we need to inform people that gifted children come in all colors, shapes, and sizes — just like all the other kids. There is a whole world out there that still thinks gifted children are skinny kids in thick glasses, whose parents went to fancy colleges.

Second, we need to insure that gifted children get the school programs they need, an equal share of the funding, and thereby an equal opportunity to learn all they are able to learn — just like all the other kids. Most people still think that gifted children are so smart that they can teach themselves. Why do they need special programs? This widely held attitude is reflected in the unequal share of money and time for gifted children provided in state legislation and local planning and budgeting.

Third, advocates of gifted children must work for the day in the near future when the climate will be such that people will value the strengths of our children, assist them in their areas of weakness, and be pleased for them to grow up and take respected places in society — just like all the other kids. We know that gifted children have superior ability and that the word *superior* makes people hostile, defensive, apathetic, or complacent.

EARLY ENROLLMENT

Most parents of gifted children ask, "What is the best thing I can do to help my special child?" Some seek information by reading everything they can on gifted children and by consulting with professionals. Some work on getting school personnel to do something different — and more suitable — for their child. Your child will probably benefit from any and all efforts you make to determine both what he needs and how you and others can better respond to those needs. But don't expect to find a single solution such as early admission to school.

According to Patricia Mitchell of the National Association of State Boards of Education, when considering early enrollment ask yourself these questions: What will my child get in the school program that I, and/or a good preschool/kindergarten teacher, cannot provide? Will being with older children help my child? Will she enjoy being with older children? Will the placement with older children be a real improvement over the current placement — or will it still not provide what she really needs? Am I certain she's capable of handling the work? If, after the most careful and objective examination, you still feel early enrollment is an important way to help your child, then you might follow these steps.

1. Find out if early enrollment is permitted in your district.

State legislatures and state boards of education usually set admission requirements for schools, including: the minimum age for enrollment in first grade and kindergarten, the date by which a child must meet the age requirements to be enrolled, and whether or not a local school board may make an exception to the age requirement.

If your district may make exceptions, then you must find out how to get them to make an exception for your child. If state policies do not permit local exceptions, then your local district cannot legally admit your child before the age set in state policy. About two-thirds of the states do *not* permit local exceptions.

2. To change your state's policy to permit early enrollment, seek additional information and support.

Changing a state policy is not easy. First approach your state association for gifted children and elicit their support. Then investigate which body (state legislature or state board of education) sets the age-of-enrollment or no-exceptions policy and what key persons in that body think about changes to permit early enrollment. If attitudes are favorable to change (or if, at least, these persons are willing to consider it), then find a respected legislator or state board member to introduce the change, and back them up in any way they suggest (visits with other policymakers, phone calls, letters) to get the new policy accepted. As policymaking processes are quite complex, make sure you read more about advocacy and invest your time in finding out who's important in *your* state's process and what they think about the early enrollment policy. Don't wear yourself out and waste your time trying to introduce a new or revised policy through a weak or ineffective policymaker to a policy body that is not interested in or supportive of the concept.

3. If local exceptions for early enrollment are permitted in your district, seek additional information on local policies and procedures.

Find out what it takes to have your child enrolled in kindergarten or first grade before the "normal" age. Do you need specific scores on specific tests? If so, how do you arrange for testing? Do you present your case to the superintendent, a staff member and/or the local school board? If so, what information and approaches did other parents use to present their cases successfully? Use this period of initial investigation to find out more than just the formal policies and procedures for early enrollment. How people respond to your inquiries about policies will give you valuable information on how they feel about early enrollment and who really decides on cases for exception to age requirements. Use this information to prepare your case so that it will appeal to the key decision makers and win their support.

4. If early enrollment is permitted, but your district has a policy of "no exceptions" to the age requirement, seek additional information and support to change local policy.

Changing a local policy is similar to changing a state policy. It's not easy, and you'll probably need the support of others to be successful. If you have a local association for gifted children, seek their support. If there is no local association, find some parents, educators, other professionals who work with young children, and/ or community leaders who will help you.

Next, investigate how, when, and why the local policy against early enrollment was made. This will give you an idea of how difficult it will be to change the policy. For example, if your school board recently made the policy, which was suggested by the superintendent and approved by a clear majority of the board, and most of those key people are still in the positions of authority, it will be difficult to change the policy.

If you decide it's possible to change the policy, find out who the most influential people are in your district, what they think about early enrollment, and what it would take to get them to support a policy change. You can begin to determine this by attending school board meetings and observing the structure of such meetings — who is asked for advice among the board members, who is most outspoken, whose opinions are deferred to most often, etc. Again, this period of investigation is worth a substantial investment of time. You will find out not only who *makes* decisions in your district, but also who *influences* the decisions. By talking with both decision makers and decision influencers on an individual basis, you may find out their personal, as well as their public, stance on early enrollment. You'll know how to present your case to maximize your chance for success.

5. *If at first you don't succeed, keep trying.*

The person who said, "Where there's a will there's a way" probably had not attempted to change a school policy. Remember that you are seeking recognition by the schools of your child's intellectual precocity and that the schools have a responsibility to help advanced learners. They may resist early enrollment for any number of reasons. For example, they may think that young children, regardless of intellectual ability, will be emotionally or socially hurt by "pushing" them ahead; or by recognizing your child's advanced abilities through early enrollment, the school will also be obligated to provide a special instructional program, and there are no resources to provide such a program; or if the school makes an exception in your case, even if well-justified, then it will set a precedent and too many parents will seek early enrollment for their children.

You might answer these objections by pointing out that emotional and social damage are not inevitable with early enrollment, and that the same cautions apply as with grade skipping (see chapter 9); encouraging the school to provide a gifted program by beginning with the resources already at the district's disposal (library, resource center, specialty teachers, etc.); assuring the school board that it is unlikely they will be inundated with early enrollment requests, but if they do get others, they will have a clear set of guidelines and procedures to follow.

If your attempts to get an exception made for your child, or to change a state or local policy to permit exceptions, are not successful, you can try again, find another way to meet the needs of your gifted child, or, as a last resort, move to another area. (Some parents have sent their children to private school, or hired a home tutor, or even started their own small school until the child had passed the particular grade level that had the age requirements.)

PARENT INVOLVEMENT AT SCHOOL

"Parent involvement at school holds the hope for renewed public faith in education," according to Gina Ginsberg-Riggs, executive director of the Gifted Child Society in New Jersey. Ginsberg-Riggs singles out seven key roles parents can take to get involved as "partners" in their gifted children's education.

1. *The Parent as Learner:* This entails becoming familiar with the educational bureaucracy by enlisting educators to help parents learn how a school works.

2. *The Parent as Helper:* The oldest and most accepted parent role, helping out in school, can range from running book fairs to taking cafeteria duty. Additionally, parents can help teachers with "busywork," so they are freed to spend more time with gifted students.

3. *The Parent as School Supporter:* Spreading positive feelings about the school among friends and neighbors will help shape supportive and productive attitudes in community members. Some points to get across: there is joy in learning; teachers are to be

respected; homework is a student responsibility; and school is a good place to be.

4. *The Parent as Source of Information:* Parents provide information about their children — home versus school behavior — and about the family and community to school personnel. This communication enables school personnel to be more sensitive to individual differences and to provide appropriate education for each student.

5. *The Parent as Resource Person:* Sharing talents and experiences, hobbies, career information, special training or know-how can be a significant source of enrichment for gifted children. Parents can make themselves available as mentors for students' projects, independent studies, etc.

6. *The Parent as Teacher:* Parents are their children's "first teachers" and have the most lasting impact on their lives. They remain teachers of their children's values until adulthood, and probably beyond. In this regard, parents should think of themselves as educators' working equals.

7. *The Parent as an Agent for School Change:* This entails exercising one's influence by standing up and being counted as supporting education for the gifted. Critical to this role is knowing who the right person is to contact and persuade (the one with power to act); the right time (when the issue is under discussion); and the right way (in large numbers and with correct information).

Ginsberg-Riggs contends that no school in the country "takes advantage of all its parent power." She maintains that "everything a school does can be done better or more economically with the help of parents in some way."

If, despite all your efforts, you don't feel the school is working well for your child, it may be enlightening for you to consider four possible types of parent-school interaction identified by Nicholas Colangelo of the University of Iowa and his colleague David Dettman in *The Journal for the Education of the Gifted*.

• *Type I — Cooperation:* Simply stated, this interaction results in open sharing of information about the child and genuine cooperation among all parties. Following the identification process, by which the child is determined to be "gifted" in one or more areas, the student is allotted ample educational opportunities matched with individual needs.

• *Type II — Conflict:* As the word *conflict* implies, this inter-action is based on conflicting opinions about just what the role of the school should be. It can be summed up, say Colangelo and Dettman, as follows, "Parents believe that their gifted child needs special programming by the school in order to develop his or her abilities. However, the school believes that the typical school curriculum is adequate in meeting the needs of all youngsters, including gifted." This is, of course, the most difficult situation and can lead to three splintered directions for parents: they may continually fight the school; they may join forces with other parents to assert their position; they may feel hopeless and withdraw from communicating with the public school system or seek out a private school.

• *Type III — Interference:* Though this interaction is closely aligned with conflict, there is a reversal of the dynamics found in conflict relationships. For example, in a Type II conflict situation, advocates of gifted programs will need to focus their energies on educating and informing the school system of the need for such programs, whereas in a Type III interference situation other parents are the audience to be convinced. Here the school is anxious to provide expanded activity and curriculum for the gifted student, but the parents are more concerned with negative effects their children may encounter from being labeled "gifted" and the impact this special attention may have on siblings who are not so iden-tified.

• *Type IV — Natural Development:* This is a partnership that develops between the parents and school based on an agreement that the school's role should be passive. The premise in this kind of interaction is that high ability will take care of itself, that "cream rises to the top."

Colangelo and Dettmann consider lack of insight into these interactional dynamics as the "single most destructive impedi-ment" to developing a working relationship between home and school for the benefit of gifted children. They suggest that parents work toward a more beneficial relationship with the school by first assessing and understanding the particular type of interaction that applies to their situation. Then they should take a logical plan of action most beneficial to both groups.

Another broadly based way you can help your school help the

gifted is to encourage and assist in the education of the community about the special needs of these special children.

Writing in the *Roeper Review*, Donovan Walling, a school public relations expert, outlines the primary objectives of a gifted program's *informational outreach activities* as developing the community's understanding of giftedness and gifted education, acquainting community members with the goals and objectives of the school's gifted program, clarifying misconceptions and myths about the gifted, and providing concrete answers to concrete questions about the gifted and gifted education.

Walling says these things can be accomplished in several ways. *Pamphlets*, for example, which are portable, simple to understand, and reach many people, can successfully convey important information if designed correctly. A pamphlet should focus on a single topic (not broad generalities), avoid educational jargon, and list a contact person for further information. "Why Gifted Education Is Important to Our Country" is an example of such a topic. The same goes for *newsletters*, he says, and both can be distributed at libraries, supermarkets, and other public places.

Bibliographies, especially annotated ones, help enlist community support and promote good will, according to Walling, as they point people in the right direction for obtaining detailed information on a subject. If possible, include in its listing where the book is available. Even better are *resource collections* of desirable materials put together by teachers or parents and housed in a convenient location — like the school or public library.

Most schools have activities throughout the year in which student work is displayed. *Visual displays* at school fairs or shopping malls allow for one-to-one interaction with community members. The display can be manned by teachers and/or gifted students who are willing to chat about their work and program. *Limited hotlines* — several hours per day or week — are another form of "interactive" communication, states Walling, allowing for direct questions and answers about giftedness and the gifted program. Likewise, parents and teachers can share the phone duty.

All of these PR activities are important not only for getting information out; they tell community members that both the parents and the schools *care*. "If schools demonstrate that they care what the community thinks," Walling states, "then the community will in turn care about the course of education and will provide the support necessary for excellent school programs."

Building community support for your gifted program depends on providing community members with the right kinds of information. And it depends on a concrete demonstration of the value of gifted education.

What do community members need to know? Not merely the philosophical arguments. At a far more visceral level, the public seeks reassurance that services for our brightest youngsters do not violate one of our country's most cherished and implicit values — that of egalitarianism. Advocates need to convince community members (and school officials, for that matter) that education for the gifted is not elitist, and this should be a major focus for "informational outreach activities."

What constitutes an elitist program? One element is what can be called the Chromosome Syndrome, the "you either have it or you don't" attitude toward exceptional ability based on the premise that giftedness is predominantly a genetic endowment. Of course the genes are involved, but so is a nurturing environment that allows — and often causes — latent potential to blossom.

Closely related to this is the sole reliance on IQ when identifying and selecting children for gifted programs. Nothing reeks more of exclusivity and does more for perpetuating the old myths than this magic number. In contrast, identification criteria should be broad, flexible, and inclusive of as many children as possible.

Gifted children need special programs to challenge and develop their special abilities. But sometimes the activities children actually do in their programs appear more like special privileges for being smart than substantive learning experiences. As Dorothy Sisk of the University of South Florida says, sooner or later we must have gifted children do more than "pretend they are leaves in the autumn wind."

A gifted program is subject to charges of elitism when it is completely segregated or isolated from the rest of the school and community. It is difficult to build support for your program when no one knows anything about it or cannot see the benefits of it.

One of the traditional rationales for gifted programs is that gifted children will make outstanding contributions to society someday. Why not today? Many gifted children — through school programs and on their own — have planned and organized special community projects to serve persons in need, such as senior citizens.

Such activities utilize the skills and talents of gifted children in a concrete demonstration of caring and can be applied to a myriad of other socially oriented projects.

It takes information to build awareness and support. But the biggest return for your dollar may come from community service.

OTHER AVENUES FOR PARENT ADVOCACY

We are a democratic country where the majority rules. If our children do not have the kinds of education we would like, it is usually because not enough people wanted a different education for them. Our path, then, is clear: we must "sell" gifted education to more people; we must convince an ever-increasing number that our cause is honorable, and that our future thinkers and doers must have an education that challenges their abilities. Several methods put together by Gina Ginsberg-Riggs are effective.

• *Educate Yourself:* We cannot effect positive change if we don't know what we're talking about. Read up on gifted children and their education. Know your state's legislation on the gifted and inform yourself about what your child's school has done — or failed to do — for gifted students. Be very sure of your facts. Lack of knowledge makes you an ineffective person; wrong information ruins your credibility. As advocates, we must see our role to provide others with the information and motivation for change.

• *Be a Joiner:* Almost everywhere parents are finally being recognized and respected as partners in the education of their gifted children. We must work supportively and creatively alongside educators to earn continued equal status. One way is through state parent associations. Most states have parent groups for gifted children. Join that group or start one if none exists where you are. One parent can get lost in the bureaucratic shuffle; a group of parents — the bigger the better — is hard to ignore. And remember, the tasks of such a group can appear awesome. Break them down into manageable pieces; set reasonable goals with reasonable timeframes.

• *Don't Overlook the Private Sector.* As parents, we can encourage and help develop community-based programs for the gifted in cooperation with the schools. The private sector is ready with people, places, things, and — sometimes — tax-deductible dollars, because it is vitally interested in student preparedness for the world of work. Gifted children are in the uniquely favorable position of being just the kind of young people the private sector needs and would like to have for its future leadership. Business and industry can be encouraged to support or initiate gifted programs, participate in mentorships, provide products or other services. An excellent book on this is *The Private Sector: New Answers to Old Budget Questions* available from the Gifted Child Society.

According to Frank Cookingham of Kent State University, writing in the *Roeper Review*, using resources within the community can help ease the burden of school districts with limited funds for special programs, curb student boredom with the regular curriculum and resultant behavioral problems, and prevent talent from going undeveloped. Cookingham points out that it is now commonplace to think of education as involving much more than formal schooling and to acknowledge that the public school system cannot meet all or everyone's educational objectives. Hence for the gifted student, as well as for their own survival and sustenance, the schools need to tap and exploit the potential of all institutional forces within the community.

• *Become a Political Animal:* As advocates, you must learn about politics. For starters, it is important to know who your state and federal legislators are and who sits on the Senate and House Education and Appropriations Committees this year. Become familiar with the mechanics of turning a piece of legislation from an idea into a law and the correct way and most effective time to communicate with legislators. It is essential to communicate with legislators, teachers, boards of education, and others in powerful places.

A state legislature can be particularly influential in education for the gifted. It can pass a law requiring special education for all gifted children, or one that encourages a local option. It can define who the gifted are, how they are to be identified, and what services they should receive. It can decide how much money will be provided for education of the gifted and how it will be distributed. It can decide if teachers should have special training. It can influence gifted education through action on other programs — such as appropriating money for more school psychologists or other special personnel.

Or . . . it can do none of these things.

To make sure that doesn't happen, advocates for the gifted must delve behind what is often perceived as the mystery of the legislative process in their states, says Lyn Aubrecht, chairperson for legislative action of the North Carolina Association for the Gifted and Talented. A member of the faculty at both Meredith College and North Carolina State University, Aubrecht is a contributor to *An Advocate's Guide to Building Support for Gifted and Talented Education*, published by the National Association of State Boards of Education.

Not surprisingly, *how* one approaches a lawmaker is just as important as *what* one has to say. Aubrecht's first advice for working through the complexities of state legislature is to find an influential "friend," preferably a legislator, who is known or presumed to be sympathetic with the cause and principles of gifted education. The reason: "They generally . . . have access to an office or department that will help to research and write potential legislation."

There are two ways to find legislators who are sympathetic and will help you, Aubrecht adds: lobby with your own legislators at home and canvass the offices of legislators when they begin their session; an advocacy campaign should encompass both methods. The "at home" approach is easier and more informal. As these solons are elected by local people, they will listen to your concerns. Either by phone or appointment, ask your legislators for their opinion on the educational needs for gifted children. Follow up your conversation with a memo outlining the main points you discussed; thank him or her for the meeting and any future support that can be given your group on behalf of these children. During the legislative session, write often, asking for an update on your cause.

If you canvass the legislature, make it a point to see legislators who have initiated or supported legislation for the gifted in the past; legislators who represent your home district; legislators who represent districts where your organization has members; legislators who might eventually support legislation for the gifted: for example, those who represent districts with large numbers of gifted children.

Aubrecht advises advocates of the gifted to be aware, when talking to legislators, of the legislator's time constraints; be brief, if necessary, and follow up with a written statement. You should also be honest, knowledgeable, and thorough — explaining what other states are doing and what you would like your state to do. Emphasize that education for the gifted needs "friends" in the legislature.

The same approach can be used with other state officials who are potential allies, Aubrecht says. These include the governor, lieutenant governor, members of the state board of education and state department of education. Local parent groups may wish to band together and share responsibilities for approaching state officials.

Lobbying for educational change is a sophisticated skill that advocates for gifted education must learn if they are to compete successfully with other constituencies for a fair share of available resources. Approaching state lawmakers is one important facet of mounting a successful advocacy campaign. There are others, including petitions, testimony, letter writing, and dealing with legislative sub-committees.

For information on these activities, write for *Lobbying and You* by Larry E. Harris, c/o Another Opinion, Inc., 3311 Garfield St., N.E., Minneapolis, MN 55418.

• *And Don't Forget the Press.* Cultivate a friendly contact responsible for education news. Use the press to keep the issue of gifted children visible. Learn how to write a publicity release, and be sure the press is informed about school programs (your school probably has a school public relations designee) and parent association activities.

WHY AND HOW TO START A
PARENT GROUP

Parents can accomplish a great deal through forming a group of advocates for gifted and talented children. Pat Davies, parent representative for New York State's advocacy machine, has suggested a number of things such a group can do:

• Help educate each other and teachers on effective strategies for working with gifted children.

• Share ideas for games and activities that spark creativity and that children enjoy.

• Help coordinate gifted programs, including review and selection of teaching staff.

• Establish parent volunteer programs for organizing field trips and other opportunities for gifted children to do things together.

• Purchase appropriate informational and instructional materials for community or school libraries.

• Coordinate services of community resources (for example, museums, businesses, mentorships) and those of local colleges or universities.

• Voice support to a school district's administration for teachers of the gifted and the need for enriching curriculum.

What about getting a local parent group off the ground? Davies says successive steps are necessary. Here are some of the most important ones.

1. A core of advocates (two or three) need to plan and conduct a public meeting to establish contact with other people sharing their concerns. (Remember to have sign-in cards: name, address, phone numbers, specific questions.)

2. Invite a speaker — a local administrator who is "pro" gifted, a professional in the field, the school coordinator of gifted programs, or a representative from another parent group.

3. Select a steering or planning committee with geographic representation. This committee will be responsible for drafting goals and objectives; a list of potential officers, board of directors, and their responsibilities; recommendations for other committees needed; a projected budget and dues required; local bylaws. This committee will also plan the program for the second public meeting. (Set a date at the first meeting.)

4. The agenda for the second meeting should include all steering committee activity; bylaws should be reviewed, revised, and adopted; nominations for officers should be presented and also accepted from the floor before voting; committee responsibilities should be described and volunteers enlisted to serve on them.

One important activity many parent advocacy groups have been instrumental in are state or local Gifted Education Weeks. Such an activity helps to increase awareness of the needs of gifted children and gets legislators and decision makers involved and in the public eye themselves. The activities below, initiated by the Harrison County, West Virginia, Association for the Gifted for their Gifted Education Week, should be a useful springboard for other groups planning such an event.

• • A mayoral proclamation was signed establishing Gifted Education Week.

• Letters were sent to state and local leaders advising them of the designated week and inviting them to participate.

• Newspaper articles were written explaining gifted education, the county program, and the organization's efforts on behalf of the students.

• Radio and TV appearances were made by some members of the group's executive committee, and public service announcements aired concerning activities for the week.

• Classroom visitations were scheduled for the public.

• Gifted students displayed examples of their work in downtown area store windows; made puppets and gave puppet shows in area schools; and wrote, produced, directed, and presented a video show for the parents' monthly meeting.

• A banquet honoring gifted students was held at the end of the week.

• A booklet of gifted students' literary writing was compiled to commemorate the week.

• The organization visited clubs, churches, the senior citizens' center, and other community resources trying to enlist the services of persons willing to share their talents and knowledge and act as mentors for gifted students.

EVALUATING GIFTED PROGRAMS

Evaluating programs for the gifted and talented is still in its infancy, but it's important for parent advocates to keep up with what is going on and learn as much as they can about evaluation. With fewer programs overall being funded with federal and state grant money, local school decision makers will have to make some hard choices concerning which programs to cut and which to maintain. Gifted programs will not be spared from this review. Nor should they be.

Unfortunately, there is some evidence that such programs are often the first to go in periods of economic hardship. The attitude that gifted programs are "add-ons" or "all frills" or "OK if somebody else is paying for them" prevails in many school districts throughout the country. Hence, parents and teachers and school board members — anyone who has a vested interest in these programs or is in a position to sit in judgment — must learn what to look for when evaluating a gifted program.

Cheryl J. Gowie, coordinator of the gifted and talented program in the Herkimer (New York) Central School District and evaluation consultant on gifted to the New York State Department of Education, offers some broad guidelines for evaluating gifted programs. Writing in the *New York State School Boards Association Journal,* Gowie acknowledges that "many of the traditional approaches to program evaluation may not be available or appropriate," but that "creative and informative evaluation strategies can be devised."

She lists four areas which should be considered when evaluating a gifted program: theoretical framework, curriculum, students' role, student products.

Framework: A gifted program should have a statement of philosophy and the school district should have a carefully thought out definition of what "giftedness" means. "Based on this definition, the identification procedures, the goals and objectives, the curriculum, and the evaluation strategies will be formulated," Gowie states. "All should follow logically from the definition and be consistent with its intent."

Gowie cites the mismatch and inconsistency of program components as the reason why some gifted programs fail to get positive results. If a program is for the intellectually gifted, for example, assessment of a student's leadership potential to select that child for the program, or a curriculum geared to develop creativity, would be "highly inappropriate." Conversely, if a district wants to foster leadership and creativity, Gowie points out, then these things should be included in the definition a school board adopts.

"Differentiated" Curriculum: This doesn't necessarily mean a separate curriculum for the gifted, but it does mean organizing and adapting the regular curriculum so that it enhances the learning of gifted children. Drawing upon the ideas of Sandra Kaplan, associate director of the National/State Leadership Training Institute of Gifted and Talented in Los Angeles, Gowie recommends that the curriculum content for the gifted be organized around an issue, some problem, or a theme — say, nuclear disarmament as part of a social studies unit. It should be broad, draw upon various disciplines, and include increasing levels of complexity and ab-

stract thinking. Curriculum content linked to a skill, such as problem solving, and something produced by a student — such as a proposed nuclear disarmament schedule involving all major superpowers — "constitutes a learning experience of value," she states.

In contrast to such a curriculum, Gowie notes, are activities such as field trips and interesting speakers that could benefit *all* children, not just the gifted. However, if gifted children are the only ones enjoying such activities, then the program is subject to charges of elitism — which is devastating to school and community support — in addition to being insufficiently modified and enhanced according to the higher ability levels of gifted students.

The Students' Role: Another consideration in evaluating a gifted program is whether the student's role as learner is expanded. Gowie is as convinced as other experts in the field that "rather than being a consumer of knowledge, the gifted student should become a producer of knowledge; rather than being merely a good test-taker or lesson-learner, the student should become a first-hand investigator of real problems."

She admonishes school board members and parents to be wary and critical of a program for the gifted that places students in the traditional roles of information consumer and regurgitator. Likewise, evaluation of "student progress" on this basis is inappropriate because the goals, objectives, activities, and student roles are different from what they are in the regular classroom.

Student Products: How, then, should one evaluate the program vis-à-vis student "achievement"? Through the quality of student products, Gowie suggests. Although school board members and other district-level decision makers will not get fully involved in student evaluation per se, the following five criteria offered by Joseph Renzulli at the University of Connecticut will help in assessing this component of the program: the product's statement of purpose and problem focus; the level, diversity, and appropriateness of resources used; the logic, sequence, and transition of ideas; awareness and consideration of intended audience; and plans for follow-up activities.

Gowie suggests for purposes of comparison that those deciding the fate of a gifted program might examine the kind and quality of student products coming from the special program alongside of those from the regular classroom.

What You Should Look for in a Gifted Program

The checklist that follows covers the important elements in evaluating or setting up a gifted program in your child's school. Also included are some reasons why these elements are important. (This information came from the *National Report on Identification*.)

I. Identification Procedures: Look for comprehensiveness and equity.
   A. Nomination for a Talent Pool
      1. Students are sought in all areas of giftedness in the federal definition: a. general intellectual; b. academic; c. creative; d. visual and performing arts; e. leadership.
      2. The talent pool is representative of the entire student population.
      3. Tests are used to include, not exclude, students from programs.
      4. Information beyond tests is used.
      5. Teachers have training in the characteristics of giftedness.
   B. Assessment: Matching Needs and Program Options
      1. Further information on interests and learning styles is sought.
      2. Data is gathered to match students needs and multiple program options.
   C. Evaluation: Improve the Program
      1. Data on individual student progress is gathered, rather than competitive evaluation.
      2. Students are involved in self-evaluation.

II. Program Design: How many of these different program options are available to identified gifted students?
   A. The regular classroom provides alternatives to students as part of the regular curriculum
   B. Homogeneous grouping is required or elective subjects
   C. Resource rooms or learning centers in a pull-out option
   D. Access to libraries/laboratories at a higher-level building
   E. Continuous progress in the basic skills
   F. Early entrance to or exit from school, or grade skipping
   G. Mini-courses, seminars
   H. Extracurricular, after school, or Saturday activities that focus on student interests

> I. Independent study
> J. Internships/mentorships
> K. Field trips
> L. Counselors with special training dealing with gifted students

III. Staff Training: Do staff in all program options, including the regular class, have some training in each of these areas of gifted education?
> A. Identification
> B. Academic needs
> C. Emotional needs
> D. Non-competitive evaluation procedures

IV. Curriculum: Does the curriculum in each program option, including the regular class, meet more than half of these objectives?
> A. Grouping:
>   At least part of the time do gifted students have time to work together in groups of 2–18?
> B. Content or Subject:
>   At least part of the time is the content modified in one of these three ways?
>   1. Accelerated — moving more quickly
>   2. Interdisciplinary
>   3. Based on individual or group interest
> C. Is the emphasis on higher-level thinking rather than just more information?
> D. Are children encouraged to apply their learning to create a variety of products rather than just tested?
> E. Does the curriculum provide for emotional growth by developing these things?
>   1. Positive self-concepts, self-acceptance
>   2. Independence
>   3. Risk-taking in creative activities or projects
>   4. Self-evaluation skills
> F. Does the curriculum develop decision-making skills?
>   1. As part of the content of the curriculum
>   2. In offering students a variety of options at each stage
>   3. By guaranteeing that students learn the objectives of every class and activity

G. Does the curriculum stimulate both sides of the brain?
   1. Does the curriculum develop spacial and visual abilities as well as verbal abilities and calculation?
   2. Are intuition, feeling, and imagination as valued as logic, scientific data, and accuracy?

1. Comprehensive identification benefits all those students included because it provides a broader experience of giftedness. With more students identified (up to 25 percent), greater variety in possible grouping by interests becomes more viable.

Disadvantaged, culturally different, and creative students are served this way as well.

2. Gifted children are as different from each other as they are from other children. They have needs for differing amounts of homogeneous grouping, grouping by ability ranges, and at various stages of development their interests differ. No single program option can ever meet all of the needs of all gifted children. A variety of combinations will go much farther toward meeting those needs.

3. Every educator is an educator of the gifted. They are involved in identifying, teaching, relating to, and evaluating gifted children. Regular classroom teachers also need to learn how to do this appropriately so both they and their students are successful.

4. Homogeneous grouping is essential for sharing common interests, stimulating each others' thinking, and learning that others can be better than they are at some things.

The ability for higher-level thinking, both critical and creative, is one of the essential characteristics of the gifted that must be developed if their full potential is to be achieved. Also, student interests are essential to galvanize gifted abilities.

We do a disservice to gifted children if we don't help with their emotional needs. The label of gifted can be a burden, unless we assist them to deal with the inevitable pressures placed on exceptional children.

A PARENT'S CHECKLIST OF EXPECTATIONS OF THE SCHOOL

Anthony Jinkinson, an elementary school teacher of the gifted in Canada, has put together this checklist to help insure a program's smooth running once it becomes implemented.

• Have meetings been arranged with the parents of those children entering the gifted program before the program begins — meetings as a group, at which time concerns can be raised and interactions between staff and parents can go on in a nonthreatening atmosphere?

• Has the school board committed itself to the continuance of the program so that, as long as the child remains in it, there will be an appropriate placement for him at his grade level?

• Has the school board established a written curriculum covering the classes for the gifted? Is this curriculum available to the parents? Is the curriculum "tight" enough to insure that the basics are covered, yet flexible enough to provide for individual learning, child interest and teacher interest?

• Is there adequate funding to equip the class with sufficient equipment, materials, supplies, and field trips without having to rely on regular school budgets?

• Is there adequate accessibility to high-tech equipment (computers, VCRs)?

• Is the class size small enough to allow the teacher opportunity to provide each child with adequate input, yet large enough to offer good group dynamics?

• Does the teacher have a diverse enough background of grades taught and interests to be able to interact with the children at their functioning level?

• Does the programming provide an emphasis on individual learning versus group learning? Is there a blend? Is there interaction between the children in groups at a sufficiently high level to promote sound learning?

• Do the teacher and school have an "open door" policy which allows parents to visit at any time without prior notification? If parents do visit, will they be accepted and perhaps even asked to join in?

• Has the school planned several evening meetings throughout the academic year to which the parents are invited to hear guest speakers talk about giftedness?

• Are there year-end reviews (besides regular parent conferences), at which time each child's suitability for the program is discussed and at which any concerns can be raised by the parent regarding the program as a whole?

GIVING SCHOOL SCIENCE
THE ACID TEST

No one doubts the importance of quality education in the sciences. It is the foundation of medical breakthroughs, national defense, and rapidly developing technology, which we've come to take so much for granted. Yet references in the news, voiced concerns from educators, and attention from government offices reflect a growing uneasiness over low student enrollment in science courses and a need for upgrading the quality of available curricula.

For gifted students, a general trend away from hands-on experience at the early ages is especially disturbing. These students — the ones who are likely to contribute the most to future scientific discoveries and advancement — are particularly ready for and need earlier challenges.

A recent survey of 80 highly successful space scientists conducted by June Scobee and William R. Nash of the University of Houston at Clear Lake and Texas A & M respectively, and reported in the Fall 1983 issue of the *Gifted Child Quarterly* pinpoints the kinds of educational opportunity the respondents feel contributed most to their own successes, and what they consider important to students.

Most important, the scientists suggest, is "teachers willing to challenge students to think for themselves" (that is, provide activities directed toward problem solving or scientific investigations). Other aspects of an effective program are "opportunities to hear experts in the field," "interaction with peers with the same or better mental capacity," "opportunity to have a mentor," "hands-on experiences with scientific equipment," and "opportunities to study or learn about interrelation among disciplines of science and/or humanities."

In addition to the above aspects, the following checklist of questions should serve as a tool for evaluating your school's existing basic science programs and a guide to needed improvements.

1. *Does science begin in the very early grades?* Young children and particularly the gifted are generally fascinated by many aspects of science. Even a teacher with little science background and a low budget should be able to harness this enthusiasm.

In addition to the traditional subject matter relating to nature and health, the basics of such concepts as measurement and spatial relationships, matter, mass, gravity, force, motion, and energy are important stepping-stones to a balanced understanding of ourselves and our environment.

2. *Is there a coordinated science program specified in writing and adhered to throughout the school district?* This is a very important factor, and the absence of such a written program can cause considerable frustration and inefficiency. For example, if sixth graders in Mrs. A's class have been concentrating on raising hamsters and bean plants and those in Mrs. B's class have been experimenting with the mathematics of floating objects, then in all probability the two groups are not going to be equally prepared for a junior high class in physical science.

On the other hand, enough flexibility must be built in to accommodate the special interests of gifted children.

3. *Does the science curriculum emphasize the scientific thought process?* Commitment of fact to memory has its place, though the survey participants rated it least important. Most important, however, students must be taught to think logically, to evaluate cause and effect, to look for alternative explanations, to plan and control change in their lives. An inquiry approach should be an important part of every district's curriculum.

4. *Does the program routinely provide hands-on experiences?* You can talk forever about how to use a ruler, but unless you actually use one, the idea remains abstract and useless. Children can read about seed germination and growth, but reading is a weak substitute for touching, watching, and nurturing a seedling. Gifted children like to learn by doing. Experimentation encourages interest through participation, enhances the remembering of ideas, and provides useful skills for the real world.

5. *Is there a correlation between actual instruction and particular aspects of a community's economics, geology, or natural history?* In other words, is there an attempt to make science relevant by relating it to real world problems? How does science relate to agriculture or industry in your area? What species of plants or animals are significant?

6. *Are science classes suited to students' abilities?* As soon as a school or district curriculum is made sequential, ability grouping of some sort automatically occurs. The simple matter of appropriate course prerequisites insures it. And ability grouping is a must for gifted learners. Classes that contain students with widely divergent

academic skills can be very frustrating to instructor and student alike. As noted by the space scientists, gifted students need to work with others of like or superior ability.

7. *Are there outside avenues for appreciation and recognition of science-related achievement?* Do local organizations reward high achievement by public awards or scholarships? Are students (and teachers) encouraged to enter contests or otherwise demonstrate both their own ability and the school's quality of science activity? Recognition for accomplishment is critically important in building a healthy self-concept.

Toys, Games, Computers, and Television

S HOULD gifted children play like other children, or would that
be a big waste of time? If play is important, what kind aids
in the development of the child's social and cognitive skills?
What toys and games may be purchased to encourage these things
as well as strategy building and imaginative thinking?

Generally the beginning age level of the games discussed below
depends on the skills of the individual child. Parents should assess
the child's verbal and math abilities, for example, in making
choices. Unless otherwise noted, the games are suitable for two
or more players.

THE VALUE OF PLAY

What may appear to be trivial "child's play" to adults can be
a complex learning experience for children. In a special issue of
Practical Applications of Research, the newsletter of Phi Delta
Kappa's Center on Evaluation, Development, and Research, four
experts on the subject were asked to provide their ideas and information on the value of play.

The educators report that certain kinds of play can help children
"clarify and master" many fundamental skills — physical, social,
and intellectual. Play is linked to intellectual development through
a process psychologists call *transformation* (defined in their context
as "the intellectual ability to change oneself into some object,
person, or situation") and communication through language.

Studies of kindergarten children have established a significant correlation between their playfulness and aspects of divergent or creative thinking. And young children observed in "free play" with specific materials have exhibited high degrees of problem solving, goal-directed behavior, and persistence.

The researchers stated that *symbolic play*, which is characterized primarily by role playing and pretending, is essential in the development of abstract thinking. "Children who engage in symbolic play," the report continues, "show advances in general emotional growth, speech fluency, persistence at tasks, an ability to distinguish reality from fantasy, cooperation with others, the ability to tolerate delays, empathy, and leadership."

PRACTICAL APPLICATIONS

Parents and teachers can cultivate symbolic play and, along with it, the intellectual development of their children or students. The report offers these suggestions.

• Watch your children play, and learn what they like and dislike, their favorite themes and interests. Encourage them to talk about their play; let them know you're interested.

• Show playfulness yourself. Children learn from imitating adults. Help them by making comments and asking questions that encourage playing. Also encourage pretending for fun and learning.

• Play with your children and help them select appropriate play materials. Support them by praising their efforts at using props and materials and their efforts at role playing.

• Plan for your children's play. Provide a place of their own to play, a place for organizing materials, and both open-ended and close-ended toys.

Word Games

Word games have always held a place of honor in educational circles. Regardless of the game, if it involves the alphabet and the kids, it has traditionally merited paeans of parental and pedagogical approval. All word games have educational value because all word games encourage the exercise and development of curriculum-related skills: letter recognition, spelling, reading, vocabulary.

In most cases, word games demand a complex blending of reasoning and language skills, far more complex than those defined by any single area in the school curriculum. For the child who enjoys playing with words, word games can become an invitation to explore and develop skills that range from pattern recognition, to abstract logic and deductive reasoning, to spacial perception. The competition for speed in many of the games involves quick reaction and flexible thinking.

ALPHABET SOLITAIRE   In this game the young child plays with the relationship between upper- and lower-case letters. The playing board is a specially designed grid of matching capital letters and "free" spaces, and the deck consists of matching lower-case letters and "free" cards. It is essential that the child have some previous mastery over the relationship between capitals and lower-case letters in order to play the game.

Alphabet Solitaire is available from the manufacturer in several forms, including just the instructions on how to make one's own game.

RAZZLE   Razzle is a game for children who are already able to read. It is purely a language arts game, involving vocabulary and spelling skills, as two players race to spell and pronounce a word that can be made from a random assortment of letters. A unique mechanical device — a holder that changes letter configurations — adds to the interest and intensity of psychological pressure as well as the demands upon the player's vocabulary skills.

CROZZLE   Crozzle involves careful strategizing as much as it involves vocabulary and spelling skills. Up to four players draw their own grids and through the play form as many words as possible in the rows and colums of the grid. Where on the grid to write each new letter is the central issue of the game. The adept player quickly becomes able to identify and select from a host of properties of word formation. The game can be difficult and, because of the many options that each player must consider, often frustrating.

SCRABBLE CROSSWORD CUBE GAMES   Forming intersecting words, as in Crozzle, is obviously a more conceptually challenging task than finding a word in a random array of letters. Scrabble Crossword

Cube Games complicate the task even further, involving computational skills, reasoning, and language skills. The set consists of fourteen wooden letter cubes, a dice cup, and a miniature hourglass timer. As in Razzle, the pressure is that of a race, but as in Crozzle, the task is much more complex. Several players can play this game.

RUNES   Runes, like Crossword Cubes, involves a complex network of skills of which language arts is but one component. Here players race to create words out of an assortment of letters, but before they can begin that leg of the race, they must first make those letters out of an assortment of shapes.

Runes is a word game that not only rewards players for a good command over vocabulary and spelling, but also challenges and develops the players' perceptual and deductive reasoning skills. It is a very different kind of word game and, as such, can be the unique path that leads the more perceptually oriented child into the world of language.

DIG-IT   This action game combines general knowledge (of the sort recently popularized by trivia games), spelling ability, and speed. Players simultaneously grab what they need from a mound of 378 letters, and the player who first completes one word in each of five assigned categories collects points.

VWLS CRAZE   Five-letter cubes show only consonants. It is up to players to combine any number of them with vowels of their choice to make as many words as possible before the sand in the timer runs out. The rules call for players to take turns, but the game is even more fun when everyone uses the same letters simultaneously. It can also be played as solitaire to sharpen skills.

LINGO   The most concise description of Lingo is "do-it-yourself-Boggle." Both games involve building words from a sequence of letters that zigzag through a grid. But whereas Boggle letter cubes fall into their grid in random order after a single toss, Lingo players make their own grid and choose where to place each letter card. The scoring rewards strategy more than vocabulary. The 54-card deck can also be used for an intriguing solitaire game.

ON-WORDS   This game, using letter cubes, is actually a number of games ranging over a wide spectrum of difficulty, from simply spelling words of a required length to levels that will challenge the linguistic specialist and the connoisseur of word puzzles and games. Adult help will be needed in studying the 84-page instruction book.

WORD WAR   Players compose their own crossword puzzles on one of nine reusable wipe-off boards, each preprinted with a different 8″ x 8″ grid and four randomly placed vowels. Players need to be aware of word structures and common letter sequences in order to place each letter most advantageously. The game can also be played as solitaire.

SCRABBLE DUPLICATE   Not only do players use all the same letters, but in this game they also use the same grid — a paper replica of the standard Scrabble board. The advantages of this version over regular Scrabble are that everyone is playing simultaneously, without waiting for others to finish their turns; luck is eliminated as a factor; and the written record of letters dealt in each sequence enables pen pals to play by mail.

Number Games

If you think of math games as games that center around logical skills, then you'll have to include Chinese Checkers and tic-tac-toe. If you insist that math games are games that involve numbers, then you wind up with anything from bingo to bridge. Probability? Chutes and Ladders, Monopoly, and maybe even backgammon. Problem solving? The puzzle of your choice. All of these games are truly math games, and it is for that particular reason that a math laboratory tends to be such fun.

The first of these games involves numbers and calculations. They're recommended for gifted kids who like playing with numbers, because the other kinds of mathematical games such as the last four, which involve construction, design, and problem solving, are better for those who don't.

DOMINOES   Dominoes are actually as chock-full of mathematical properties as Cuisinaire rods. The game that most of us are familiar with, according to Frederick Berndt, author of *The Domino Book*, is actually called Muggins. Muggins, it turns out, is an excellent, but merely introductory, game in the world of "dominoledge." Berndt describes 19 more domino games, each more complicated, each involving more convoluted calculation. *The Domino Book* also includes solitaire games, and 136 domino-arithmetic puzzles.

DAVY JONES' DEEP SEA GAME   This game demands fast, if somewhat elementary, calculations. It uses five dice, housed in a transparent, liquid-filled cylinder, with a different figure on each of their faces: sharks, octopuses, porpoises. The game demands quick calculation of value of dice rolled according to various factors. Though the task may seem simple to an older child, competitive pressure from his peers will quickly restore interest and challenge. The game, one of the Gurgle series, is available from most large toy stores.

TRIBULATION   Tribulation makes far more complex demands on the ability to make rapid calculations. The board is a holder for a 7″ x 7″ matrix of cardboard tiles. The tiles are numbered 1 to 9. There are also number discs, numbered from 1 to 50. Players compete in a real test of their abilities to make rapid calculations and also challenge their perceptual skills.

CRAZE   Craze is an even deeper challenge to arithmetic skills. It is a very complex game, not only because of its demands on computational skills, but also because of the multiple strategic considerations that arise from being able to pick target numbers by position and point value.

PASCAL-TYPE CALCULATOR   This close facsimile to the mechanical calculator invented by Blaise Pascal in 1642 lets children see and understand how a base-10 calculator works. Inside a plastic see-through case are four interconnected wheels that look like telephone dials. Add by dialing clock-wise; when the total on any wheel passes 10, it trips a lever that adds 1 to the next wheel on the left — a physical reenactment of the arithmetic function of "carrying." Dialing counterclockwise illustrates subtraction and "borrowing." An optional set of 24 activity cards offers a more structured guide and shows how to multiply and divide.

PATTERN BLOCKS   Geometric shapes enable children to explore size and pattern relationships, fractions, congruence, and angles. The most common ones, known as parquetry blocks, are based on the square. Slightly more intricate and versatile are the colored pattern blocks developed under a grant from the National Science Foundation to help children learn the skills needed for mathematical and scientific thinking. These wood blocks with 1″ sides are based on the hexagon and include triangles, trapezoids, and both wide and narrow rhombuses. An optional addition is a set of three mirrors for exploring design and symmetry.

MATH GO-ROUND   Imagine a wheel divided like a spider's web into concentric rings and spokes, and 48 cardboard tiles, each showing either a number or a function sign, which fit into the spaces between the threads. The challenge is to arrange all the tiles so that they form 20 interlocking equations — 4 going around each ring, and 8 from the circumference to the inner ring. When correctly solved, all 20 equations will be arithmetically correct, and each will be connected to others, somewhat like a round crossword puzzle. Turn the tiles over, and a second puzzle awaits solution. For one person, but suggested variations permit two or three to play cooperatively.

NUMBER RINGS   Each corner of the playing tray has a cluster of cones numbered from 1 to 18. The object of the game is to encircle all the cones in one's own sector with rings. The strategy is to manipulate the numbers by various combinations of addition, subtraction, multiplication, division, square roots, or powers to arrive at a needed number. There's also a solitaire challenge: to ring all the bases in twelve rolls of the dice.

Games of Logic and Critical Thinking

If the object of logical reasoning is to reach a valid conclusion, then the ultimate logician must be the "detective," who searches for clues, assesses their relevance, draws inferences from them, tests hypotheses, and finally solves the case. It is not surprising that many games of logic and critical thinking involve crime and detection.

CONSULTING DETECTIVE GAME   Fans of Sherlock Holmes are offered 10 cases in which to match wits with the master sleuth. Investigating all the clues will eventually reveal the solution. But the goal, of course, is to avoid the red herrings and zero in on the vital clues. Players can verify their solutions in the Quiz Book and read Holmes's detailed analysis and explanation in the solution section of the Case Book. For one to six players.

CLUE   "Mr. Boddy" is found dead in his nine-room mansion, represented by the game board. The names of 6 suspects, 6 weapons, and 9 rooms are each on a separate card. One card from each group is concealed at the start of the game and is the "solution" to the crime. The rest of the cards are dealt to all the players, who attempt to solve the crime by making "suggestions" aimed at discovering which cards are in other players' hands and, by process of elimination, which are part of the solution. Making inferences from the other players' suggestions can be just as revealing as one's own suggestions. An old favorite and a good game to begin with; for three to six players.

SAFECRACK   Players compete to find the combination to the safe by using information found on an ingeniously designed set of cards. They learn such facts as that the first number is a multiple of three. Knowledge gained from one's own cards and hints derived from the placement of opponents' cards on the gameboard will help players deduce the three-number combination. There are enough variations of combinations and clues to offer a fresh challenge no matter how frequently the game is played. For two to six players.

MASTERMIND   One player secretly arranges a row of colored pegs behind a shield and the other attempts, in the fewest tries possible, to duplicate the pattern without seeing it. Players discover their own strategies for extracting information. The standard gameboard, with four holes and six colors, is soon outgrown; a wiser purchase would be the advanced set with 5 holes and 8 colors, which can be simplified at first by arbitrarily using fewer holes and colors.

GRIDLOCK   A grid of round, square, and cross-shaped projections is to be completely covered by tiles containing two or three matching-shaped cutouts. Success depends on looking ahead to avoid being left with unusable shape combinations. Tiles for 50 puzzles fit inside the compact playing board, making this self-contained game a good choice for summer travel. This is a puzzle to be solved solitaire, but the gridlock is also a fine one to do cooperatively.

Strategy Games

The purest strategy games are those in which there is no element of luck. Both players start with the identical equipment, the only possible advantage accruing to the player who moves first. Among the classic games, chess, checkers, Go, and Othello are good examples. Most of the following games are in this category. All are for two players unless solitaire applications are noted. Good strategic game playing involves thinking ahead, analyzing the options at each move, anticipating the opponent's response to each, visualizing the appearance of the board after subsequent plays, and keeping the ultimate goal in mind.

LEAP   This is a game like chess. The handsome wood gameboard is a 6″ x 6″ grid, surrounded by felt-lined troughs that hold 36 numbered disks. The 18 odd numbers are on dark wood; the 18 even, on light. Two-player games, based primarily on knight's leaps or checker-jumping variations, pose such challenges as exchanging positions of light and dark teams or blocking the opponent's next play. Solo puzzles (each with multiple variations) include chessboard problems, shape transformations, and multiple-jumping solitaires in which the object is to end up with only one disk remaining on the board. The accompanying 29-page booklet includes strategy hints and theoretical discussions.

DOMAIN   This is a game of spatial and perceptual strategy which requires visualizing the relationship (which changes at each move) between playing pieces (two-sided geometric shapes) and open spaces on the board, and selecting a play that will simultaneously touch an opponent's piece and prevent the opponent's next play from touching one's own. It is highly recommended for combining simple rules with complex strategic possibilities.

VIS-À-VIS   This is another game of perceptual strategy, this time based on symmetry. One player tries to form mirror-image patterns of colored disks in vertical and horizontal rows, while the other player attempts to prevent their being formed.

PENTE   Sharing some elements of tic-tac-toe, Go, and Othello, Pente is nevertheless unique in its playing qualities, and an Oklahoma State University researcher is currently using Pente in experiments on sequential logic, abstract thought, and geometric design. Although the game is simple enough to enjoy on the novice level, advanced theories of play can be explored in two published strategy books.

Manipulative Puzzles

The phenomenal success of Rubik's Cube several years ago sparked a new interest in manipulative puzzles.

Adaptations, variations, and completely new puzzles now abound. The best of them are a perfect integration of aesthetic appeal, kinesthetic pleasure, and mental challenge, like the ones below.

The cautious way to approach a new puzzle is to devise a system of notation in order to keep track of moves and be able to reverse them if necessary. Once the puzzle has become randomized, its solution depends on analytical skills, a logical approach, memory, and an ability for sequential visualization. A dash of creative intuition wouldn't hurt!

TSUKUDA'S SQUARE   In a square base there are 16 numbered tiles, which are moved by means of plungers. Finding the solution depends on analyzing the effects of various sequences and combinations of moves and experimenting to find the shortest way of interchanging tiles.

A more difficult version replaces the numbers with squares divided diagonally into red and white halves. This version will stimulate visual perception, pattern recognition, and reasoning.

RUBIK'S REVENGE   Mastery of the original Rubik's Cube gives one a head start on solving this larger 4″ x 4″ x 4″ version, but in no way guarantees easy success. With each face containing 16 cubelets, there are no longer center pieces to maintain the orientation of the cube. All cubelets rotate independently of the others, and while some of the algorithms from the smaller cube have the same effect, others don't.

Analytical skills, three-dimensional visualization, and the ability to anticipate the result of a sequence of moves are all put to the test in restoring the cube to its original solid-color state.

INVISIBLE MAZE The first problem is to find the maze. Enclosed within a transparent acrylic box are a steel ball and a 13″ x 13″ array of clear pegs. The challenge is to roll the ball down the right path from one corner to the diagonally opposite one. It requires sharp visual acuity to detect the minuscule variations in spacing, as well as manual dexterity and coordination to tilt the maze so the ball rolls in the desired direction, and a good memory in order to backtrack each time the ball encounters a new barrier. This maze offers a new challenge when the box is rotated or turned upside down.

BACK IN THE BOX Turn the box upside down, and out tumble 17 tetrahedrons. As its name implies, the object is to replace them, a seemingly impossible task because each edge of the largest tetrahedron is longer than any edge of the container. Several approach strategies are possible. The child with a sense of design and spatial construction will be able to visualize how the pieces should be grouped and positioned. One who applies logic to puzzles can sort and categorize the shapes into equivalent groups, and thereby deduce their correct placement. The mathematician can work it out as an exercise in geometry.

The accompanying instruction folder explains the mathematical formulas of geometric solids for those so inclined, and shows the step-by-step replacement of the pieces for those of little patience.

THE ORB The Orb is a sphere horizontally transected by four grooved, circular tracks each of which contains beads of a different color. After the beads are scrambled the challenge is to return those of the same color to their separate concentric circles.

The puzzle is a study in symmetry that can be solved by visual analysis.

DOO-MEES These are intriguing topological puzzles made of wire. To solve them the child must separate two shapes that are completely separate, but seem inextricably intertwined. The pieces, though somewhat flexible, are not to be bent. The solutions must be arrived at through careful observation and experimentation, inspecting each of the intertwined loops and moving them from position to position. The puzzles are available in various orders of complexity, and the simpler ones help the player develop insights which are useful in solving the more complex. In buying a series of puzzles of differing orders of difficulty, the parent is providing the child with an actual curriculum in topological thinking.

MAGNA-TEASE   Magna-Tease is an exceptionally difficult, but enjoyable, puzzle made of magnetized cubes. The faces of each of 12 acrylic cubes bear magnetic disks. The object is to make the cubes fit back into the box. The cubes are uniform, so there are, in fact, no visual clues. To solve this puzzle, the player must experiment with each block, establishing the polarity of each side and classifying blocks by polarity and position.

AMAZING MAZES   These three-dimensional maze posters by Larry Evans are works of cunning perspective and intricacy. The "Posterbooks" unfold to 25″ x 34″ posters. The Fantastic Journey is an intricate fairyland of castles and monsters and meandering paths. The Space Maze and City of Tomorrow are each studies of perspective and interwoven paths.

Science "Playthings"

Consider science not as a series of separate disciplines (physics, chemistry, biology, etc.), but rather as a way of thinking. It starts with curiosity and planning a strategy for answering the question "why?"; it continues with observing, predicting, pursuing hunches, and testing results; it concludes with finding the answer to the problem. But always the *process* of exploration and discovery is far more important than the resulting factual knowledge. As children become involved in their investigations, they develop their ability to devise ways of testing their ideas and problem solving.

The best science playthings, such as those that follow, are open-ended: that is, they pose a problem that each child will approach in his or her own way. Be wary of kits that leave nothing for the child to do but follow directions.

SUNPRINT KIT   The Sunprint Kit, developed at the Lawrence Hall of Science at the University of California, uses only water and light-sensitive paper to make art and nature prints.

Creativity and appreciation of natural forms are stimulated as children combine forms of artistic or surrealistic effects, or experiment with three-dimensional objects to produce images with graduated shadings.

TOPTICAL   Toptical combines the play of a top with the science of optical illusions. The heavy hardwood top is 4½" tall with a 3½" diameter base on which a variety of colored disks can be placed singly or in combination. When each disk is slit along a radius, they can be superimposed and slid together to expose different amounts of each color. Spinning the top produces the visual illusion of mixing the colors; varying the proportion of each color changes the resulting blend.

The instruction folder contains guidance and will spark self-devised investigations. Playing with Toptical will promote inventiveness in using everyday materials to seek answers to questions. Ages 5 and up.

MINI-LABS FINGERPRINT KIT   Here are the materials and procedures for detective role playing. There's enough graphite and talcum powder to make more than a thousand prints, feathers and holder for brushing the prints, tape squares and classification cards for preserving and comparing them, a magnifying lens for examining them, and a carrying pouch. The instruction folder is a masterpiece of clarity. It combines factual information with opportunities for independent observation, pattern recognition, logic, reasoning, and an introduction to punch-card sorting. Ages 7 and up.

SUPER MICROSCOPE   It doesn't look like a traditional microscope, but it does all that a microscope does, and more. In its simplest configuration, it is a 30-power magnifier. Add the zoom lens, and it becomes a microscope of 50X to 100X power. Remove the mirror assembly, and transparent specimens can be viewed by holding the microscope up to the light like a kaleidoscope. Add the masking frame, and project specimens through a 35mm slide projector.

The microscope comes with two prepared slides, five blanks with cover slips, instructions on making slides, and ideas for experiments that go beyond the simple "gather and look."

CREATIVE MOMENTS INVESTIGATIONS This is a packet of 50 science challenges, each in a separate reusable folder. The introductory folders describe investigation techniques: observing, making a hypothesis, testing it, recording the results, and reaching a conclusion. Once children learn these techniques, they are ready to apply them to such investigations as "Could you lift yourself off the ground with a piece of string?" or "Where does the water go after it rains?"

Each folder suggests a procedure for conducting the investigation and then poses a number of variations, related activities, and advanced challenges based on the preliminary investigation. The areas of investigation include the physical world, nature, and psychology. Most of the activities use readily available materials. Kit No. 3, ages 10–14.

SCIENTIFICS "Fun with fundamental science" is the overall description of these little kits, whose intrinsically motivating contents nearly leap out of their clear polyvinyl bags and tempt a child to try them. The series includes *Magnetism* (with four bar magnets, six ring magnets, and instructions for making them float in the air and for making a compass); *Mirrors* (with instructions for constructing a periscope, kaleidoscope, and teleidoscope); *Bi-Metal Thermodynamics* (with a set of jumping disks); *Color* (with color filters, polarizing filters, and a diffraction grating that breaks up light into the spectrum colors); *Weather* (with materials for building a barometer and forecasting weather); *Illusions* (with an electric motor and four illusion cards).

SKY CHALLENGER Six interchangeable wheels turn stargazing into a series of cosmic adventures. Each wheel is designed for a different activity and can be rotated in its slipcase to reproduce the sky view on any day of the year in any Northern Hemisphere location. Besides several star charts, there is a clock for telling time by the stars, and an astronomy newsletter.

THINGS OF SCIENCE   *Things of Science* is a series of kits devoted to a different field of science every month. Each includes a booklet with detailed background information, instructions, and all necessary materials for conducting an average of 20 experiments. Hundreds of different kits have been produced since 1940, all designed to provide concrete experiences that bring even the most esoteric subjects down to earth. Examples are the laws of probability, pinhole photography, gravity, and fossils. Ages 10–14. For information on membership and a list of available topics, write Things of Science, R.D.#1, Newtown, PA 18940

CRITTER CONDO   Studying little creatures close up requires a proper container to house them. Rather than buying a succession of single-purpose environments, this clear plastic 9½" high, dome-topped cylinder includes supplies for observing and experimenting with many kinds of flora and fauna. Numerous activities and experiments are also suggested (and mail-order sources for material given) for studying ants and caterpillars, raising beetles from mealworms, hatching praying mantis eggs, growing "living fossils" from pond soil, and for using the condo as an aquarium, terrarium, cactus garden, or for growing carnivorous plants.

ELECTRICITY EXPERIMENTS   This collection of electrical components provides unlimited opportunity for budding inventors to experiment with complete safety. Everything except batteries (which you can buy more cheaply locally) is included: lengths of pre-stripped insulated wire, bulbs, battery holders, compass, buzzer bar; also switches and bulb holders specially designed with all their working parts exposed to view, Fahnestock clips for instant attachment of wires, and forty open-ended questions that give youngsters just enough insight to figure out by themselves how to produce light, heat, sound, and magnetism.

Games of Deception to Build Social Interaction

The role of game playing in the development of social interaction skills is a subject of great relevance to parents of gifted children — especially if there is more than one child in the family. Most gifted children are able to understand abstract issues such as rules and winning much sooner than they fully develop their abilities to be compassionate, and they can use their understanding to confound even the most patient of parental attempts at establishing an understanding of justice.

It is from the concept of fairness based on agreed-upon rules that an understanding of the rudiments of justice derives.

The apparent subject of the following games is the wrongful act: lying, betraying, dissembling. Yet the paradox is that games of deception can cement peer and family relationships. Under sometimes profound psychological pressures, a player can simply bow out, refuse to play. Players must, therefore, develop sensitivity to each other, being careful not to overstep the bounds of fair play and discretion, causing the entertainment element of the game to evaporate.

DIPLOMACY   The classic "serious" bargaining game is aptly named Diplomacy. This game, for 3 to 7 players, models a setting in which one attempts to gain world domination merely through the art of making and breaking alliances. Though a significant portion of the play involves strategic positioning of one's forces on a map of the world, the players spend most of their time engaging in writing, passing secret messages, and making complex deals. To win, it is necessary to make certain promises that you don't actually intend to keep. Given the foreknowledge that deception is more or less a rule of the game, the construction of an alliance is in itself a highly skilled achievement.

I DOUBT YOU   This is a traditional children's card game, played with a regulation deck, which allows a family to play with deception in a more rudimentary and hilarious form. Players (three or more) have to lie to fulfill the object of getting rid of cards equally distributed. They lay cards face down on the table stating what they are. If you think a player is lying you say, "I doubt you," and the accused player must reveal the cards he has just played with positive consequences for the truth and negative for a lie. The game involves bluffing, risk-taking, and calculation regarding when to call another person's hand. Play builds social interaction and participation skills.

HOAX   For those who wish to play with the subtler delights of the "social arts of deception," the game Hoax offers an opportunity in depth. Hoax, like I Doubt You, is a lighthearted game, but, like Diplomacy, involves cunning and sophisticated social interacting and strategizing.

The object of the game is to discover the true identity of the other players without revealing yours. There are six different possible identities. Each identity has certain powers which are useful in gaining tokens, which are in turn used to gain information about other players.

The task of discovering who's who is challenging and entertaining and demands deductive reasoning, keen observation, good recall, and pokerlike bluffing. The psychological value of the game lies in assuming and testing divergent social roles and presenting them in a convincing manner.

No-Cost Family Games

Some of the most appropriate games for gifted children don't cost anything. The bright child tends to be intrigued by the following kinds of games that take only paper and pencil and/or imagination. They like to devise new rules and variations. Games like these provide a chance for the family to interact and have fun, and they can be played anywhere — on a long car trip, for example.

SUPER-DUPER-GHOST   Super-Duper-Ghost is based on a spelling game called Ghost in which players, taking turns, say letters. The rule is that the new letter must, when taken with the rest, spell out the beginning of a word. On the other hand, it must not spell a complete word. Whoever finishes spelling a word has to start the next round. In another variation, a new letter can be placed either in the beginning or at the end of the string of letters. For example, the response to A, M, P, L, instead of being E, bearing the onus of completing the word *ample*, could be X, A, M, P, L. If a player believes that another is bluffing, providing letters with no real word in mind, you can "call" his bluff and require that player to reveal the word and its definition.

SAFARI   This is the name for a version of a guess-my-rule word game such as Fannee Dollee, in which Fannee Dollee likes things that have double letters — eggs and jelly — in their names, but hates things without them — ham and jam. In Safari, the problem poser can make up any rule at all: for example, only things with antennae, or only green things, or only words that begin with vowels. The Safari leader begins the round by saying, "I'm going on a safari and I'm taking a . . . ," filling in the blank with a word that exemplifies the rule. Players randomly or in turn ask if they can take other words or objects and are told "yes" or "no" depending on whether or not the words used fit the pattern. Creative thinking is encouraged as well as inductive and deductive reasoning.

THE MINISTER'S CAT   The Minister's Cat is a chanting game that can be played in the car or around the table with a group of just about any size. A rhythm is more or less established, everybody clapping hands or hitting knees or something like this in cadence. One player begins the game by saying "The Minister's cat is an *angry* cat," or any kind of a cat as long as the adjective begins with the letter *a*. The next player, without breaking whatever rhythm exists, must use a different adjective, also beginning with the letter *a*. This continues until a player can't think of an unused adjective beginning with *a*. The punishment for this failure is that the player must now start with a *b* adjective. The game continues in this manner as far through the alphabet as everybody can stand. In addition to the obvious "language arts" practice, the game challenges the players' ability to coordinate motor and cognitive elements at the same time.

IN THE MANNER OF THE ADVERB   This is a game of the charades type. One player, or preferably two players go out of earshot while the remaining players select an adverb. The excluded players then attempt to deduce the adverb by asking anybody or everybody to perform certain actions in the *manner* of the adverb: "Talk in the manner of the adverb," or "Drink your coffee in the manner of the adverb," or get up, or shake hands, or recite Shakespeare. The way we play it, the round continues until the adverb is somehow guessed. If the guessers get too frustrated, hints are generally freely and imaginatively offered.

FICTIONARY/DICTIONARY   Fictionary, or Dictionary, depending on who teaches it to you, is an often hilarious challenge to creative writing skills. You need a dictionary and pencil and paper for everybody. One player selects the most obscure word he can find. Usually, that player suggests a few different words until one is found that absolutely nobody knows. All write down the word on a piece of paper and next to it write the most dictionary-sounding definition possible. While the players do this, the word-finder also writes down the real definition. When everybody is done (which can take quite a while), the definitions are gathered, shuffled, and read one at a time. The definitions are read once more. If playing for points, each player votes for the definition he thinks actually came from the dictionary. You get a point if you vote for the correct definition and if somebody else votes for yours. Usually, however, the players just try to guess who wrote what. Both vocabulary and writing skills are enriched.

ADDITIONAL RESOURCES

There are many and varied resources for a true wealth of games that are wholesome, challenging, and of real value to the social and psychological development of a family of gifted children. The following are a few of our favorites.

The New Games Book. Dolphin/Doubleday, 1976.

More New Games. Dolphin/Doubleday, 1981.

Handbook of Recreational Games, by Neva L. Boyd. Dover Publications, 1975

Coin Games and Puzzles, by Maxey Brook. Dover Publications, 1973.

Parlor Games, by Nora Gallagher. Addison-Wesley, 1979.

Deal Me In, by Margie Golick. Jeff Norton, 1973.

Toy Book, by Steven Caney, Workman, 1972.

Gamut of Games, by Sid Sackson. Pantheon, 1982.

COMPUTERS AND COMPUTER SOFTWARE

According to *Instructor Magazine*, the largest periodical for elementary school teachers, the fastest growing area of computer use is elementary school, and the use of computers in gifted programs is rampant. Increasing numbers of families now own video games or computer systems.

How should computers be used for gifted children? Notwithstanding their limitations, what is their ultimate promise, their use at its best?

Although these questions will remain open for debate, computers are no mere fad to be ignored. They have, as John Tashner of Appalachian State University says, the possibility of changing the way we process information — that is, how we think.

Writing for the American Library Association, Tashner, an associate professor in the Department of Secondary Education at the university, outlines several ways in which the computer can serve as an educational *tool* for the gifted. He says this high-speed technology can give students practice in skills such as analysis, synthesis, and evaluation.

In addition, computer-assisted instruction (CAI), in teaching specific subject-matter concepts and processes, can help enhance a gifted student's problem-solving abilities as well as creative expression using graphics, sound generation, and intricate programs. In short, Tashner says that computer literacy so defined is "uniquely suited" to gifted students as it enables them to use and develop higher-level thinking skills by working with multiple variables simultaneously.

Are the students themselves learning to take advantage of the full dimensions of this technology and thereby develop *their* potential to the fullest?

The answer is probably no in most cases. Using the computer solely as an electronic teacher does justice to neither the technology nor the student, according to some experts in this field. Alan Kay, director of research at Atari, is one who holds this view. In an interview by Herbert Kohl in *Learning*, Kay is quoted as seeing the true meaning of "computer literacy" as gaining enough understanding and fluency with the medium itself to allow one to create (or model) "mini-worlds" in which a variety of simulations and scenarios can be played out.

Seymour Papert, a colleague of Piaget, expresses a similar view in *Mind-Storms: Computers and Powerful Ideas*. A major benefit of computer technology, he says, is the opportunity to enter a "what if" world where without risk one can freely experiment with hypotheses.

Thus, at its best, the computer can help gifted children do what they need to do anyway: envision many possible worlds and then build a sensible one. "We have to learn to think of the computer," Kohl writes, "as a system maker and not a basal text book." In this way we may hope to prevent the computer from becoming "yet another dull vehicle for exercise, drill and boredom."

Software That Challenges

There are exemplary software programs that seem particularly oriented toward the gifted child. Much of the plentiful drill-and-practice type ("educational") software is neither aimed at gifted children nor does it inspire children to learn much more than workbooks do.

In the parenthesis after each program are listed the publisher and after the dash the computers the program runs on. Ad. stands for Coleco's Adam, Ap. for Apple II, At. for Atari, Comm. for Commodore 64, and PC for IBM PC. All Atari programs run on Atari computers only.

CREATION   One of the most stimulating uses of the home computer concerns the creation of art and music. With good software, the computer allows tremendous freedom of self-expression by taking care of the technical aspects of drawing pictures or writing music.

Almost every major software house has published a piece of computer graphics software. Some, like *Paint Magic* (Datamost — At., Comm.) and *Fun With Art* (Epyx — At., Comm.), are controlled by moving the "brush" with the joystick. A few like *Paint 'N' Sketch* (Tech Sketch — At.) use a "light pen" to draw directly on the screen, which is closer to the act of drawing but tiresome on the arm holding the light pen stylus.

The most notable new entry is *AtariArtist* (Atari), very similar to *Koala Pad* (Koala Technologies) in that it uses a special drawing tablet. You can draw on the rectangular tablet's vinyl surface with your finger, a wooden stylus, or the special pen that comes with it, and your pattern will appear on the screen exactly as you drew it on the tablet.

The *AtariArtist* software used with the tablet lets you do much more than freehand drawing, too. There are two screens — a blank "canvas" for drawing and a "palette" or menu of functions. The user can toggle back and forth at will without affecting his or her picture. The palette selections include commands for drawing straight lines, boxes, or circles of any size, checkerboard patterns and solid colors, filling enclosed areas, and choosing among nine different brush sizes. You can even call up a magnifying glass that enlarges your drawing and lets you work on fine details.

Most of the new software designed to inspire or enhance musical talent is aimed either too high or too low. However, *Music Construction Set* (Electronic Arts — Ap., At., Comm.) and *SongWriter* (Scarborough Systems — Ap., At., Comm., PC) will have the strongest and longest lasting appeal for the gifted child. *Music Construction Set* uses real musical notation — whole through sixteenth notes, rests, sharps and flats, time signatures, etc. — that the user "drags" into position on two musical staffs by moving the joystick. Notes or measures can be cut from one place and pasted into another, allowing for a great deal of experimentation. Youngsters can save compositions of up to 700 notes on a blank disk for future editing or listening.

SongWriter is less of a system for exploring the workings of musical composition than it is a highly sophisticated musical toy, but it gets the attention of everyone, even the tone deaf. Basically, one selects notes by positioning little squares on a roller, in much the same way that player-pianos work. With the notes in place, the user is free to experiment with playback at different speeds, in different keys, etc. *SongWriter* may lack the educational value of *Music Construction Set*, but it is a bit more fun and easier to play with.

Last in this creative, fine arts category of software is *Movie Maker* (Reston — Ap., At., Comm., PC), a wonderful tool for making your own animated computer cartoons complete with music and sound effects. There is an enormous amount to learn with the *Movie Maker* animation system, but much of it is mnemonic and virtually anything you wish to do with the program is only a few keystrokes away.

For example, you may not want to begin by drawing your own shapes; instead you can use the characters stored on the disk. To make a dog run across the screen, you simply select the dog file from the menu to get a screenful of the same dog in a dozen different positions, press "S" to tell the computer you are defining a sequence, use the joystick to move a window over the dog shapes and press the action button to "pick up" each one in the order you want the computer to display them, and press "A" for action to make your dog run in place. You can then turn on the recorder and use the joystick to move the dog, capturing up to 300 frames per cartoon. Depending on the rate of frames per second you select, 300 frames translates into cartoons of thirty seconds to two minutes. You can use up to six different actors in the same cartoon.

With *AtariArtist, Music Construction Set,* or *Movie Maker,* parents can stimulate an interest in art, music, or animation by giving children access to their creative disciplines without requiring the technical abilities those disciplines traditionally demand. The ability to save these creative compositions and show them to family and friends makes these tools much more valuable than the toys some people perceive them to be.

EXPLORATION   As the mass markets have opened up for home computers, consumers have broadened their taste in software beyond video games. A great many publishers are focusing on what is best described as "activity software" — broad-ranging programs that represent systems for exploring new experiences. Rather than using the power of the computer *against* the player in a game scenario, these activity programs transfer that power *to* the player by giving him or her a world to explore and the tools to do so.

AtariLab (At.), the first interactive science experiment kit, is one of the best efforts I've seen in this direction. The starter set contains an interface module that plugs into a joystick port, a temperature sensor that plugs into the module, and the temperature experiment cartridge that plugs into any Atari home computer. A very well designed and lengthy manual teaches the explorer how to use the software and how to design, perform, and record scientific experiments with temperature. For example, the sensor displays the temperature, or change in temperature, on the computer screen when it is immersed in a liquid or held between thumb and forefinger. This program gives the child the opportunity to design an experiment, do it, and record the results for future comparison or study.

Turtle Toyland Junior (H.E.S. — Ad., Comm., PC) is a wonderful introduction to computer programming for young children because all of its activities are controlled through simple manipulation of the joystick. The child can draw background pictures and animated shapes, compose musical melodies, and store them all in a "toybox" for future playing. These various elements can be combined in endless ways to create "filmstrips," which are actually fundamental computer programs. Graphics, animation, sound effects, and logic are the components of computer programming, and this program puts them all within reach of the gifted four- or five-year-old.

Turtle Toyland Junior is a barrel of fun as an electronic playground, but it is also a high-level, visual programming language. Though its structure steers the child through its principles, each activity focuses the child on using the computer to express creativity.

Older or more advanced children will benefit from more extensive programming languages such as the new *Turtle Graphics II* (H.E.S. — Ad., Comm.) and *Atari Logo* (At.). Both are descendants of the programming language Logo that was developed by Seymour Papert of M.I.T. To teach children or first-time users about the operation of a computer, it lets them program a turtle to draw shapes on the screen. The beauty of these languages is that they are extensible, which means the user can build complex programs by combining small routines.

For example, it would be difficult for a young child to write a program to draw a square on the screen in BASIC language because it requires that many commands be combined *by the user.* In Logo, the child would only have to create a small program to draw a line, another to turn 90 degrees, and then join them under the single computer command DRAW SQUARE, which could then be used as the foundation for another even more complex program and so on.

RECREATION   Games are still the most popular home computer programs, but lately there has been a trend away from arcade types of games and toward more mentally oriented challenges. The following new games and others like them will give your kids some terrific fun and stimulate mental growth.

The Seven Cities of Gold (Electronic Arts — Ap., At., Comm.) may be the best example of the more challenging type of game. Action takes place during the historical age of discovery from 1492 to 1540, and translates into at least twenty hours of game time. The object is to explore the uncharted New World (North and South America) and to discover the legendary Seven Cities of Gold.

You set sail from Spain after hiring men and purchasing supplies for an expedition.

The graphics initially show nothing but water surrounding the ship, and, like Columbus, you have no maps. Your instruments of navigation are latitude markers and dead reckoning, at least until you hit land. You can then take a landing party ashore and explore for many months at a time. You'll encounter various terrains and villages whose natives' temperaments range from belligerent to servile. You can trade with the natives — goods for gold and food. You can also pull out your sword and try to beat them into submission, but the Crown takes a dim view of violence, and when you return home to Spain your rating will decline.

You will be surprised at how difficult it is to identify your location, even though you might know the geography of the continents pretty well. Playing *Seven Cities* inspires the use of an atlas to identify rivers, mountain ranges, lakes, coastline, etc., because nothing is labeled. The voluntary learning fostered by this unique and wonderful game turns it into an outstanding lesson in North and South American geography. And the order in which the information is discovered and what type of information is discovered is up to the child. Seven Cities is both a game and a system of discovery.

At first glance, it's easy to miss the potential of *The Game Show* (Computer Advanced Ideas — Ap., At., Comm., PC). This game for one or two players works like the television show *Password*. It concerns vocabulary and information on fifteen different subject areas. Questions, answers, and clues are programmed on the game disk. Some of this information is relevant and important; some is trivial. But the disk also includes a mini-authoring system that allows the user (or the parents) to create his or her own categories, writing the questions, answers, and clues into the blank format; this turns *The Game Show* into much more than a game. It is an interactive system of learning that can be used on as many levels as you are willing to create.

Story Tree (Scholastic Wizware — Ap.) is a fantastically openended learning tool that children and parents can use to create interactive stories with multiple branches and many different conclusions. The reader or player of a story receives the text one section at a time and is given a number of choices about how the story will continue.

But *Story Tree* can also be used as an interactive data base, a very useful function of computers. For example, a young philatelist can enter information about a stamp collection. The reader would first make a choice between foreign or U.S. stamps, then between several time periods, specific dates, denominations, and finally would reach a paragraph or two of information describing the particular stamp being researched. *Story Tree* is also useful for writing interactive articles in which the reader is free to skip from section to section in any order.

Nonfiction Computer Gaming

Operation: Frog (Scholastic — Ap., Comm.) is the quintessential example of nonfiction computer software, a cross between a puzzle and a biology simulation that is entirely controlled by the joystick. The left side of the screen shows the outline of the frog with its three layers of internal organs, which must be removed *in proper order* and placed in the examination tray on the right side of the screen. To accomplish this, the player uses the joystick to move a little hand to one of four tools: a probe, surgical scissors, forceps, and a magnifying glass. Probing an organ reveals the exact location to snip with the surgical scissors, and, once snipped, an organ is moved to the tray with the forceps.

Once a piece has been removed to the examination tray, an animated illustration accompanied by a text description of each organ can be viewed by using the magnifying glass. The frog can be reconstructed after it is completely dissected. *Operation: Frog* will not replace the real dissection process, but it is surely an inviting preparation.

U.S. Adventure (First Star Software — Comm., At. 800, Ap.) is a novel approach to the adventure-game format. It takes place on three different screens: a map of the United States, a time machine, and a main menu. From the menu, using either joystick or keyboard control, the player can elect to travel from state to state, travel in time, pick up historical events, or drop events to make room for new ones.

The object of the game is to make a path around the map that visits all 50 states in the order in which they were admitted to the Union. As the player succeeds in admitting states to the Union, more historical events are revealed, such as the First Continental

Congress or Lincoln's assassination or Jimmy Carter's inauguration, plus a few bogus events to make the player think. If one tries to pick up a bogus event, one loses all the events being carried.

Each event is indicated as past, current, or future, depending on the year to which the player has traveled. With a little computation (and possibly some "cheating" in reference books), the player can manage to place events and earn points. *U.S. Adventure* is not a game that will be solved in a week or even a month without a lot of learning taking place. Furthermore, it's fun for the whole family and is the kind of game for which the more the merrier holds true.

Dinosaur Dig (CBS — Ap., Comm., PC) is all about dinosaurs — when they lived, what they ate, their size and habits, and much more — and is presented with beautifully drawn color illustrations for each of two dozen different dinosaurs. The package includes a vinyl overlay that fits over the keyboard so that the child merely presses a key to get a picture of or information about, say, the archaeopteryx, rather than having to type in the entire name. There is a lot of information about the time period of the dinosaurs, too.

Once the player is familiar with all the dinosaurs, he or she can flip the program disk to the reverse side and play several games. These games are based on information contained on the first side of the disk, giving the children the ability to brush up after a severe loss. It isn't really possible to play the game well without having looked through the information on side one of the disk. Fortunately, there are plenty of color graphics, animations, graphs, and charts to maintain users' interest.

Timebound (CBS — Comm.) is a joystick-controlled romp through the last 2,000 years of recorded history: real history divided into 11 different categories such as politics, sports, inventions, and architecture. As the player sets the time machine in motion, the years begin ticking away and events begin appearing briefly in the 11 event windows where the player can position him- or herself. Only when the player is positioned in a window during the year when an event occurs can that event be caught.

Whenever the player catches an event, he or she will receive a clue to the whereabouts of a character named Anachron, who hops from one event in time to another every few moves. Suppose the player is properly positioned to catch the invention of the microscope in 1590 and gets the clue that Anachron is with Genghis Khan. He or she would have to know or learn the direction in which to travel, forward or backward in time, to reach Genghis Khan. And if the player makes too many stops along the way by checking too many dates, Anachron will have changed location. *Timebound* is good for the whole family and is so much fun to play that even young children can't help absorbing some important chronologies.

Computer Construction Sets

Robot Odyssey I (The Learning Company — Ap.) is an adventure game with a unique twist. The player finds him- or herself lost within the enormous city of Robotropolis, many levels below the surface of the earth, and the object is to find a way home. Interestingly, the player is a brain with no body and cannot solve the adventure's puzzles directly. Instead, the player must build a special robot for each task. For example, to retrieve a key, the player must build a robot that can sense the presence of a key, move to it in the maze, and pick it up. If the key is along one wall, the child might build a robot that hugs walls as it travels. Of course, there are almost as many solutions to any puzzle as there are children.

Each robot contains four thrusters for motion in eight directions, a thruster switch, four bumpers that detect walls, an antenna to send and receive coded messages, an object grabber, a periscopic eye, and a battery. These can be wired together in thousands of different ways to form circuits, which can be copied onto computer chips and incorporated into more complex circuitry, and on and on. *Robot Odyssey I* is a brilliant equation of Boolean logic and game play that can be reduced to a single element: fun.

Adventure Construction Set (Electronic Arts — Ap., Comm.) is just what it sounds like: a kit of objects and tools that allows the user to program original graphics and text adventure games — and a great deal more. Objects, characters, and terrains can be "cut and pasted" together from the disk library, or can be created from scratch with the graphics editor. And all of the program construction is accomplished by selecting items from a simple menu system. Original adventures can be as large as 250 rooms or locations, can employ as many as 500 different creatures and characters, and can hold more than 5,000 objects.

The disk also includes seven mini-adventures, small games that illustrate what can be done with the construction set, and the player is free to change or experiment with these designs. There is also a full-blown adventure called Rivers of Light, set in the Middle East near the dawn of humanity, that will take months of play to solve. Rivers of Light can also be changed and reprogrammed by the player. Of course, the real thrill is creating original games for friends and family members, tailored to their skill levels, needs, and interests. *Adventure Construction Set* is a powerful utility with its only prerequisite being a creative spirit.

Mr. Pixel's Cartoon Kit (Mindscape — Comm.) is a simple-to-operate set of graphics and animation tools that lets children design and assemble their own cartoons. Every aspect of the program is controlled with the joystick by selecting items from an ever-present visual menu at the bottom of the screen. The child can select background scenery and characters (or draw them from scratch), and then animate each character individually. At any point during the creation process, the cartoon can be "rewound" and played back, either continuously or one frame at a time. Only three characters are allowed on-screen simultaneously, but they can be exchanged for others, so up to ten characters may appear during a cartoon. Of course, complete cartoons or portions can be stored on blank disks for future viewing or editing.

Mr. Pixel's Cartoon Kit is the first in a series of six programs that cover drawing, music composition, story writing, and game creation. Whereas animation software generally requires programming skills, the menu-based system of this program is wonderfully simple and powerful enough to engage adults for a while, too. And for those players who don't know where to start, there are three completed cartoons on the disk that can be viewed and then changed. The important thing is that *Mr. Pixel's Cartoon Kit* keeps pace and grows with the user.

Light Waves (CBS — Comm.) is a kit for creating and saving "computer action puzzles." The best way to begin is by playing the 30 that come pre-programmed on the disk. The screen displays a rectangular border track in which light pulses flow in one direction, counterclockwise. The player's character, called the *light rider*, moves automatically along this track. Inside the track are a number of light beam segments, some adjacent to the edges of the track, some adjacent to other light beams. Each beam segment, shaped either like an L or a straight line, also has a unidirectional light pulse. If the light rider comes in contact with the beam, it will be sent in the direction of the pulse.

By tapping a key, the player can select a light beam, and by tapping another key, the player can rotate the beam in 90-degree increments. Thus, the player builds a circuit of light beams over which the light rider travels. The object of each puzzle is to lead the light rider to a special energy square, whereupon it advances to the next, slightly more difficult, puzzle.

The graphics and sound effects of *Light Waves* are stunning, almost mesmerizing, and the visual puzzles are cunningly designed. But what really makes *Light Waves* a treat is its game generator system. The child can create unique puzzles at any level of sophistication through a simple method of placing the light beam segments on the screen and selecting the few other game parameters from menus. *Light Waves* is for either one player or for two players who can work against each other for the best total score or with each other to solve the most frighteningly complex puzzles.

TELEVISION

We all know the evils of too much television watching for children. Yet, since gifted children particularly crave novelty and stimulation, the TV set beckons temptingly to them with its offerings of words and pictures, companionship of sorts, knowledge of the unknown, and exploration of adult situations. It's only too easy for them to get used to being entertained at will without any interaction.

The best way to turn your television into an ally for the development of your gifted child's mind and psyche is to make the process of watching an *active* one. Critical viewing is qualitatively different from passive addiction, since one's own perceptions are brought to the task. You can teach your child the habit of healthy criticism and of giving credit where it's due.

First, in order to alert the whole family to how much time is spent watching, keep a journal for a few days. Keep track of who turns the set on, who watched, and *what* programs were seen. However, don't use the log to criticize unduly any family member who is a heavy watcher. Next, begin perusing the TV schedule together and choosing the week's programs. If homework is getting done well and on time, outdoor play is sufficient, interaction with friends is comfortably frequent, and family members are in touch with each other to your satisfaction, you can be more lax than otherwise in allotting TV time.

The way to turn television to best advantage for your gifted child is to spend time watching it with her until critical viewing becomes a habit. Talk about what's happening on the screen. No need to be overly didactic or direct with older kids; they'll rebel at lectures.

At appropriate moments, discuss the following:

• *Stereotyping:* Studies show that women, the elderly, and minorities are very stereotyped on prime time and Saturday morning programs, and that heaviest watchers believe most in these stereotypes. Pinpoint examples. Are young people stereotyped too? The handicapped? Gifted children?

• *The Appeal of TV Heroes:* What qualities are we led to believe make people worth idolizing? Are they superheroes, doctors, rock stars, police officers? In what ways are these portrayals accurate or inaccurate?

• *The Various Emotions Some TV Shows or Movies Create in Us.* Discuss words for these emotions and how people are affected differently. To what extent does this emotional fabric affect our perceptions of reality?

• *The Ways Television Families Differ from Ones You Know:* How do people on TV use their leisure time? What careers do most people on shows pursue?

• *The Ways Problems Are Solved on Television Series:* Are the methods employed realistic, effective? Discuss alternative endings, perhaps less violent solutions, less pat resolutions.

• *The Unreality and Irresponsibility of TV:* For example, people rarely wear seat belts; alcohol is frequently imbibed, but people stay sober, slim, and safe; birth control is never mentioned during love scenes, etc.

• *Old Movies and Sitcoms:* Watch them together and discuss the historical periods involved. Notice outdated language and styles. Compare shows made back then with shows made now depicting former times.

• *Tender Topics, Such as Birth, Death, Sex, Disability, Drug and Alcohol Use, as They Are Broached on TV Programs.*

• *Social Values:* How do different characters handle conflict: seriously, humorously, ironically? Notice the interactions of characters — do they help, share, support each other, or do they belittle one another? Do people talk about their feelings? What about their environments — do you see books and musical instruments and art in their rooms?

Discussion provides a good basis for active TV viewing, but sometimes it doesn't go far enough. Here are some suggestions for more active involvement:

• Plan ahead and have your child read the book before seeing the program on which it is based. Another time have him read the book after seeing the show. Compare these experiences. Ask him what he thinks are the pros and cons of each medium.

• If a play is going to be broadcast, try to obtain the screenplay and compare the written with the performed version. How has TV affected the production?

• Your child can do a TV favorites survey among family members, friends, and classmates and analyze the data by age and sex.

• Encourage your child to try to beat the contestants on quiz shows. You and she can then make up questions to try to stump each other.

• Play an observation and memory game: together watch a show during which you take written and mental notes on visual and spoken details. Quiz each other afterward.

• Have your child imagine she's a visitor from another country or planet, and have her compose a description of the "typical American" as portrayed by an hour's or an evening's TV programming and commercials. How does this description compare with her own perceptions of the "typical American"?

• If your child wants to watch a favorite sitcom you don't like, watch with him and have him review it for you, as if to "sell" you on its merits.

• Visit a TV studio to learn about and demystify the processes involved in TV production.

• Follow up on what your family watches. If a concert on TV

is enjoyed, buy the record. Look up references, names, vocabulary words that are unclear. Locate places and names on a map.

• Discuss the limitations of TV biographies and docudramas by comparing them to written versions. What is emphasized? What is left out? Have your child imagine what it's like to have her life televised. Suggest that she can write the script.

• Talk about the preponderance of violence on TV. To increase awareness, break the violence down into types as you watch.

• Have your child choose a new program now and then: sports events, telethon, opera, nature study, talk show, something aimed at an age or ethnic group not his own. Breaking habits permits children to gain fresh viewpoints.

• Read, discuss, and analyze TV reviews by critics. Encourage your child to compose her own reviews, which can be sent to the stations or read aloud. Talk about the criteria for judging quality. Are the performances real, moving? Is attention paid to detail? Is the plot complex, lifelike? What about the setting? Is there a point, a moral, to the program? What feelings are you left with?

• Watch the news together. Discuss the effect on us of news events taking place elsewhere. Talk about the importance of the individual editor's judgment as to what appears on a particular newscast. Compare news and editorials. Compare the depth of TV news coverage of a topic with that of a newspaper and news-magazine. Have your child make up a news bulletin or an entire program. She might like to do a mock interview with a "celebrity" or "accident victim."

• Get a book about how television works. *Your World: Let's Visit a Television Station* by Billy N. Pope is a photo book for the young child. Jeanne and Robert Bendick's and Eurfron Gwynne Jones's *Television Magic* explains the production of a program.

• *The Illustrated TV Dictionary* by Carolyn Handler Miller contains many starting points for discussion. Find examples of the following as you watch together: cliffhanger, dissolve, teaser, reverse angle shot, freeze frame, laugh track, instant replay, voice-over, pacing, credits, flashback, fadeout, point of view.

And Now a Word from Our Sponsor

Commercials provide unlimited opportunities for learning to be a critical viewer. Try these ideas.

• Point out that men's voices are most often used to sell products ("the voice of authority"), but that women's bodies are often used to adorn products and attract the eye. Discuss the trickiness of selling techniques. *Thirty Seconds* by Michael J. Arlen is a book-length account of the creation of a half-minute commercial (AT&T's "Reach Out and Touch Someone"), highlighting the incongruous and absurd details.

• Teach your child how to decode commercial messages. Catch the fallacious reasoning, the overuse of superlatives, the irrelevant claims and statements.

• Ask: Is this commercial honest? Should this product be sold to children? Is the jingle catchy but meaningless? Are the values shown ones we want to emulate? Do the testimonials mean anything? Is this product really useful? Essential? Dangerous?

• Make a list of claims made for a toy, household product, or food. Compare these to reality. Using the scientific method, do your own comparison tests on such items as paper towels.

• Notice the public service ads. Have your child think about what causes are most deserving of public service time and design their own commercials for them.

The Last Word

Gifted children can become excellent critics in the best sense of the word. With the appropriate tools for objective evaluation and learning viewed as an enjoyable and stimulating family activity, TV viewing needn't be feared as an ominous IQ monster that gobbles up your child's intellectual points in direct proportion to his personal Nielsen Ratings. Instead, it can become a challenging interactive medium.

One final activity is worth mentioning. Once gifted children gain some experience in evaluating TV programs and commercials, they may wish to make their views — likes, dislikes, and reasons — known to producers and sponsors. The addresses of the major networks can be found in most weekly program guides.

Reading for
Gifted Children

W ITHOUT a doubt, one of the most critical activities in the development of a gifted child is reading. Almost without exception do the biographies and autobiographies of gifted individuals allude to the importance of reading in their early lives. Not only does reading develop and challenge cognitive skills, it opens up worlds of potential interest and involvement — areas in which the gifted often later excel. More often than not, children who are intellectually advanced come from homes where reading is highly valued.

The book reviews in this chapter have been condensed from the original full-length reviews that were published first in *Booklist*, a journal of the American Library Association, copyrighted by the American Library Association. The books were selected by Barbara Elleman and Betsy Hearne, contributing editors of *Gifted Children Monthly*, who chose them for their complexity, advanced thinking level, and themes of intrinsic value or interest to gifted children. The books are divided into fiction and nonfiction, and by age level. The ages cited, however, are guidelines only. Appropriateness should be determined by your child's reading level and interest.

A special section is included in this chapter: "Biographies for the Gifted"; biographies are especially important in providing re-alistic successful role models.

A sharing experience that many families enjoy is a read-aloud time when everyone can join in, whether it be around the backyard picnic table, family campground, or family-room fireplace. Too often abandoned when children master reading skills, reading aloud not only offers the opportunity for discussion, it can also enlighten young minds whose mental promise allows early grasp of vocabulary, but whose lack of experience inhibits a grasp of complex themes. Two books written especially for parents on this subject are Butler's *Book for Babies* and Hearne's *Choosing Books for Children*, both of which the library should have. Or for a more personal approach in selection help, ask your librarian.

FICTION

Across the Stream by Mirra Ginsburg, pictures by Nancy Tafuri (Greenwillow, 1982), ages 2–4.

A strikingly simple story line works perfectly in the company of crisp, clear, full-color scenes that depict its action one step at a time. The simple shapes and strong colors are tailor-made for the younger picture-book audience, who will find the story's action tuned right to their sensibilities.

Moonlight by Jan Ormerod (Lothrop, 1982), ages 3–5.

Ormerod has taken the simple ritual of bedtime and without words portrayed it in a way children can appreciate. Her realistically colored washes show shrewd observation of home life, from fruit rinds in the kitchen sink to toothpaste escaping from its tube.

Peter Spier's Rain by Peter Spier (Doubleday, 1982), ages 3–6.

This wordless picture book celebrates a brother and sister's experience of a rainstorm, from first drops to clearing skies. A comic book format with various-size scene frames offers a wealth of detail, and it's Spier at his richest in color and composition.

Bear's Adventure by Brian Wildsmith (Pantheon, 1982), ages 4–6.

A big brown bear crawls into a balloon basket for a nap; instead he finds himself on the airways to high adventure when he lands in the middle of a big city parade. Bright vibrant circus colors highlight the amusing oversize pictures.

Do Not Open by Brinton Turkle (Elsevier-Dutton, 1981), ages 4–6.

This simple story of a lady who finds a bottle on the shore is lifted above the ordinary by Turkle's impressive illustrations executed in vibrant color. When Miss Moody finally opens the bottle marked Do Not Open, a truly frightening monster pops out. Children will appreciate such an appropriate conclusion; everyone will enjoy such a lovingly designed book.

The Mystery of the Stolen Blue Paint by Steven Kellogg. Pictures by the author (Dial, 1982), ages 4–8.

Kellogg's multicolored mystery series takes on blue, as a dog, a gang of kids, and a can of paint romp through this funny, lighthearted tale. Kellogg's black line drawings accented with blue are deftly and enthusiastically drawn with childlike expressions that are right on target, and background details add funny scenes that readers will enjoy following.

A Rose for Pinkerton by Steven Kellogg. Pictures by the author (Dial, 1981), ages 4–8.

Kellogg, whose *Pinkerton, Behave!* gave Great Danes their own special place in picture books, brings the dog back in a zesty tale that is delivered with splendid flourish. Mellow shadings of color, unusual use of light, and effective crowd placement provide background for a funny and well-placed story that complements and is complemented by the dexterous illustrations.

When I Was Young in the Mountains by Cynthia Rylant. Illustrated by Diane Goode (Dutton, 1982), ages 5–7.

The author's recollections of an Appalachian childhood are nicely wrought in Diane Goode's muted scenes of a pair of children and their grandparents who live together in a four-room house. Goode's soft colors and fine textures give the setting a pristine glow that's as warm as the rosy memories.

Yeh-Shen: A Cinderella Story from China by Louie Ai-Ling. Illustrated by Ed Young (Philomel, 1982), ages 5–7.

In this variant of Cinderella (which predates its European counterpart), Yeh-Shen, servant of her stepmother and stepsisters, lives a life of drudgery. Her only friend is a beautiful fish that swims in a nearby pond and shares her meager rations. The pastel and watercolor intensities vary from soft to vibrant, and the whole work has a misty, dreamlike air.

The Wild Swans by Hans Christian Andersen. Retold by Amy Ehrlich. Pictures by Susan Jeffers (Dial, 1981), ages 5–8.

Soft textures and soothing color give Jeffers's ambitious spreads a quiet power that well suits Andersen's tale of love and sacrifice. Minute, feather-light cross-hatching and restrained hues are responsible for the pictures' soft appearance and subtle shadowing.

The Little Girl and the Big Bear by Joanna Galdone. Illustrated by Paul Galdone (Houghton Mifflin/Clarion, 1980), ages 5–8.

A blond, pigtailed girl, picking berries with her friends in the forest, becomes lost and takes refuge in a lonely hut. Galdone's line drawings are washed in lively colors, providing a spirited complement to this old Slavic tale.

Suho and the White Horse: A Legend of Mongolia by Yuzo Otsuka. Adapted from the translation by Ann Herring. Illustrated by Suekichi Akaba (Viking, 1981), ages 5–8.

Spacious paintings lift the reader into the heart of Asia and into a story that unfolds the fundamentals of good versus evil through the love of a young herdsman for his white horse, which is killed because of a noble's greed. The Mongolian steppes stretch wide across double-page spreads, with clay hues effectively shaped into figures by surrounding color of thick outline, always skillfully balanced by the focal white horse.

Nicholas Bentley Stoningpot III by Ann McGovern. Illustrated by Tomie de Paola (Holiday, 1982), ages 5–8.

Bored with his life of traipsing around a yacht with his wealthy parents, preppy-looking Nicholas Bentley Stoningpot III longs for adventure. This clever story should catch the fancy of young Robinson Crusoes and inspire dreams and conversation about their own would-be island adventures.

The Hunter and the Animals by Tomie de Paola (Holiday, 1981), ages 5–9.

A bright blue bird alerts his friends that a hunter is entering the forest, and in fear the animals quickly hide. When the discouraged hunter falls asleep, the animals secrete his pouch and gun and alter the look of his surroundings. In this wordless story, speckled backgrounds, interconnecting shapes, and acorn-laden stylized trees provide a unique background for the rust-colored foxes, gray beavers, beige deer, and forest-green owls that peer from the pages.

Ming Lo Moves the Mountain by Arnold Lobel. Illustrated by the author (Greenwillow, 1982), ages 6–8.

Ming Lo and his wife love their house, but they don't love the mountain that towers over them, since it sheds both rocks and rain and also blocks the sun. Ming Lo consults the village wise man for advice on how to move the mountain. Illustrated in earthy tans, grays, and greens for a subdued look that is a subtle counterpoint to the story's sharp wit.

The Golden Serpent by Walter Dean Myers. Illustrated by Alice Provensen and Martin Provensen (Viking, 1980), ages 6–8.

In this tale set in India at the turn of the century, the king summons the wise man Pundabi to solve a "mystery." Although children may need help interpreting this abstract tale, they will be drawn to the delicate, finely toned art. The sand-baked hues of the buildings contrast well with the hazy mountain backgrounds and stylized characters, creating a smooth integration of art and story.

The Dragon Kite by Nancy Luenn. Illustrated by Michael Hague (Harcourt, Brace, 1982), ages 6–9.

Determined to steal the golden dolphin on top of the shogun's castle, Ishikawa, a Robin Hood figure of the later 1600s Japan, schemes to reach the high promenade with the help of a magnificent kite. Against a gray-green patterned border photographed from an antique kimono, Hague's captivating full-color illustrations expand the lyrical tale into an accomplished integration of story and art.

Aladdin and the Wonderful Lamp retold by Andrew Lang. Illustrated by Errol LeCain (Viking, 1981), ages 7–8.

Lots of deep, brooding color and extensive rococo ornamentation fit both the story's Middle Eastern setting and its undertones of evil and foreboding. The pictures dominate the book thanks to the large page size and the drama projected by form and color.

The Balancing Girl by Berniece Rabe. Pictures by Lillian Hoban (Elsevier-Dutton, 1981), ages 7–8.

The story concerns a raven-haired paraplegic named Margaret who delights in balancing things. It's her way of asserting her independence and getting other people's respect; it's also the key to her money making idea for the school carnival. Hoban's smudgy charcoal sketches of moon-cheeked little kids give a homy warmth to Rabe's characters and their grade-school setting.

Hosie's Zoo by Leonard Baskin. Pictures by the author (Viking, 1981), ages 7–9.

The uneven poetical murmurings here are the barest of frames on which go Baskin's fierce, intense portraits of an eclectic mix of wildlife. This is an album of pictures rather than a picture book.

But the pictures are compelling, prone to evoke the inherent power of each species.

Where the Buffaloes Begin by Olaf Baker. Illustrated by Stephen Gammell (Warne, 1981), ages 7–9.

In this softly remembered and elegantly told tale, a boy named Little Wolf journeys to a fabled lake where the buffalo are born and thereby saves his people from enemy attack. Gammell's misty, ethereal illustrations are powerful accompaniments to the story. Their soft edges and wispy details contribute to the tale's mood of mystery and awe.

The Silver Cow: A Welsh Tale by Susan Cooper. Illustrated by Warwick Hutton (Atheneum/Margaret K. McElderry, 1983), ages 7–9.

Cooper tells of a greedy farmer who reaps the rewards of his son's forbidden harp playing in the form of a silver cow sent by magical lake powers. Both the writing and the painting for this Welsh tale are beautifully balanced between the concrete and the mystical. Hutton's rich watercolors are the soul of the work.

A Visit to William Blake's Inn: Poems for Innocent and Experienced Travelers by Nancy Willard. Illustrated by Alice and Martin Provensen (Harcourt, Brace, 1981), ages 7–10.

Willard's collection contains both inventive nonsense and lyrical poetry, light humor and profound points. The paintings accompanying the verse also have a dreamlike air, yet are anchored by their steady eighteenth century propriety. Dominant hues of tan, gold, and warm brown combine with patterns and designs that make each illustration absorbing to look at.

Two Pairs of Shoes by Pamela L. Travers. Illustrated by Leo and Diane Dillon (Viking, 1980), ages 7–10.

Abu Kassem's tattered slippers are the hallmark of his miserliness. In contrast, the ragged sandals of the king's chief adviser, Ayaz, are treasured symbols of his humble roots, a fact that reaffirms the king's faith in him. Marbleized backdrops set off intricate scenes where splashes of patterning play nicely against outsize turbans and brilliant pants.

Hambone by Caroline Fairless. Illustrated by Wendy Edelson (Tundra, 1980), ages 7–10.

To ease his hurt when Hambone, his pet pig, is slaughtered, Jeremy plants a memorial tomato seedling. His tomato plant —

christened Hambone — becomes a prolific bearer, providing the right sort of happy finish to a story that treats tender feelings gently. Longer than a picture book, but shorter than a novel, *Hambone* is a good choice for reading aloud.

Mustard by Charlotte Towner Graeber. Illustrated by Donna Diamond (Macmillan, 1982), ages 8–10 (younger for reading aloud).

A meaningful story about the death of a pet. Very true to life, this is an accurate portrait of an illness and the grieving process; it is also refreshing to have the parents visibly moved by this experience rather than just portrayed as supports for the children. Diamond has provided simple, exceptionally effective pencil illustrations.

The Dragon of Og by Rumer Godden. Illustrated by Pauline Baynes (Viking, 1981), ages 8–10.

Sharp, vital characterization gives this deft fantasy unexpected color and momentum. The Dragon of Og is a quiet beast who troubles no one till he runs afoul of Angus of Og, the stubborn new lord who has come to rule the castle lands. The story of how the dragon is slain and revived occurs against a vivid setting that pays attention to the squalor and poverty of the times as well as the glories.

Knock at a Star: A Child's Introduction to Poetry compiled by X. J. Kennedy and Dorothy M. Kennedy. Illustrated by Karen Ann Weinhaus (Little, Brown, 1982), ages 8–11, especially for reading aloud.

Fresh in both selection and presentation, this includes more than 150 poems, most of them rare in anthologies. There is in most of the poems a combination of brevity with depth of feeling or a twist of invention that takes the reader by surprise. A good many of the verses will make the reader laugh, though occasionally there is a heart-stopper. An afterword to adults and a note to people working with groups of children both contain direct, sensible advice.

Pot Belly Tales by Mary Haynes. Pictures by Michael J. Deraney (Norman Lothrop Enterprises, 1982), ages 9–10.

In 1888, Susanna Packer watches her father cast a potbelly stove in his foundry. That stove becomes the unifying factor in ten subsequent vignettes that follow the stove's ownership down through the years until sometime after 1978, when the sturdy old heater turns up at an antique auction. Softly shaped and shaded pictures feature expressive, real-looking faces and detailed interior and exterior backdrops.

The People in Pineapple Place by Anne Lindbergh (Harcourt, Brace, 1982), ages 9–11.

Reeling from his parent's recent divorce, ten-year-old August Brown takes an immediate dislike to his new home in Washington, D.C., until he meets spunky April Anderson and her strange apartment friends from Pineapple Place. Lindbergh's true theme is one of adjustment to divorce and to a new relationship with a working mother, which shines through with warmth and understanding.

Offbeat Friends by Elfie Donnelly (Crown, 1982), ages 9–11.

This English translation from the German concerns an eleven-year-old Viennese girl, Mari, who befriends Mrs. Panacek, an old lady who lives at a mental home. When Mrs. Panacek runs away, Mari harbors the old lady overnight in her apartment, where she is discovered by the girl's amazed parents. They, however, are touched by Mrs. Panacek's vulnerability, too, and soon the whole family has reached out to help her.

Salted Lemons by Doris Buchanan Smith (Four Winds, 1980), ages 9–12.

Darby is the new girl in town, but she's feisty enough to meet and match the challenge of the neighborhood and eventually build her own niche in the local hierarchy. World War II colors the story and provides much of its philosophical substance.

The Cricket Sings: Poems and Songs for Children by Federico García Lorca. Translated by Will Kirkland. Illustrated by Maria Horvath (New Directions, 1980), ages 9–14.

Of special interest to discerning students of poetry or Spanish, this book features 25 lyric poems from Spain. The English translation faces each poem, and stylized, toylike black-and-white translations decorate almost every page.

Scary Stories to Tell in the Dark: Collected from American Folklore by Alvin Schwartz. Drawings by Stephen Gammell (Lippincott/ Harper, 1981), ages 10–12.

Sure to provoke chills along the spine, this collection of short selections about witches and ghosts include "jump" stories as well as macabre songs, modern-day psychic tales, and frightening legends from the past. Gammell's smudge drawings are not for the timid; their horrific tone expands the atmosphere in a ghoulish, though always skillful, manner.

Mystery Madness by Otto Coontz (Houghton Mifflin, 1982), ages 10–12.

In this madcap mystery, twelve-year-old Murray calls his sister, Blanche, for a ride home from the dentist; he hears a shot, a scream, and Blanche pleading with the housekeeper, Maria, to forgive her. From this, Murray deduces his sister and her friend Harold have accidentally done in Maria.

The Night Journey by Kathryn Lisky. Drawings by Trina Schart Hyman (Warne, 1981), ages 10–13.

Each afternoon thirteen-year-old Rachel spends time keeping her great-grandmother, Nana Sashie, company. This trial they both must endure turns into the highlight of their lives when Nana decides to share with Rachel the story of her family's escape from Tsarist Russia.

This Time of Darkness: A Novel of the Future by H. M. Hoover (Viking, 1980), ages 10–13.

Using as her setting a future underground city where rats, over-crowding, and authoritarian automation intrude on living, Hoover builds a tale of gripping suspense. Eleven-year-old Amy, ignored by her mother and unhappy with her life, determines to escape when she meets the captive Axel, who tells her about his home outside that has rain, sunshine, and real food.

Footsteps by Leon Garfield (Delacorte, 1980), ages 10–14.

Riddled with guilt for a past misdeed in connection with a mysterious Aldref Diamond, David Jones leaves his sickbed each night to pace the floor, while below, his son William listens in fear. Even after Jones's death, the footsteps continue, and William vows to ferret out his father's former partner.

Calling B for Butterfly by Louise Lawrence (Harper, 1982), ages 10–14.

Self-centered Sonja; shy, timid Ann; scholarly, intensive Matthew; and belligerent Glyn are the only survivors, along with baby Benjamin and his younger sister Caroline when an asteroid smashes a starliner to pieces, leaving the six alone in life ferry B (B for butterfly).

The Refugee Summer by Edward Fenton (Delacorte, 1982), ages 11–13.

The summer of 1922 is a strange one for young Nikolas, who lives a simple life in Kifissia, an elegant suburb of Athens. Son of the Villa Pandora caretaker, he is blissfully drawn into a world of noble deeds with the Pallikars, a secret society.

Frankenstein's Aunt by Allan Rune Petterson (Little, Brown, 1981), ages 11–14.

In this hilarious spoof of the Frankenstein-Dracula-werewolf stories, Frankenstein's cigar-chomping, no-nonsense aunt returns to the scene of the crime, where the monster was created, to restore respect to the family name. Finding the castle in ruins, she decides to reconstitute the defunct creature to help in the rebuilding process.

The Haunting by Margaret Mahy (Atheneum/Margaret K. Mc-Elderry, 1982), ages 11–14.

Shy and withdrawn eight-year-old Barney becomes extremely frightened when he begins receiving supernatural messages from an uncle the family has long believed dead. Mahy handles suspense adroitly and characters with aplomb, enriching her story with well-drawn relationships — especially between the children and a much adored stepmother.

The Sword and the Circle: King Arthur and the Knights of the Round Table by Rosemary Sutcliff (Dutton, 1981), ages 12–14.

The age-old stories about Arthur, the knights of the Round Table, the sword Excalibur, the magician Merlin, and the days of Camelot effortlessly flow from the hands of a master storyteller. Using the tales' inherent magic, Sutcliff weaves freshness and clarity into her tellings, providing a rich storehouse for reading aloud or sharing aloud.

Don't Forget to Fly: A Cycle of Modern Poems collected by Paul B. Janeczko (Bradbury, 1981), ages 12 and up.

Thematically clustered in groups of two, three, or four, the 130 mostly short poems run a broad gamut of styles and moods and treat subjects as diverse as morning, night, suicide, friendship, love, parents, marriage, Sundays, insomnia, cats, crows, cars, war, movies, and poetry. Recommended for young adult as well as junior high and high school collections.

NONFICTION

Let's Play by Satomi Ichikawa (Putnam/Philomel, 1981), ages 1–4.

In this picture book for very young children, the point is to look — and look and *look* at the familiar toys Ichikawa features, first alone, and then as part of a scene in which children play with them. The pictures are softly colored, clean-looking depictions of slightly antique interiors and fresh rural-looking backyards.

On Market Street by Arnold Lobel. Pictures by Anita Lobel (Greenwillow, 1981), ages 2–6.

Children just learning the alphabet, as well as those already expert with letters, will appreciate this merry display of ABC's.

Dinosaurs Beware! by Marc Tolon Brown and Stephen Krensky (Atlantic Monthly Press/Little, Brown, 1982), ages 3–5.

At last, a painless way to teach children safety rules (unless they hurt from laughing so hard!). Some pages feature several tips, others one large one, but in all cases the message is clearly stated and the vividly colored pictures will make that message stick in a child's head.

Tool Book by Gail Gibbons (Holiday, 1982), ages 4–6.

Gibbons takes everyday tools and, through maximum use of graphics and minimum text, gives young children a fine introduction to how things work. The art, striking in its simplicity, makes use of plain perspectives and jelly-bean colors that will rivet attention.

A Winter Place by Ruth Yaffe Radin. Paintings by Mattie Lou O'Kelley (Atlantic Monthly Press/Little, Brown, 1982), ages 5–7.

A slight poetic text provides the framework for fifteen lovely pieces of primitive-style art. The pictures, charming pastoral scenes with intense colors, innovative patterning, and hidden surprises, and the lilting language combine to make a captivating book.

Giorgio's Village by Tomie de Paola (Putnam, 1982), ages 5–8.

The covered boards that are the gates to Giorgio's village unfold, and viewers enter an awakening Italian square as the sun rises over the green hills. The day progresses through five other different foldout scenes — the markets are set up, siesta time arrives, the children play in the fountain, a puppet show comes to entertain, and the village settles down for the night under a moon that glides across the sky.

Anno's Britain by Mitsumasa Anno (Philomel, 1982), ages 5–8.

Continuing the successful format used in *Anno's Journey* and *Anno's Italy*, the author-illustrator shows a blue-clad wanderer washed ashore, beginning his travels through Great Britain. The meticulously crafted watercolors are full of scrumptious detail and humorous asides; a pair of caring adult eyes might help ensure a rewarding book experience.

A Duckling Is Born by Hans-Heinrich Isenbart. Translated by Catherine Edwards Sandler. Photos by Omar Baumli (Putnam, 1981), ages 7–9.

Isenbart uses color photography to chronicle the development of a duckling to its first swim. The photography throughout is eye-catching, compelling attention and juxtaposing well with the spare, informative text.

Dinosaurs! A Drawing Book by Michael Emberley (Little, Brown, 1980), ages 7–10.

Using the same straightforward method found in Ed Emberley's popular how-to-draw books, his son demonstrates how making simple, appropriate lines — added a few strokes at a time — can lead to the drawing of specific creatures.

Seeds: Pop, Stick, Glide by Patricia Lauber. Photography by Jerome Wexler (Crown, 1981), ages 7–11.

The wonder of nature is exemplified in this lucid exploration of the many byways of the traveling seed. Carefully composed photographs help children understand the seeding process and, along with the author's concluding suggestions, motivate youngsters to observe growing plants closely.

Anno's Medieval World by Mitsumasa Anno. Adapted from the translation by Ursula Synge (Philomel, 1980), ages 7–11.

With meticulous detail, Anno depicts a medieval time when people were awakening to the concept of a round earth. The full-color drawings, presented on parchment-looking paper and bordered with a trellis motif, abound with jugglers, shipbuilders, farmers, peasants, and astronomers in fascinating displays.

If You Are a Hunter of Fossils by Byrd Baylor and Peter Parhall (Scribner, 1980), ages 8–10.

With lyrical prose and sea-color scenes that stretch across the pages, Baylor and Parnall describe how a mountainous area must have looked long ago. The familiar style and tone add to the craftsmanship and sensitivity of this presentation that will capture reader's attention.

A Horse's Body by Joanna Cole. Photography by Jerome Wexler (Morrow, 1981), ages 8–10.

The horse has a body that "seems to have been designed especially to run." Cole elaborates on that observation, showing the horse's evolution from eohippus, and analyzing its leg and foot construction and its various gaits. With clear, well-chosen black-and-white photographs, the connection between the animal and its environment becomes clear.

Marco Polo by Gian Paolo Ceserani. Illustrated by Piero Ventura (Putnam, 1982), ages 8–10.

In broad strokes, Ceserani's text recounts Marco Polo's life against the enthusiastic backdrop of Ventura's minutiae-filled spreads. The pictures elaborate on the words, so that readers will absorb considerable information on locales, dress, and social organizations.

Cars and How They Go by Joanna Cole. Illustrated by Gail Gibbons (Harper/Crowell, 1983), ages 8–10.

This picture-book explanation of how a car works is an interesting example of how a complicated topic can be rendered in basic terms without sacrificing key concepts. Here, things are made simple as Cole lets Gibbons's crisp, pure, sunny illustrations do a good deal of explaining.

Secrets of the Venus Fly Trap by Jerome Wexler (Dodd, Mead, 1981), ages 8–11.

How does a Venus flytrap capture its prey, grow, and multiply? Wexler's pure, close-up black-and-white photographs and inquiry approach show readers the particulars.

Lobo of the Tasaday by John Nance. Photos by the author (Pantheon, 1982), ages 8–11.

Photojournalist Nance focuses on Lobo, a Tasaday boy who was about ten years old at the time, to reveal a little of the daily lives of this Stone Age people. Both photos and the very idea of these happenings are at once riveting and bittersweet, for readers will know, as the Tasaday here do not, that their lives will change forever.

Wildlife Alert! The Struggle to Survive by Gene S. Stuart (National Geographic Society, 1980), ages 8–12.

The plight of numerous animals around the world and the steps being taken to help them form the substance of this attractive book, which features handsome full-color photographs. The text is somewhat choppy, but the pictures are appealing. Accompanied by a booklet of projects and puzzles and a wall poster.

Creatures of Paradise: Pictures to Grow Up With by Bryan Holme (Oxford, 1980), ages 8–12.

This collection brings together drawings, paintings, and sculptures of beautiful animals and birds from many times and countries. Care in the reproduction as well as in the placement of pictures makes this an appealing introduction to the world of art.

Bridges by Anne and Scott MacGregor (Norman Lothrop Enterprises, 1981), ages 8–12.

Three kinds of bridges — beam, arch and suspension — are described in crisp terms and delineated with large, precisely executed drawings that sweep across the page, providing panoramic views as well as historical and architectural points of reference. Detailed instructions for making models and variations of the bridge types are based on actual engineering principles and turn *Bridges* into a fine combination of fact-and-craft book for would-be engineers.

Behind the Scenes of a Broadway Musical by Bill Powers (Crown, 1982), ages 8–12.

Using Maurice Sendak's musical *Really Rosie* (taken from his book, *The Sign on Rosie's Door*) as its basis, Powers goes behind the curtain to detail the various aspects of getting a show ready to open on Broadway. The work of the casting agent, choreographer, director, costume and set designers, and light crew, as well as the six children who were the main characters, is clearly evoked in both commentary and photographs.

Messing Around with . . . Baking Chemistry, Drinking Straw Construction, Water Pumps and Siphons (three books) by Bernie Zubrowski. Illustrated respectively by Signe Hanson, Stephanie Fleischer, Steve Lindblom (Little, Brown, 1981), ages 9–10 (younger with adult help).

These elementary science books do an excellent job of introducing the processes with which they're concerned. All rely on easily obtained items, and the investigations can be conducted on the home front with little problem. Humorous pen-and-ink drawings add a light touch to the straightforward, personable text.

The Long Journey from Space by Seymour Simon (Crown, 1982), ages 9–11.

Spectacular space photographs, elegant design, and a clean, straightforward text make Simon's introduction to comets and meteors a sure pick for the astronomy shelf. A companion to *The Long View into Space*, this describes in nontechnical language what comets and meteors are, how we came to know about them, what their special characteristics are, and, via the superb photographs, what some of the more famous of them look like.

Tic Tac Toe and Other Three-in-a-Row Games from Ancient Egypt to the Modern Computer by Claudia Zaslavsky. Illustrated by Anthony Kramer (Harper/Crowell, 1982), ages 9–11.

This would certainly come under the heading of everything you ever wanted to know about tic-tac-toe. There is also a section on computers and ways to program for tic-tac-toe. The gray-wash illustrations and informative diagrams are a plus.

The Magic of Color by Hilda Simon (Lothrop, 1981), ages 9–11.

A carefully "stepped" text, in conjunction with demonstration pictures, explains color visions as the result of light reflection, with experiments along the way to prove points about afterimage reversal of primary and complementary colors. Also described are optical illusions by color juxtaposition and the process by which printers mix four-color screen for full-color illustrations.

Many Friends Cooking: An International Cookbook for Boys and Girls by Terry Touff Cooper and Marilyn Ratner. Illustrated by Tony Chen (Philomel, 1980), ages 9–12.

A companion volume to *Many Hands Cooking*, this collection gives children the opportunity to duplicate authentic recipes from 33 countries. Fine line drawings heightened with distinctive colors enhance the book, which, although spiral bound, is strong enough to withstand the use it will undoubtedly receive.

Dinosaurs of North America by Helen Roney Sattler. Illustrated by Anthony Rao (Lothrop, 1981), ages 9–12.

Arranged by broad geologic time periods (Triassic, Jurassic,

Cretaceous), this carefully researched book features more than 80 different types of dinosaurs native to North America. The drawings, many full- and double-page spreads, are executed in gray-green tones and skillfully shaded to emphasize the creatures' size.

The Weaver's Gift by Kathryn Lasky. Photography by Christopher G. Knight (Warne, 1980), ages 9–12.

Author and artist follow the course of woolmaking from the birth of a lamb to shearing, carding, spinning, drying, and weaving. Excellent black-and-white photographs show most of the tasks involved in the months-long process. Much detail about the traditional methods of preparing cloth is included in the text, making the whole production a fine documentary of a dying art.

National Geographic Book of Mammals edited by Donald J. Crump (National Geographic Society, 1981), ages 9–13 (younger for photos).

Well organized and lavishly illustrated, this comprehensive album of mammals of the world will make an excellent library and home reference source. Included for each species is a world map inset that shows the mammal's range; a boldface fact list that includes height, weight, habitat, food, life span, pregnancy length, number of young, and the animal's order; and a light, straightforward essay.

Faces on Place: About Gargoyles and Other Stone Creatures by Suzanne Haldane (Viking, 1980), ages 10–12.

This photo-essay about gargoyles and other architectural carvings can be used to motivate children to raise their eyes and observe the buildings around them as well as those they may see on vacation. The black-and-white photographs are clear, well composed, and nicely coordinated with the brief text.

The Ideas of Einstein by David E. Fisher. Illustrated by Gwen Brodkin (Holt, Rinehart and Winston, 1980), ages 10–12.

Discussing the theory of relativity in 60 pages, Fisher offers necessarily abridged information but nonetheless makes clear that Einstein's questions about the nature of time, space, speed, and energy were very important, and that his answers — the theory itself — laid the groundwork for modern physics. There are diagrams and a glossary.

The Crest and the Hide compiled by Harold Courlander. Illustrated by Monica Vachula (Coward/McCann, 1982), ages 10–12.

A sparkling collection of 20 African tales marked by wit and verbal economy. The majority are brief (only a few stretch beyond the two-to-three-page average length) and make salient comment on matters of friendship, goodness rewarded, the merits of wisdom, or the price of indulgence.

Women Who Work with Animals by Bill Gutman (Dodd, Mead and Co., 1982), ages 10–12.

The author profiles six women whose affection for animals has led to successful careers of working with them in a variety of settings. Gutman's narrative style occasionally becomes awkward, but overall the accounts are straightforward and lively. The book's relatively large print may make it attractive to reluctant readers, with occasional black-and-white photos of women at their work.

The Kids' Whole Future Catalog by Paula Taylor (Random House, 1982), ages 10–12.

Although this is a hodgepodge, readers who enjoy sending away for things (some free, some not) will welcome it as another source of information. The topic here is technology of the future. The book is copiously illustrated with black-and-white illustrations and photographs.

A Children's Almanac of Words at Play by Willard R. Espy. Illustrated by Bruce Cayard (Clarkson N. Potter, 1982), ages 10–12.

Wordplay for everyday — that's Espy's beguiling offer in this compendium of stories, jokes, puns, riddles, poems, nonsense, and general good fun. Dedicated to his six grandchildren, whose own wordplay penchants are highlighted intermittently, this collage of verbal fun teaches and challenges as well as amuses.

The Secret Life of Hardware: A Science Experiment Book by Vicki Cobb. Illustrated by Bill Morrison (Lippincott, 1982), ages 10–13.

Soaps, polishes, paints, a hammer, a saw — who would think they're the stuff of an instructive, entertaining science lesson? As she did in *The Secret Life of School Supplies*, Cobb casts an appraising eye at the body of scientific knowledge that's implicit in these common, everyday materials and objects.

The Cat's Elbow and Other Secret Languages collected by Alvin Schwartz. Pictures by Margot Zemach (Farrar, 1982), ages 10–13.

The lure of secret languages is perennial among kids. They may have heard of Pig Latin, but how about "Iggity" or "Kinyume," which East African kids play around with, or "Ku," which was spoken by the children of Chernovtsy in southwestern Russia.

Dollmaker: The Eyelight and the Shadow by Kathryn Lasky. Photos by Christopher G. Knight (Scribner, 1981), ages 10–13.

The dollmaker's world is filled with measurements and calibrations, minuscule tools, and the desire to replicate in dolls the light in a child's eye. Lasky and Knight take readers on a photographic journey through the world of one particular dollmaker, Carole Bowling, and the voyage is no less than amazing.

Man's Place in Evolution by The British Museum of National History (Cambridge University Press, 1981), ages 10–14.

This logical and concise exploration of *Homo sapiens*' place in the scheme of evolution explains how and why scientists arrived at their current opinions, and acknowledges the uncertainty surrounding some links. Photographs, drawings, and diagrams predominate, clearly illustrating outlined principles and distinctions in relation to human anatomy.

Thunder, Singing Sands and Other Wonders: Sound in the Atmosphere by Kenneth Heuer (Dodd, 1981), ages 10–14.

In a straightforward manner, Heuer discusses the reasons for the sounds of nature, such as crashes of thunder, breaking of waves, humming of telegraph wires, and murmuring of forests. He cites primitive superstitions and beliefs as well as early scientific theories, and encourages readers to stretch their awareness about the environment. Accompanied by striking black-and-white photographs and a brief bibliography.

Working Kids on Working by Sheila Cole. Photographs by Victoria Beller-Smith (Lothrop, 1980), ages 11–13.

In this collection of interviews, junior high age children tell about their work experiences in different locales throughout the country. Ranging in age from nine to fifteen, they are babysitters, stable hands, file clerks, farm workers, models, actors, dockhands, newspaper carriers, dishwashers, dancers, and computer programmers.

Jupiter: King of the Gods, Giant of the Planets by Franklin Mansfield Branley (Elsevier/Nelson, 1981), ages 11–13.

Branley reviews what's known of Jupiter's size, composition, and major satellites, Io, Europa, Ganymede, and Callisto. He also discusses the planned Galileo spacecraft that will aim to penetrate Jupiter's atmosphere and allow scientists to see if conditions are favorable for life to evolve. A Jupiter fact list, metric conversion tables, and list of further reading are appended.

Rescue from Extinction by Joseph E. Brown (Dodd, Mead and Co., 1981), ages 11–13.

As Brown reports, scientists estimate that one out of every six species is threatened with extinction; reasons include overhunting or crowding out by domestic competitors, but the principal cause is the destruction of habitat. A discussion of the extinction process considers the question of why some animals bounce back from dwindling numbers and others don't. The text's informal, straightforward style makes it easy to read, and there are frequent black-and-white photos for illustration.

National Geographic Picture Atlas of Our Universe by Roy A. Gallant (National Geographic, 1980), ages 11–16.

Beautiful as well as encyclopedic, this atlas contains a profusion of full-color photographs, paintings (including speculative scenes on other planets and satellites, and portraits of life forms that might appear on other worlds), diagrammatic drawings, maps, and charts.

Thorny Issues: How Ethics and Morality Affect the Way We Live by John Langone (Little, Brown, 1981), ages 12 and up.

The author of a number of issue-oriented books for young people now tackles ethics — perhaps the thorniest issue of all. Stressing that the study of ethical problems around questions that, for the most part, have no definitive answers, Langone does indeed raise a host of questions, to evaluate critically their own values and those of others.

Flight: A Panorama of Aviation by Melvin Zisfein. Illustrated by Robert Andrew Parker (Pantheon, 1981), all ages.

This compilation of milestones in the history of aviation should appeal to airplane lovers, young and old. Parker's large watercolor illustrations are deceptively childlike while engendering feelings of motion and power.

BIOGRAPHIES FOR THE GIFTED

"Biographies are but the clothes and buttons of the man," scoffed the humorist Mark Twain, but this very reservation about the effectiveness of biography points to the need for careful scrutiny of the written portraits we give to impressionable children.

Too often, under the guise of entertainment or teaching a lesson, authors stray from the facts to present a glorified, sensationalized, or stereotyped image of their subject. This is dangerous because children — even the gifted — who have neither the background nor the experience to separate fact from fiction, are inclined to take what they see in print as truth.

It is imperative, then, that a biography be evaluated threefold: as a book of history, as an account of a person's life, and as a piece of literature.

Just as we expect accuracy, authenticity, and objectivity in history books, so should these be major ingredients in a biography. Documentation, once thought unnecessary in juvenile works, is now becoming recognized as a signal of careful research.

Authors who fictionalize through heavy use of dialogue, pass off legendary exploits as truth, use biographies to teach morals, or present only the worthier aspects of a character's life, cheat children out of experiencing the full dimension of a person's individuality. The subject's uniqueness becomes distorted or lost.

Biographies must also succeed as literature. The materials should be well written, smoothly flowing, free of triteness, and appealingly presented in a suitable tone and appropriate style. The best kind of biography recreates living, breathing men and women in their particular niche in time, and brings new insights and lasting impressions to the children who are meeting these people only through the pages of a book.

Biographies are often used in programs for the gifted to present case studies of individuals who exemplify outstanding achievement, persistence in the face of overwhelming odds, strong conviction, and standards of excellence. They can also be used to spark in a gifted child an interest in some area of human endeavor or period of history.

The Many Lives of Benjamin Franklin by Aliki. Illustrated by the author (Prentice-Hall, 1977), ages 6–8.

Children may have their notions of Franklin firmed up here in an equally humorous but more broadly concerned biography. Aliki's captioned cartoons — lightly lined and washed — expand or punctuate her easy text, which sketches Franklin's life from child-hood on.

Jane Goodall by Eleanor Coerr. Drawings by Kee de Kiefte (Put-nam, 1976), ages 7–9.

A look at four-year-old Jane Goodall gives way to an intelligent, straightforward recounting of how Goodall eventually comes to her career despite her lack of formal training — a situation that she later chose to remedy by attending Cambridge University.

P. T. Barnum by Anne Edwards. Pictures by Marylin Hafner (Putnam, 1977), ages 7–9.

Humorous black-and-white drawings on nearly every page and large print aim to insure approachability for young readers on their own. The text portrays Barnum as a clever youngster who went on to develop his world-renowned circus.

Along Came the Model T! How Henry Ford Put the World on Wheels by Robert Quackenbush (Parent's Magazine Press, 1978), ages 7–9.

Henry Ford's obsession with building a "smaller, lightweight horseless carriage" is traced from his childhood delight in fixing watches and repairing toys, through his early experimentation to his success with the Model T.

Dr. Beaumont and the Man with the Hole in His Stomach by Samuel Epstein and Beryl Epstein. Illustrated by Joseph Scrofani (Coward-McCann, 1978), ages 8–11.

A combination of accurate history, interesting science, and vivid storytelling, this is the account of a pioneer researcher and the man upon whom he based his discoveries. Egotistical, ambitious Dr. Beaumont happens to save the life of Alexis St. Martin after a shooting accident leaves the voyageur's stomach exposed. Pen-and-ink drawings spark the text, and a selected bibliography attests to reliable sources.

The Secret Soldier: The Story of Deborah Sampson by Ann Mc-Govern. Illustrated by Ann Grifalconi (Four Winds, 1975), ages 8–12.

When Robert Shurtliff joined the revolutionary forces in 1782, marched across New York, suffered through hard winters with little food, was injured by the enemy, and bravely helped fallen soldiers, no one suspected that Robert was really a twenty-year-old girl named Deborah Sampson. Unusual and interesting bold line drawings decorate the text.

I Am a Stranger on the Earth: The Story of Vincent Van Gogh by Arnold Dobrin (Warne, 1975), ages 11–14.

A brief but perceptive biography of the great impressionist artist who vacillated between torment and exaltation. Reproductions of the artist's paintings and drawings appear opposite the text, captioned with appropriate quotations from Van Gogh's letters to his brother — an effective way of incorporating the artist's work and feeling into his life story.

Bibliography

THE FOLLOWING resources have been selected to supplement the topics covered in *Parents' Guide*. Although by no means exhaustive, the list offers a broad range of texts that can serve as background materials or occasions for additional reading on subjects of particular interest.

Allen, Steve. *How to Think* (record album). Sewell: Gifted and Talented Publications, Inc. (P.O. Box 115, Sewell, NJ 08080), 1982.

Canfield, Jack, and Wells, Harold C. *100 Ways to Enhance Self-Concept in the Classroom: A Handbook for Teachers and Parents.* Englewood Cliffs: Prentice-Hall, 1976.

Clark, Barbara. *Growing Up Gifted.* 2nd ed. Columbus: Charles E. Merrill Publishing Co., 1979.

Coffey, Kay. *Parentspeak on Gifted and Talented Children.* Ventura: Superintendent of Schools (Ventura County Schools, 535 East Main St., Ventura, CA 93009), 1976.

Cumming, Robert. *Just Imagine: Ideas in Painting.* New York: Charles Scribner's Sons, 1982.

Delisle, James R. *Gifted Children Speak Out.* New York: Walker and Company, 1984.

Delp, Jeanne, and Martinson, Ruth. *The Gifted and Talented: A Handbook for Parents.* Ventura: Superintendent of Schools (535 East Main St., Ventura, CA 93009), 1975.

Eberle, Bob, and Stanish, Bob. *CPS for Kids: A Resource Book for Teaching Creative Problem Solving to Children.* Buffalo: DOK Publishers, 1980.

Ehrlich, Virginia Z. *Gifted Children: A Guide for Parents and Teachers.* Englewood Cliffs: Prentice-Hall, 1982.

Feldman, Ruth Duskin. *Whatever Happened to the Quiz Kids: Perils and Profits of Growing Up Gifted.* Chicago: Chicago Review Press, 1982.

Felker, Roberta M., ed. *A Parent's Guide to the Education of Preschool Gifted Children.* Washington: National Association of State Boards of Education (444 North Capitol St., N.W., Washington, DC 20001), 1982.

Fischer, Robert. *Trick Photography: Crazy Things You Can Do with Cameras.* New York: M. Evans and Co., 1980.

Galbraith, Judy. *The Gifted Kids Survival Guides.* Minneapolis: Free Spirit Publishing Co., 1983.

Gallagher, James J.; Kaplan, Sandra N.; and Sato, Irving S., ed. *Promoting the Education of the Gifted/Talented: Strategies for Advocacy.* Los Angeles: National/State Leadership Training Institute for Gifted and Talented (316 West Second St., Suite PH-C, Los Angeles, CA 90012), 1983.

Gallagher, James J. *Teaching the Gifted Child.* Boston: Allyn and Bacon, 1975.

Gallagher, Richard P. *Learn How to Study: A Study Skill Program.* Philadelphia: self-published (416 Comly St., Philadelphia, PA 19120), 1984.

Gardner, Richard A. *Therapeutic Communication with Children.* New York: Science House, 1971.

Gifted Child Society. *The Private Sector: New Answers to Old Budget Questions.* Glen Rock: GCS (90 Rock Road, Glen Rock, NJ 07452), 1983.

Ginsberg, Gina, and Harrison, Charles H. *How to Help Your Gifted Child: A Handbook for Parents and Teachers.* New York: Monarch Press, 1977.

Goertzel, Victor and Mildred. *Cradles of Eminence.* Boston: Little, Brown, 1962.

Grost, Audrey. *Genius in Residence.* Englewood Cliffs: Prentice-Hall, 1970.

Hall, Eleanor G., and Skinner, Nancy. *Somewhere to Turn: Strategies for Parents of the Gifted and Talented.* New York: Teachers College, 1980.

Holme, Bryan. *Creatures of Paradise: Pictures to Grow Up With.* New York: Oxford University Press, 1980.

Janson, H. W. *History of Art.* New York: Abrams, 1977.

Kaufman, Felice. *Your Gifted Child and You.* Reston: Council for Exceptional Children (1920 Association Dr., Reston, VA 22091), 1976.

Khatena, Joseph. *The Creatively Gifted Child: Suggestions for Parents and Teachers.* New York: Vantage, 1978.

Krueger, Mark. *On Being Gifted.* New York: Walker, 1978.

Lipman, Matthew, and Sharp, Ann M. *Philosophy for Children.* Montclair: Institute for the Advancement of Philosophy for Children (Montclair State College, Montclair, NJ 07043), 1980.

Mitchell, Patricia Bruce, ed. *An Advocate's Guide for Building Support for Gifted and Talented Education.* Washington: National Association of State Boards of Education (444 North Capitol St., N.W., Washington, DC 20001), 1981.

Moore, Linda Perigo. *Does This Mean My Kid's a Genius?* New York: McGraw-Hill, 1981.

Osborn, Alex F. *Applied Imagination: Principles and Procedures of Creative Problem Solving.* 3rd ed. New York: Scribner, 1979.

Parnes, Sidney J. *The Magic of Your Mind.* Buffalo: Creative Education Foundation (437 Franklin St., Buffalo, NY 14202-1301), 1981.

Perino, Joseph, and Perino, Sherla C. *Parenting the Gifted: Developing the Promise.* New York: Bowker, 1981.

Renzulli, Joseph S. *The Enrichment Triad Model.* Mansfield Center: Creative Learning Press, Inc. (P.O. Box 320, Mansfield Center, CT 06250), 1977.

Richert, E. Susanne; Alvino, James; and McDonnel, Rebecca C. *National Report on Identification: Assessment and Recommendations for Comprehensive*

Identification of Gifted and Talented Youth. Sewell: Educational Information and Resource Center (P.O. Box 209, Sewell, NJ 08080), 1982.

Roukes, Nicholas. *Art Synectics: Stimulating Creativity in Art — A Teachers Guide.* Worcester: Davis Publications, Inc., 1982.

Shallcross, Doris J. *Teaching Creative Behavior: How to Evoke Creativity in Children.* Englewood Cliffs: Prentice-Hall, 1980.

Shlesinger, B. Edward. *The Art of Successful Inventing.* Washington: Kelly, Hafner Associates, 1973.

Silberstein-Storfer, Muriel, with Jones, Mablen. *Doing Art Together.* New York: Simon and Schuster, 1982.

Strom, Robert D. *Growing Through Play — Readings for Parents and Teachers.* Monterey: Brooks/Cole, 1980.

Tannenbaum, Abraham J. *Reaching Out: Advocacy for the Gifted and Talented.* New York: Teachers College, 1980.

Torrance, E. Paul. *The Search for Satori and Creativity.* Buffalo: Creative Education Foundation (437 Franklin St., Buffalo, NY 14202-1301), 1979.

Vail, Priscilla. *The World of the Gifted Child.* New York: Walker, 1979; Penguin, 1980.

Vincent, Carole. *Teach Yourself Painting and Drawing.* New York: Sterling, 1983.

Webb, James; Meckstroth, Elizabeth; and Tolan, Stephanie. *Guiding the Gifted Child.* Columbus: Ohio Psychology Publishing Co., 1982.

Whitmore, Joanne. *Giftedness, Conflict, and Underachievement.* Boston: Allyn and Bacon, 1980.

Index